STAGE MAKEUP

HERMAN BUCHMAN

STAGE MAKEUP

DEMONSTRATION PHOTOGRAPHS BY SUSAN E. MEYER

WATSON-GUPTILL PUBLICATIONS / NEW YORK

Published in USA by Watson-Guptill Publications
a division of Billboard Publications
165 West 46 Street, New York, New York
All Rights Reserved.
Manufactured in Japan
No portion of the contents of this book may be
reproduced or used by any other means without written
permission of the publishers.
ISBN: 8230-4910-8
Library of Congress Catalog Card Number: 72-145412

To the memory of my parents who could never really understand my "crazy business."

ACKNOWLEDGMENTS

I am grateful to many dear people for their help in the creation of this book: first to Joseph Rizzo who conceived the need of this work, and to Sid Walters, a former student and now t.v. director, who remembered and recommended me to Mr. Rizzo; to Don Holden, editor of Watson-Guptill Publications, for the courage to expand the work to its present size.

I am indebted to my models Linda Strouchler, Ernestine Eppenger, and especially Lawrence DuKore for their patience and endurance.

I owe many thanks to Robert Kushner of Ira Senz Wigs for the use of their wonderful wigs and hairpieces.

In particular, I am grateful to Susan Meyer for her fine photographs of the teaching stages in this book, and for her great skill as editor.

I am deeply indebted to my dear wife Dian and my daughter Cathleen for their patient endurance during the three years I wrestled with this work.

Finally, this book could never have been written except for my parents, who suffered me through many years as I perfected my craft and became a professional. How happy they would have been if they had lived to see this work.

A NOTE ABOUT THE MODELS

You will note that most of the demonstration photographs use a male model. This was not an intentional slight of the female performer. I felt it would be most effective to show all the techniques worked out on the same face to illustrate the practical intent of the book. By happy accident, the male model, Lawrence DuKore, had the patience and endurance that this taxing job called for. I trust that all the female students will realize that all the techniques shown here relate to them exactly as illustrated on the male model.

CONTENTS

FOREWORD

I wish I were able to introduce you to the author of this book; I mean introduce him personally. Alas, that is not possible; it is something you will just have to miss, which is a pity, because Herman Buchman is a very charming man and I am sure you would like him. He never failed to charm me, and that is saying a great deal, because for days on end we met each other in an uncomfortable New York film studio at the most God foresaken early hour in the morning. We were making the film of *The Long Day's Journey Into Night* by Eugene O'Neill, and I was playing the father and Herman Buchman made me up.

As a matter of fact, I don't like being made up anyway; I am accustomed to doing it myself. But in the film world it is the absolute tradition to have the makeup man. I think this tradition springs from the early days of film making when they employed real cowboys and not actors, and to ask a cowboy to put on makeup or even to powder his nose would have put him into a dead faint.

Well, I am not at my best when being made up at dawn in a beastly studio, but Herman always soothed me and cheered me up with his happy personality and by his skill at his work. When having one's hair cut or being at the dentist, I think one can always sense, at once, at the first touch, whether the operator knows his job or not. And Herman has the touch of the master.

I think in making me up as the father in this film, Buchman must have had one of his most difficult assignments. The father is a portrait of a very handsome looking man. Now I am possessed with a countenance like a bun, with two small currants in it for eyes. I never saw the film, I don't know how I looked, but at the end

of our work the producer presented me with a gold watch and chain. I think I should have given it to Herman!

Now, dear Reader, I know that the author of this book is an authority on his subject, and in venturing to express to you and to the author best wishes, I can confidently say that this book is not only the best book on the subject, but that it is also the only book existing on stage makeup.

Ralph Richardson

Sir Ralph Richardson

Sir Ralph Richardson as Falstaff. Photo, John Vickers.

INTRODUCTION

The demands made of the performing artist are infinite. In addition to natural talent and a good general education, many specific skills must be developed as well. The actor must learn how to walk, talk, dance, fence; he must study different styles of acting, improvisation, and develop a good knowledge of theater history. The singer must, in addition to the above, spend endless hours in voice training, phrasing, and breath control. He must learn foreign languages and many roles, if opera is his target. The dancer must study mime and spend constant hours in body work.

When all these skills have been perfected, the performer must then rely on his body, and in particular his face, to project the physical role to the audience. The vital link between the artist and the audience is stage makeup. This final tool, when properly used, allows the performer to utilize his face to project his role to the audience. Without this skill, all other aspects of his training are badly undermined.

The art of stage makeup, so respected and widely practiced in Europe, has fallen into sad disuse in the United States. For years Europe has enjoyed the support of the performing arts by the governments, and as a result national repertory companies abound, a fact that demands each performer be capable of making up for a variety of roles. Much of the fault in the United States rests with Broadway and type casting but the American theater is now entering a renaissance, an upsurge in regional community and university theater, in addition to the development of repertory companies. The American actor has available to him a range of acting roles as never before. In order to fully utilize this opportunity, the need to develop skill with makeup is more important than ever.

This book is designed to teach all performers how to develop this skill, and how to use this knowledge to communicate effectively to the audience. The experienced professional has as much to learn as the rank beginner. There is no magic to stage makeup. It is an acquired skill, which consists of painting, sculpting, understanding facial structure, and imagination. There are sound artistic principles underlying each step of the learning process. The beginner has, in fact, one advantage over the professional: he need not unlearn the vast mountain of nonsense that constitutes most contemporary performers' knowledge of this art.

This book pushes aside the mountain of nonsense, and places the art of stage makeup on a firm foundation, consisting of art techniques, tools, and proper application.

I look forward with delight to the thought that each of you will learn how effective these techniques are. My greatest regret is that I cannot be with you during this period of learning. How marvelous it will be for you, and for me, when you walk on the stage without worrying how you look because you know that you have created the appearance of your role.

CHAPTER ONE
MATERIALS AND TOOLS

Knowing the necessary tools and materials is basic for any artist. In this art form, your own face will be the canvas. All the materials you will apply to this canvas and the implements you use in the application are broken down into appropriate categories and listed below. Although the tools and materials are produced by a large number of manufacturers, I recommend manufacturers whose products I consider best. At the back of the book you will find a full list of suppliers where these materials are available.

The following materials represent everything you will need for applying makeup properly and creatively. They constitute the components of the actor's makeup kit.

MAKEUP BASES

The makeup base is a cosmetic that creates the desired skin color. There are many kinds of bases manufactured in a variety of consistencies: hard grease sticks, soft grease paint, liquid, and pancake. In this book, you will be using practically all of them.

Hard grease paints These are available in a complete range of colors. These paints come in stick form and are approximately 5″ long and about 1″ thick. Although this base requires a bit more effort to apply, when done properly it has a better and longer wearing quality than any of the others.

Soft grease paints These are available in a complete range of colors for use as makeup base. Manufactured in a toothpaste type tube, soft grease paint has a creamy texture and is quickly and easily spread. Soft grease paint tends to shine excessively because of its cream content and, moreover, does not survive body heat as well as the hard grease paint.

Pancakes These are also available in a complete range of base colors. This paint is supplied in a compressed form in a flat, round container, and is applied to the face with a moistened sponge. Pancakes dry quickly and have a matte finish and, therefore, form a difficult surface for further detailed makeup work. This base is the least effective for theatrical use because it dissolves under heat and perspiration. It is much more practical for film and television work because it can be repaired continuously.

Liquid base colors These are available in bottles and used primarily as a body—as opposed to face—base. Liquid base dries quickly, which makes it impractical for use as a facial base.

LINING COLORS AND ROUGES

Lining colors are the grease paints which will be used for all shadowing and highlighting effects and are applied on top of the base color. They come in all shades of gray, from white to black, in maroons, browns, blues, etc. Lining colors also come in all the reds and are called *moist rouges.*

Lining colors are available hard in sticks, and soft in tins. I prefer the tins, because the texture blends more easily. The range of colors is limited to the stronger primary hues, but any color needed can be achieved by mixing.

Dry rouges are supplied in small tins of compressed red powder and are available in various red hues. These are used primarily to touch up details after the makeup has been powdered, almost impossible to do with moist rouges.

EYE MAKEUP

To sketch in eyebrows and to outline the eye we use eyebrow pencils. They are colored soft wax in a pencil form. Although many colors are available, black and brown are the only ones you will need for your kit.

Mascara is applied to the eyelashes to darken them. It can be purchased in tubes or blocks with brushes, or in roller form. For theatrical purposes, I recommend the hard block form, because it holds up better under heat and perspiration. Waterproof mascara comes in tubes, which I recommend only for performers who are extremely active on stage, such as dancers. Otherwise, I find the waterproof too harsh for the eyes. Black and brown are the basic colors you will need for mascara.

False eyelashes may be necessary in accenting the eye. Modestly priced lashes are frequently better than the expensive ones and are worth buying.

CLEANSERS

Cleansers are various substances used in cleansing and preparing the face for makeup and also for removing makeup. There are few true differences between cleansers in a liquid and solidified state. Liquid oils and solid vegetable substances are much admired by some actors, but I think they have several disadvantages. Liquids, on the whole, are messy to use, tend to splatter, and frequently soil clothing. Solid vegetable oils, while they are among the purest of the cleansers, must be refrigerated to prevent them from turning rancid. Various brand cold creams differ little in substance, except for the amount of perfume and air whipped into them. I prefer unscented Albolene to all the other cleansers. Unscented Albolene lacks any perfume, an ingredient that tends to act as a drying agent, which is undesirable. This cream cleanses well, is never gritty, and will last for a long time.

Acetone is a strong solvent which is used to dissolve and remove any gums or adhesives used in makeup. It is also used to remove wigs glued to the head, and to clean the wigs of any spirit gum residue. You can buy acetone at any hardware store.

APPLICATORS

To apply makeup, you'll need a number of applicators designed for specific tasks.

Flat red sable brushes   These will be your most useful tool for basic painting work on the face. They can be purchased in any artist's supply shop. You will need three bristle brushes, one each of nos. 4, 5, 6. Most brushes come with 18″ wooden handles. Cut the handle down to about pencil size for added convenience.

Japanese writing brushes   These provide the finest painting point possible and are to be used whenever fine detail is required. They are available at artist's suppliers. You will need two of these brushes. Buy the one with bristles 1″ long and ¼″ thick at the widest point.

Foam rubber sponge   Used for spreading liquid base onto the hands or body, the foam rubber sponge is available from either upholstery shops or from pillow departments of variety stores. This is a very inexpensive sponge and can be discarded after use. Buy any convenient size sheet at least 1″ thick and cut into rectangles 1″ x 1″ x 2″ for convenient handling use. Since you will use each rectangle only once, you will need a large supply for various makeup jobs.

Natural sponges   These are used for applying pancake makeup and wet application of dry rouge. They come in various qualities. The best for makeup purposes are called *silk* sponges. You will need one. The size most easily grasped in the hand generally costs one dollar and is available in most drug stores or dime stores.

POWDER AND POWDER PUFFS

Powdering is the way in which you will set your makeup. Powders should be purchased in transparent, colorless form. White baby powder is fundamentally transparent and is excellent for makeup purposes. Buy any large powder puff from a drug store or variety store.

PUTTIES

Putty is used for building up facial features. Both *nose putty* and *mortician's wax* are used to build up false features when necessary and are a requirement for all makeup kits. These are available at drug stores that carry theatrical makeup. Mortician's wax may be obtained from a funeral parlor if such a drug store is not available in your town.

ADHESIVES

Adhesives are used for makeup effects and for attaching face hair and wigs. There are two basic types of adhesive you will use: surgical adhesive and spirit gum.

Surgical adhesive is a natural liquid rubber (latex) available in small tubes. It is a versatile item and can be used as an adhesive for applying false eyelashes, and for creating disfiguring marks.

Spirit gum is a fast drying bottled adhesive. It is used to glue wigs, hairpieces, false hair, or rubber pieces to to head or face. It is available in the original gum arabic form, or in newer plastic versions. It can be quickly removed by application of acetone.

LOOSE FACE HAIR

You will probably do a great deal of work involving the creation of additional face hair. Here are the varieties available to you.

Crepe wool This is a wool-like material that comes in an assortment of colors. It is extremely inexpensive, can be applied quickly, and gives very satisfactory results. For more detailed, realistic work, yak hair, or human hair must be used.

Yak hair This is a coarse animal hair and is available in all usable colors. It can provide very satisfactory results and is fairly inexpensive.

Human hair This is the most expensive of the available hairs and requires the greatest technique in application. It can be purchased in various texture qualities and it provides the most satisfactory results. Because of the expense and the detailed labor involved, these individual human hairs can only be used for single performances or a short run. For a longer run, it is more practical to use a hairpiece. Hairpieces come in a variety of styles.

FACE HAIRPIECES

Face hairpieces are ready-made pieces to be used as mustaches, beards, sideburns, and eyebrows. (We will discuss wig hairpieces in the next section.) Face hairpieces are available in silk base or lace net.

The *silk base* hairpiece is the least expensive and is the sturdiest and the longest lasting of the pieces. For this reason, it is advisable for large groups, pageants, and choral work. All the hairs are sewn into the silk material for mustaches, sideburns, Van Dykes, and even full beards. However, because the hairs are sewn on a fabric, the hair piece has no transparency, and although it will last for an exceptionally long time, it is not good enough to be used on a principal player or for work requiring reality.

The *lace net* piece is advisable for leading performers or wherever fine results are demanded. The hairs are tied by hand onto a transparent piece of net gauze. There are many different qualities in the net gauze. All these pieces must be handled with extreme care, as the net material cannot tolerate abuse. A well made mustache, beard, or sideburn on net will come closest to achieving a completely natural look.

WIGS

Now that we have discussed the face hairpieces, let's consider the wig hairpiece. Wigs are sewn on cloth bases for strength. (Of all the cloths, silk is the best quality.) The finer wigs will have a net front attached to allow for a natural transparent hairline. These will help create a realistic effect.

For realistic baldness, use an all silk wig; the silk material helps to simulate the bald pate.

ADDITIONAL MATERIALS

You will need a mild soap for a final washing and a gentle astringent, either an after shave lotion or witch hazel. You can use any kind of towel and cleansing tissue, of course.

BASIC MAKEUP KIT

Practically speaking, you will need a box to store and carry your materials. Any one of a number of suitable containers may do, from suitcases to handbags, but for efficiency and orderliness, fishing tackle boxes are most practical. They are available in several sizes and vary in the number of sectional trays they contain. The trays are excellent for holding the many small items in the basic makeup kit. A photographer's gadget bag also serves very well as a kit. However, you can use any box that enables you to carry your materials in such a way that they do not jumble, spill, break, or spoil, and that makes it easy for you to lay your hands on whatever you want.

Here is a checklist of materials I suggest you buy for your kit. I suggest alternatives in the manufacturers because one product may be more accessible in one location than in another. However, the products are equal in quality, so buy whichever you find most easily available.

Two towels

One square plain silk (for putting on wigs)

Bar of soap and soap container

Barber type shears

Box of cleansing tissues

Bottle of acetone

Bottle of astringent (after shave lotion or witch hazel)

Cleansing cream

Colorless powder or talc container

Two powder puffs

Silk sponge

Three flat red sable brushes, one each nos. 4, 5, 6

Two Japanese writing brushes, 1" long and ¼" thick at widest point

Black eyebrow pencil

Brown eyebrow pencil

Soft graphite artist's pencil

Lipstick (women only, two colors, one 3 shades darker than the other, any preferred brand)

Dry rouge (any blush-on rouge can be used, Max Factor's Light Technicolor and Dark Technicolor preferred)

Mascara in black and brown (Meyer and HSG cake preferred; in tube or roller, use Max Factor, Stein, or Leichner)

Eyelashes (women only), one pair black; one pair brown

Hair (optional for women) in crepe wool (Stein), one braid each in black, brown, gray, blond, white

Hard grease paint

STEIN	OR	LEICHNER	OR	MAX FACTOR
#14		#15		#7A
#27		Chrome yellow		Chinese

Soft grease paint (men only)

STEIN	OR	LEICHNER	OR	MAX FACTOR
#7		#4½		#7A

Soft grease paint (women only)

STEIN	OR	LEICHNER	OR	MAX FACTOR
#5½		#3		#4½

Lining colors

	STEIN OR	LEICHNER	OR	MAX FACTOR
DARK GRAY	#5	#32		#6
DARK CRIMSON	#13	#25		Red on Red
DARK BROWN	#7	#28		#2
WHITE	#15	#22		#12
BLACK	#17	#42		#1

Moist rouge

STEIN	OR	LEICHNER	OR	MAX FACTOR
#3		Carmine II		Red on Red

Pancake (men only)

MAX FACTOR

Tan #2

Natural

Light Egyptian

Pancake (women only)

MAX FACTOR

Tan Rose

Natural

Light Egyptian

Adhesives

Spirit gum (Max Factor, Stein, or Leichner)

Johnson & Johnson Duo Surgical Adhesive

The tools combined in this kit are the tools of an artist. The techniques you need to develop combine the arts of painting and sculpture. As stated earlier, you will work on a three dimensional canvas, your face.

Increasing your tactile sense will be of great advantage to you. You must learn to sketch, using soft pencil, charcoal, and pastel, since these art forms require blending with the fingers. In addition, a modeling sense can be developed by using soft modeling clay to sculpt faces and figures.

This kit with its implements, plus the acquired skill of painter and sculptor, will prepare you for the work to follow.

CHAPTER TWO

BASIC MAKEUP TECHNIQUES

Throughout this book we will be using basic makeup techniques. These techniques will apply in all the roles you will be playing and in all the makeup problems you will be solving in the following chapters. Wherever possible, I have described the techniques as part of a demonstration, but I have included in this chapter some miscellaneous techniques you will be encountering again and again. This is a kind of a "catch-all" chapter, then, one I hope you will refer back to whenever you encounter difficulty in the demonstrations to come. First I will describe some of the aspects of makeup base and base color which you should know before you begin, then I will discuss the specific techniques you will be using continually: blending and shading, highlights, shadows and wrinkles, painting the eyebrows and mouth.

CLEANSING THE FACE

Oddly enough, an important technique in stage makeup is cleansing the face completely before makeup is applied. Dip two fingers into the cleansing cream. Remove a dab about ½" in thickness and apply this to your forehead, nose, cheeks, and chin. Spread the cream gently and evenly with the fingertips. After your entire face has been covered, cleanse your fingers with tissue and with fresh cleansing tissue carefully remove the excess cream from your face. Do not rub your face dry. Leave a thin film of cream on the skin. This will act as a protective covering and will aid you in the removal of makeup at the end of the performance. Be sure, however, that it *is* a thin layer. If you leave too much on, this will soften and spoil your

makeup. With practice and experience you will learn the correct amount.

BASE COLOR

Base or base color refers to the skin color most suitable to the role you will play. The range of human skin tones extends from the palest Caucasian to the blue-black of the Australian aborigine. Through practiced observation you, the performing artist, must become aware of the vast range of hues in the Caucasian and Negroid and Oriental skin tones.

It is important to realize, however, that cosmetic manufacturer's colors are only approximations of skin tones, and are rarely usable as they are made. In the greatest number of instances, you will have to mix different colors in order to arrive at the base color you need. This will be demonstrated in detail in Chapter 3.

For theatrical purposes, you will be using hard stick base and soft grease paints for your base more than any of the others. In Chapter 3 the application of the soft grease will be demonstrated in detail and in Chapter 4 the application of the hard stick.

APPLYING PANCAKE BASE

Since pancake base is used very little in the theater because it does not hold up under lights, is thin in color effectiveness, and is usually used by lazy performers, or those lacking theatrical imagination, I have not included its application in any of the demonstrations. I will describe it here, in case you should ever

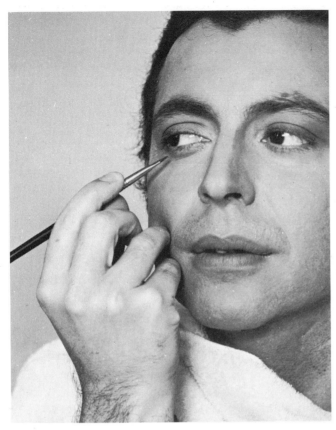

1. Hold the brush in your hand as if you were about to write on your face. Rest the little finger against the face.

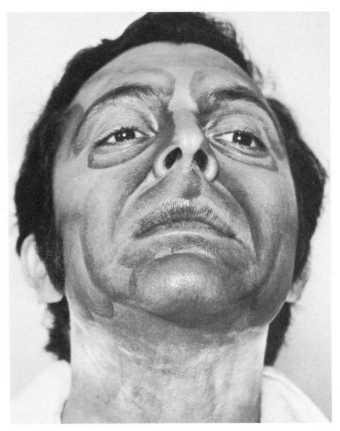

2. Starting at the base of the neck, where the makeup ends, lay on a layer of powder until the puff is empty.

have reason to use it, since in an emergency it's better than no base at all.

Pancake base is applied with a silk sponge. First moisten the sponge and squeeze out most of the water so that the sponge is still moist. Rub a corner of the sponge across the pancake until a small quantity of makeup is picked up on the sponge. Use a smooth back and forth motion to apply the pancake to the face. The amount you have picked up will cover only a portion of the face, so repeat the process until the entire face is covered.

HOLDING THE MAKEUP BRUSH

For application of almost all painting effects, you will use the brush. The most important factor is controlling the brush, and the way you hold it will aid you in your control. Hold the brush as you would a pen or pencil close to the head. Use the little finger of your hand as a fulcrum, resting it lightly on the face—carefully to avoid smearing your makeup—and use the edge or flat of the brush as if you were writing or painting. (See Fig. 1.)

FINISHING THE SKIN COLOR

When you have completed your facial makeup, always look at it critically and reexamine the skin color. No skin has a single even color throughout. Most roles call for a healthy, robust skin tone. You can kill two birds with one stone by heightening the healthy effect

of your base with the addition of some rouge on the cheeks, nose, chin, and forehead. This action also breaks up the evenness of the makeup and produces a more natural effect (demonstrated in Chapter 3.)

The male actor must also evaluate the amount of beard tone he wishes to project. Every man, even when clean-shaven, has a darker skin tone in the beard area than in the rest of the face. To create the effect of a beard tone, Caucasians and Orientals use a dark blue-gray lining color, and black performers use a dark brown or black lining color. With a small amount of paint on the fingertip, gently pat the color on through the beard and mustache area. Be careful not to destroy the work you have just completed. Add the color in light dabs and only enough to add a beard hue to your skin tone. Don't forget to carry it down onto the neck and be careful to avoid smudges or clumps of paint.

You should achieve no more than a clean-shaven effect. For more growth you will have to put hair on the face, which will be discussed in Chapter 8.

POWDERING

Powdering is a method of setting the makeup you have already applied. This seemingly simple process, if done carelessly or incorrectly, may damage or destroy what you have worked so hard to achieve.

First be sure that you use only a transparent or very lightly colored powder. The purpose of powdering is to *set* your makeup, not to discolor it, which is exactly what a colored powder will do.

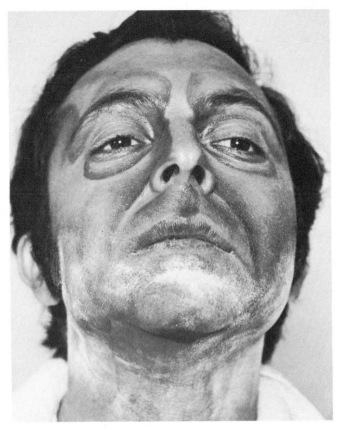

3. Carry the next layer up further onto the face.

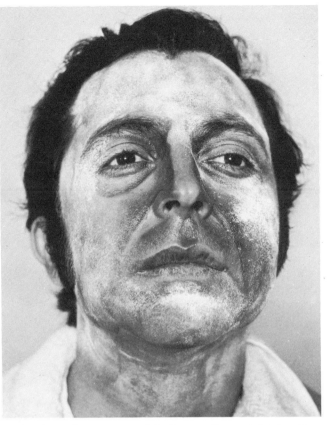

4. Continue the process of laying on the powder in steps up the face.

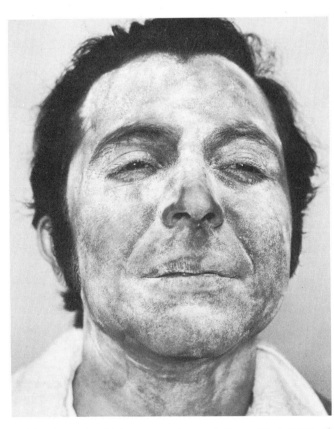

5. The face should be covered completely with a layer of powder.

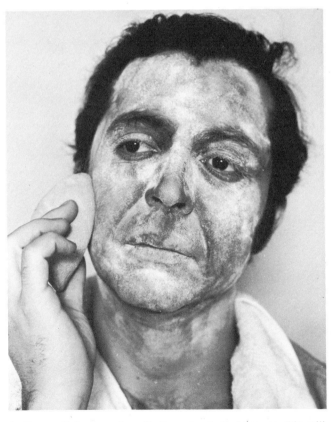

6. Now roll the powder off. Do not rub it, because this will destroy the work. Press and roll until all the powder is removed by the puff. Then wet your hands with water and pat off the excess powder film.

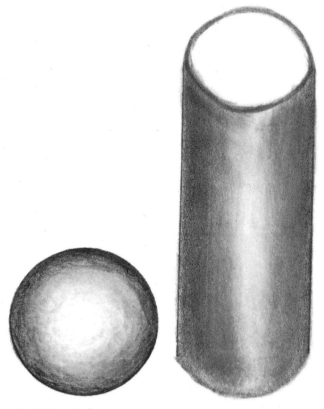

Pick up a quantity of powder on your powder puff. Fold the puff and roll the powder into it. Then open the puff and lightly shake off any excess powder. Starting at the neck, use a slight slapping motion to pat a layer of powder onto the base (Fig. 2). Move the puff up the face to an unpowdered area and repeat the patting until all the powder is used up. Now re-load the puff and repeat the patting until the entire made up area of the face is covered with a good layer of powder. (See Figs. 3 to 5.)

Now shake the excess powder from the puff. Fold the puff around your index finger. Then, with a rolling motion, press and roll the excess powder from the face onto the puff (Fig. 6). Shake the puff clean at intervals and repeat this process until nothing but a very thin film of powder remains on the face. Remember, *always roll* the excess powder off. Do not rub the puff across the face. Do nothing that might streak the makeup.

The remaining film of powder is easily removed. Using a moist silk sponge, pat off the powder film. Blot the face dry of water, check the eyebrows and hairline to see if they need a touchup, and you are finished.

Now take a hard, critical look at the makeup. Since the powdering will have set it, you may become aware of splotches, edges, streaks, and areas that should have been blended more skillfully. Look hard and observe what went wrong so that you don't repeat the error. And also look hard at those parts of the makeup that went well. They should look real and natural, a worthwhile compensation for all the hard work.

7. (Left) Try blending this form in makeup: shade darkest at the edge and blend to the lightest tone in the center. This creates the effect of a round ball. **8.** (Right) This blending uses the same idea as Fig. 7, but the shape is elongated, much the way you would shade a wrinkle.

REMOVING MAKEUP

The greatest harm you can do to your skin is to rub it excessively, leave grease on your face, and then go out into cold weather. To remove makeup correctly, apply cleansing cream to the face. Rub it well, but gently. Using soft cleansing tissues, remove much of this from the face, without irritating the skin. Then apply more cream to the face and remove this, again as carefully and gently as possible. When all the makeup is removed, wash your face with a gentle soap and with warm water. Close the pores with cold water or a mild astringent, such as witch hazel.

BLENDING OR SHADING

In your makeup work, you will constantly be creating illusions: you suggest sinking, swelling, pouches, wrinkles, illusions which demand that you master the art of blending or shading. Blending (or shading) is more frequently done than any other process and is the most important technique in makeup application. Blending means graduating the intensity of a color—whether it is dark (shadow) or light (highlight)—from its strongest color to its lightest tone, until it disappears into the base. So important is this technique, in itself, that you should practice blending before you go onto to creating the illusions to come.

Practice this technique *constantly.* Start by applying a quantity of paint (it doesn't matter how much) with the fingertips to the skin (it doesn't matter what color) and, by gently patting the fingertip, gradually reduce

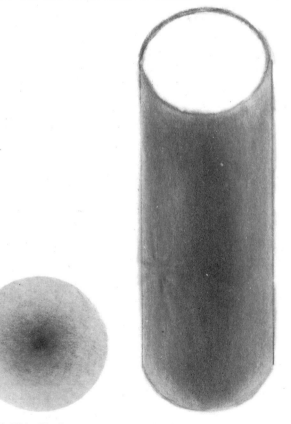

9. (Left) This illusion also creates the impression of roundness, but the shading is darkest at the center, grading to light at the edges. **10.** (Right) Blending in the same way as in Fig. 9, the illusion is one of a cylinder or tube, a technique used in painting cheek rouge.

the amount of the paint from the darkest point of application to where you can make it fade into the skin. Pat to remove all spots or blotches. This technique is the key to *all* your future work.

Once you have mastered the technique of blending, try to create some abstract illusions. Study the illusions illustrated in Figs. 7, 8, 9, and 10, to see what you can achieve with blending. In Figs. 7 and 8 the shading is darkest at the edge, blending toward light at the center, to give the illusion of a round ball or a round cylinder. We use this kind of shading in makeup whenever an edge is permissible, such as in wrinkles and skin folds. In Figs. 9 and 10, we get the effect of roundness or of a tube by blending darkest at the center and grading out to disappear at the edges. We use this kind of blending whenever we cannot have any edges showing at all, in cheek rouge and highlighting, for example.

STRUCTURE OF THE HEAD

In all your makeup work, you will be starting from the actual structure of the head. It is important to understand that structure in order to alter the head with makeup. (See Fig. 11.) The bone structure of the head includes the prominent high points of the bone masses —the forehead, cheekbones, jawbone—as well as the cartilage of the nose, the eyeball of the eye socket, and the teeth. The face has two major sinkings: the cheek sinking between the prominences of the cheekbone and the jawbone, and the depression behind the region of the temple bone. These prominences and

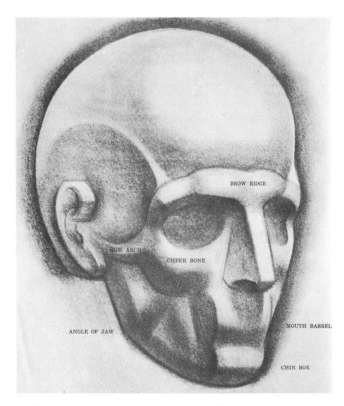

11. Study the structure of the head, making note of the areas of depression and the prominent areas in the face. You will use these for effect in your makeup work. From *Drawing The Human Head* by Burne Hogarth; Watson-Guptill.

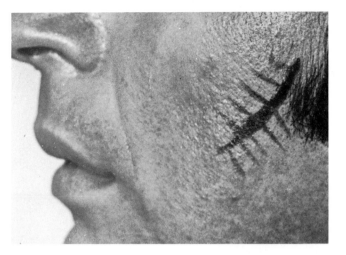

12. To sink the cheekbone, apply shadow mixture between the cheekbone and the jawbone. Always shade from the heaviest application to the lightest. Note: in these demonstration photographs, the short "crow's" lines indicate *direction* of blending. They are *not* to suggest that you apply the painting this way. Here, for example, the direction of blending is on both sides away from the center. This system is used throughout the book.

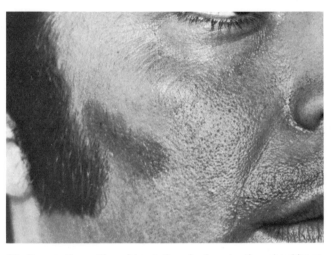

13. By gently patting, blend the shadow to the cheekbone and jawbone.

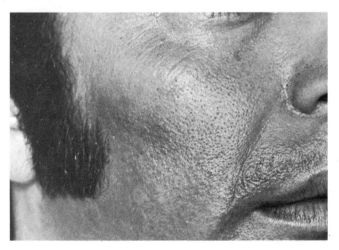

14. The cheekbone sinking has been blended.

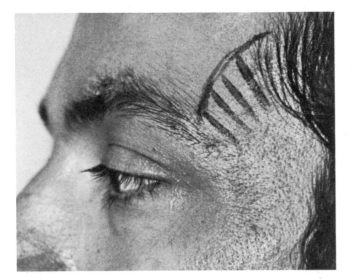

15. To sink the temple, apply the shadow mixture directly behind the temple bone.

16. Begin to blend back towards the hairline and ear.

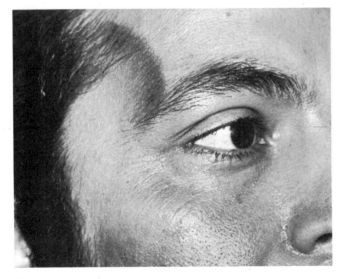

17. The temple sinking has been blended.

depressions are used to create the illusions we are after in makeup work.

The illusion of sinking can be created with painted shadows running from one prominence into the hollow, and then out to another prominence. We use this technique to sink the cheekbone, for example. Let's actually begin to create the illusion of the sinking cheekbone. (The following examples have been taken from the demonstration of aging—Chapter 4—but they apply to all the makeup problems you will encounter.)

SINKING THE CHEEKBONE

With a fingertip, apply a small quantity of brown lining color (in its deepest intensity) at a point equidistant between and parallel to the cheekbone and the jawbone. About 1″ to 1½″ in length, this shadow does not extend back to where the jawbone and the cheekbone join, and is not to extend forward to where it would intrude into any of the fleshy folds around the mouth. (See Fig. 12.)

Clean off the paint from your finger and then—with a patting technique—blend the shadow up to, but not on to the cheekbone, down but not on to the jawbone, back but not to the cheek and jawbone junction, and forward, but avoiding the fleshy folds of the mouth. (See Fig. 13.) This blending must graduate the paint so that its greatest darkness and intensity is in the center, graduating until it fades into the skin.

When the entire shadow has been blended, its total size should be no more than about 2″ in length and 1″ in width (Fig. 14). To achieve this properly demands a considerable degree of practice and care.

SINKING THE TEMPLE

To give the illusion of the temple sinking is a technique that varies greatly from the above. Unlike any of the other facial bones, the temple bone is the only one having a specific edge. Therefore apply the brown paint with the fingertips directly behind the temple bone with a patting touch (Fig. 15). The illusion is comparatively sharp, but is not a straight line, since we are trying to show the skin sinking into the back of the bone edge. As always, clean off the fingertips and, with a patting technique, blend the paint back towards the hairline and ear, carrying the graduation about ½″ in width at the top, and extending perhaps 1″ to 2″ over the ear (Fig. 16). The grading of the paint must be perfect so that when you look at yourself in the mirror, face front, you see a shading and a sinking that has no sign of artificiality and, when viewed from the side and profile, is also satisfactory. (See Fig. 17.)

PAINTING SKIN FOLDS

Painting a wrinkle involves a specific technique that includes all of the variations of skin folds denoting age. These are called wrinkles, folds, jowls, bags, or pouches. In all of these, the sinking or painting is deepest, therefore heaviest, along one specific line. In addition, each fold has a beginning point and an end point which starts small, widens to its widest

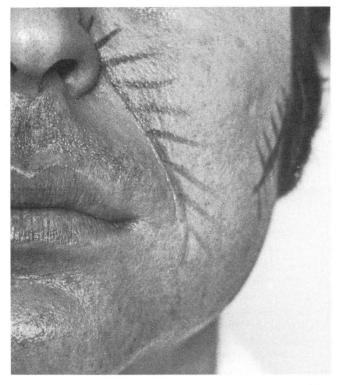

18. To start the painting of the wrinkle, first establish the line of the wrinkle and blend towards the ear.

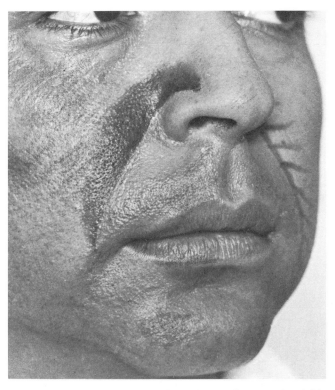

19. The wrinkle is blended, from the darkest at the fold, diminishing into the face. The width of the wrinkle is narrowest at the two origins, widening out in the center.

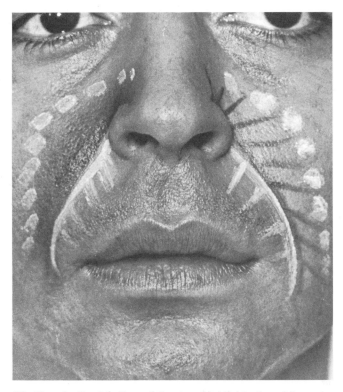

20. Here is the location of the two highlights found in every wrinkle: the high point highlight along the crest of the fold and the contrast highlight, located just below the darkest line of the fold.

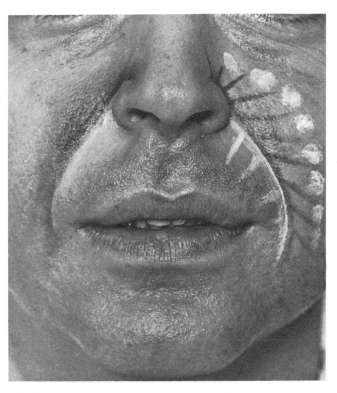

21. The high point and contrast highlights have been blended: the former blended in all directions, the latter blended away from the fold.

point, and diminishes until the fold disappears into the face.

In painting these structures, the shadow is applied with a brush most darkly along the line of the fold. (Let's examine the painting of the nose wrinkle, for example.) With the flat of the brush, the paint is blended in the direction of the fold. Its shape starts at the point of origin, widening, then diminishing to the point where it disappears into the face. (See Fig. 18.) This application of paint is then blended with the fingertip so that the color grades from the darkest to where it blends into the base (Fig. 19). Refer to the optical illusion (Figs. 9 and 10) illustrated earlier in this chapter so that you can see the ultimate effect of this kind of blending.

Painting the wrinkle is never complete until the appropriate highlights are applied. Each wrinkle or fold requires two highlights. The first—the *high point* highlight—is applied along the crest of the fold, following its shape for the full length of the wrinkle. This highlight is applied in its greatest strength a short distance just above the point where the shadow has been blended into the base. The highlight is itself blended in all directions so that it gradually disappears into the base. Experience and knowledge will teach you how to limit the highlight area so that it does not intrude into other fold areas of the face which you plan to work on later.

The second highlight is called the *contrast* highlight, and is applied with a brush directly next to, and along the darkest part of the shadow. This highlight is blended with the brush away from the shadow. The blending is then completed with the fingertip which makes the highlight grade and disappear into the base. (See Figs. 20 and 21.) The location of shadows, wrinkles, and highlights will be shown specifically in appropriate chapters, but the principles and technique described here apply to all wrinkles and folds.

PAINTING THE MOUTH

The two most expressive features of the face are the mouth and the eyebrows. These features are in constant motion and their forms are easily defined and reshaped to suggest a variety of expressions.

The mouth consists of an upper and a lower lip, each of which can be dealt with as a separate expressive entity. By considering each lip a three dimensional area, you can obtain the most potential from this expressive feature. Take a look at the mouths around you. Notice that lips are composed of various round shapes. The upper lip is always darker than the lower. This happens because the upper lip is undercut and therefore creates its own shadow. Ordinarily—for a natural lip color—a brown shadow mixture will do for the upper lip and a maroon tone for the lower. When you wish to suggest a woman wearing lipstick you should use a tone two or three shades darker for the upper lip than for the lower.

Now we approach the most important and difficult art of shaping and painting the lips. You can select and paint any shape mouth that serves your purpose, unless your own lips have uncommonly sharp edges of their own. Once again, observe mouths around you. For example, the upper lip may be extremely thin, in which case it may be painted almost as thin as a line. Or the upper lip may be full and round. The lower lip has as many shapes and as much variety as the upper lip. It may be long and thin, short and bulbous. The technique of painting the mouth is illustrated in great detail in Chapter 5.

It helps to sketch out the mouth you want on a sheet of paper and to experiment before you finally select the one you consider suitable. (See Fig. 22.)

PAINTING EYEBROWS

The eyebrows are the second feature of the face that offers the greatest variety for expression. Stop and look at eyebrows around you (Fig. 23).

The technique of painting the eyebrows is very close to that of sketching with a pencil on paper. In these photographs, for example, I have sketched an eyebrow on my hand.

Use an eyebrow pencil of the desired color, light brown, dark brown, black, red, etc. Sharpen the pencil (Figs. 24 and 25). Using the lighter color, first sketch in the hairs in the direction of their normal growth. Continue the sketching first for shape, then for density at the heavier growth. Make the hairs darker with your darker color until you create the desired shape and color (Figs. 26 to 28). The most used color combinations would be light brown and dark brown and black, gray and black, gray and white, light brown and red.

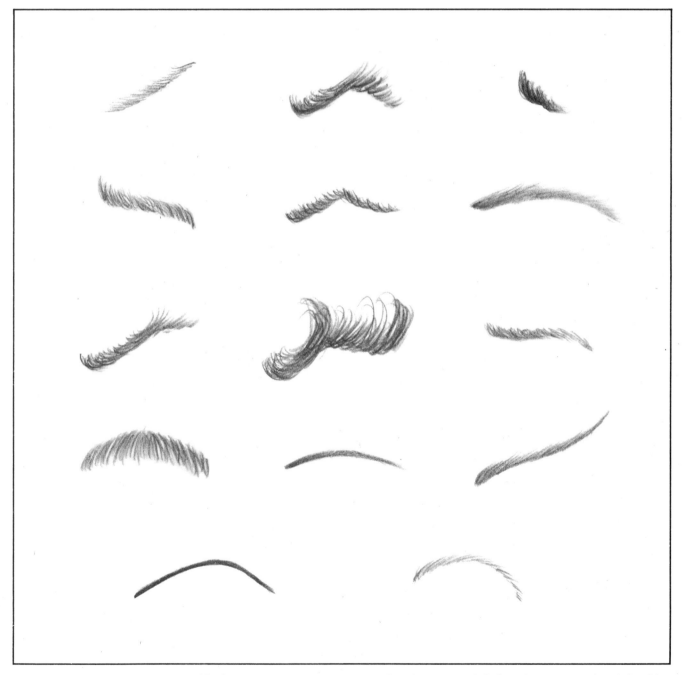

23. Study eyebrows around you and make a note of their various contours and densities.

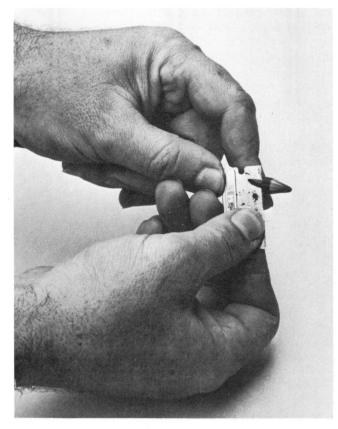

24. To sharpen the eyebrow pencil, press the razor blade through the wood with your thumb.

25. Continue to shave the pencil until you get a sharp point. The pencil is soft and will break if not sharpened with care.

26. To illustrate the technique of sketching in the eyebrow, I have drawn on my own hand. First begin to sketch in the shape very lightly.

27. Add to the intensity by applying more and more strokes of the pencil. Lift the pencil at the end of each stroke to get the feathered effect of real hairs.

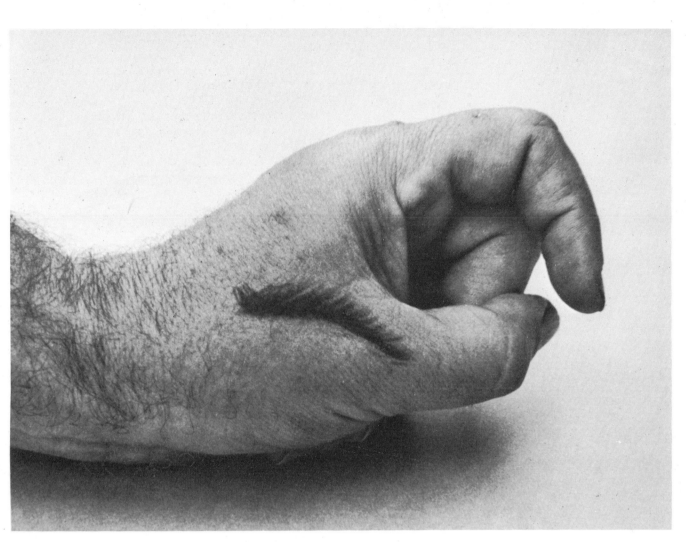

28. By applying the strokes in the direction of the natural growth, you can simulate new eyebrows of almost any size or shape.

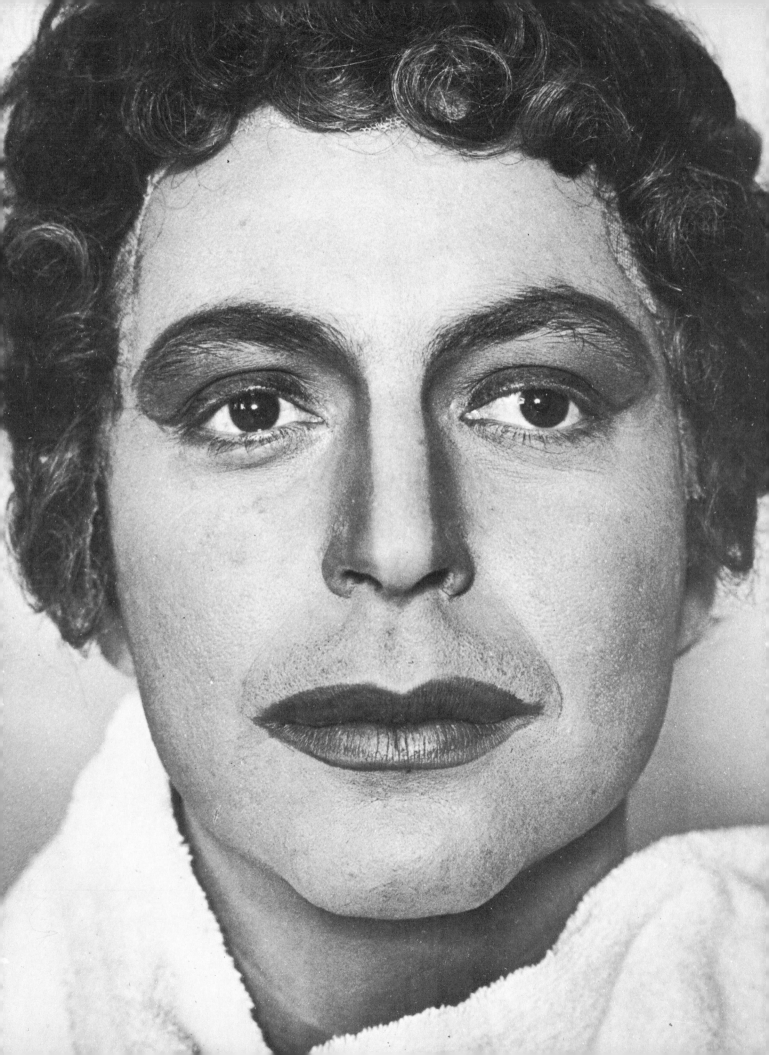

CHAPTER THREE

CLASSIC GREEK

Classic Greece brings to mind an ancient period of history, famous for the beauty of its architecture, its philosophers, its city governments, its unsurpassed paintings and sculptures. My use of the term *classic Greek* relates to the sculpture and to the standards of beauty created during this period. These standards were unique, since the features of the face and its proportions were rigid and exact, and resulted in a mask-like quality. (See Fig. 29.)

PURPOSE OF THIS TECHNIQUE

As a contemporary actor, you may very well ask, of what possible use will a mask-like makeup of rigid features be to me, especially when I will have so little occasion to play Greek roles? The question is a good one, and the answer is not simple.

Making up for the classic Greek role means that you will have to alter your face to conform to the classic Greek proportions and to project the quality of youth. In many roles, you change your appearance by building up artificial features; in this technique, you learn to alter your face with optical illusions. You will idealize your face so that you can project the image of the perfect youthful face. This is not to say that you ignore your actual face. Your own face and features must be fully utilized. To make it possible for you to utilize your own face and features to their best advantage, you must be able to project these features to your audience. Furthermore, you must be able to alter your own features to the degree called for by the role. These are skills you will need for every makeup job you attempt.

To sum up, then, the techniques and skills you learn in Classic Greek will teach you three things: how to project your *own* features and face; how to *alter* your features and face (thereby making it possible to create many variations of your own face); and how to project the appearance of youth.

Its final application is in translating this makeup to contemporary roles. The initial work is directly usable primarily in classic roles of antiquity. But its value lies in teaching you fundamental skills for contemporary work. With the current upsurge of regional and repertory theater—which requires the performer to assume many faces—the techniques learned here will prove invaluable.

SYMMETRY OF THE FACE

The Greeks envisioned their gods in human form. They were heroic in size and beautiful in their form and symmetry. Let's look at the face we are about to emulate: oval in shape, wider across the cheekbones and narrower at the chin, somewhat egg-shaped. This oval is divided lengthwise into three areas of equal size. The first, extending from the center of the hairline to the eyebrows, the second from the eyebrows to the tip of the nose, and the third from the tip of the nose to the end of the chin. These three areas are exactly the same in length.

The width of the face is divided into five equal eyes. The distance, from the sideburn to the corner of the eye is exactly the same size as the eye itself from corner to corner. The third area of equal size is the space between the eyes, and then again the next eye,

29. Here is an excellent example of the classic Grecian face with its symmetrical proportions and mask-like features. (Head from a fragmentary statue of the Diadoumenos, Courtesy, Fletcher Fund, The Metropolitan Museum of Art.)

and then again the space from the corner of that eye to the sideburn.

The last measurement of conformity involves the size of the mouth. The mouth is wide enough so that if an imaginary line were drawn straight up, it would extend from the corner of the mouth and bisect the center of the eye's pupil.

Finally, the nose is in the exact center of the face. It is absolutely straight and the nose is as wide as its bridge.

MEASURING YOUR FACE

If at all possible, get a photograph of yourself enlarged to 8" x 10" and make your notations directly on the photo. If this is impossible, take a large sheet of paper and make your notations on the paper.

Evaluate your face for its oval shape. Use your hairline as the top part of the egg shape. Place your hands along the contour of your face, your fingertips at the hairline, your chin resting between the thumb and palm, and your thumb beneath your chin. (See Fig. 30.) This will give you a blocked in idea of the shape of your face. Note this down on your sketch.

Let's first consider the proportions relative to the length of the face. Using your brush or a pencil as a measure, place the tip at the start of the hairline, and vertically down the forehead, measure the distance from the hairline to the eyebrow (Fig. 31). Marking this point on your stick or holding that point with your fingers, move the stick down the face so that the tip now rests at the point of the eyebrow you have just measured and runs vertically down the bridge of the nose (Fig. 32). Compare this measure to the forehead measure. Is it the same, shorter, or longer? Make the appropriate observation on your sketch pad and, using the same measure, take the measuring stick down to the end of the nose above the lip (Fig. 33) and compare this measure to the nose and to the forehead, measurements you've just made. Once again, make the proper notation on your sketch pad.

Now let's evaluate these measurements. If the measurements are exactly equal, congratulate yourself on having uncommonly regular proportions. If, however, like most of us, you are not exactly evenly proportioned, you must now consider how to compensate for this irregularity. With makeup, using optical illusions, we can create the effect of symmetry. At the same time, we learn how to adjust the face to our needs, a technique that is essential for every role we play.

If the chin and nose areas are equal, but the forehead area is much larger, you can adjust this by applying a wig or hairpiece that would begin at the point on the forehead that would give you the equal proportions. If the chin and forehead areas are larger than the nose area, again you must compensate. We make the nose area larger by lifting the eyebrows into the forehead and extending the nose up. This also deaccentuates the length of the forehead. We also make the mouth fuller to cut into the chin area. (We cannot diminish the size of the chin by shading it. This creates a weak receding chin effect, most undesirable for Grecian makeup.)

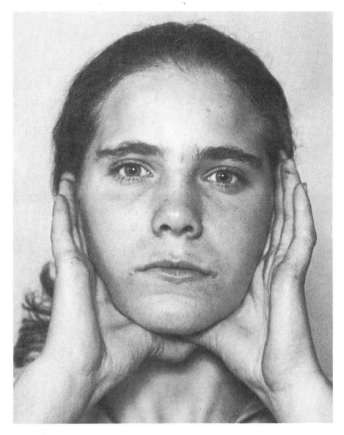

30. To evaluate the contour of your face, place your hands along the side of the face, fingertips at the hairline, chin cupped between thumb and palm, and thumb beneath your chin.

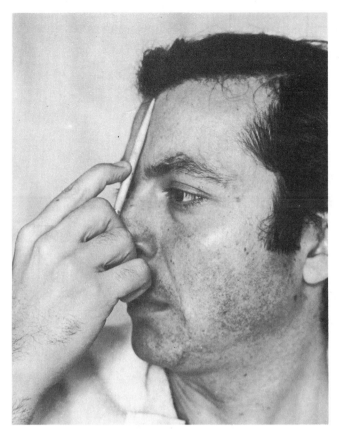

31. To evaluate the length of the face, first measure from the hairline to the eyebrow.

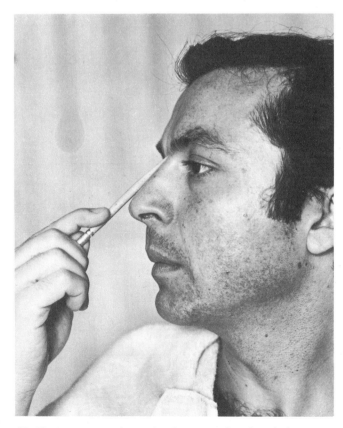

32. Next measure from the brow to the tip of the nose. Compare this with the forehead measure.

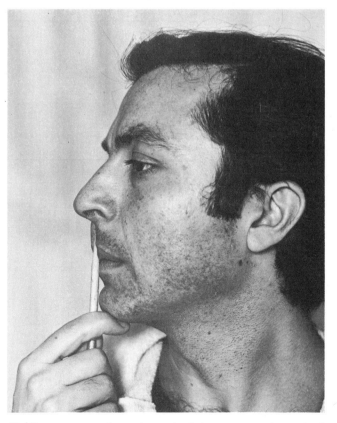

33. Now measure from the end of the nose to the end of the chin, and compare this to the first two measurements.

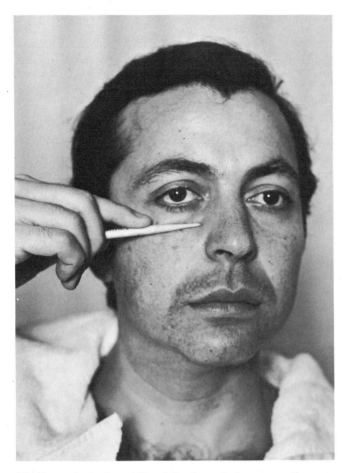

34. To evaluate the width of the face, first measure the eye.

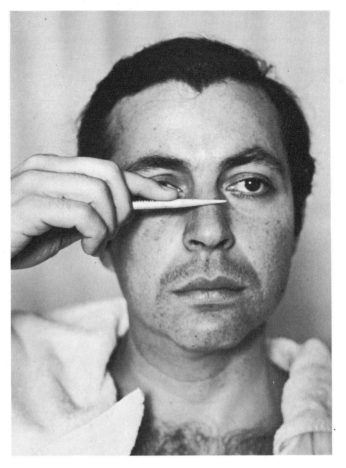

35. Gauge the space between the eyes.

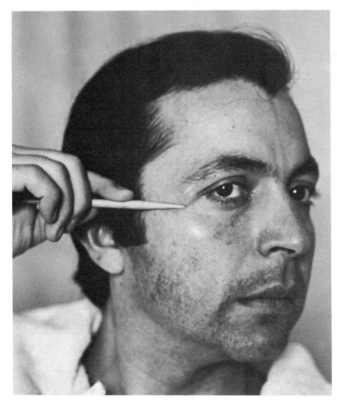

36. Next measure the space from the eye to the hairline.

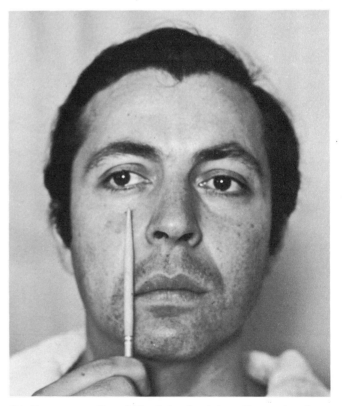

37. To measure the width of the lips, place the marker from the corner of the lips vertically to the eye.

If the forehead and nose areas are larger than the chin, we can cut down on the forehead by lowering the hairline, and we can also shorten the nose. (You cannot readily enlarge the chin area, any more than you can diminish it.)

Next, using a brush or a pencil as a gauge, let's consider the proportions in relation to the width of the face. Measure the face for its five eye widths (Figs. 34, 35, and 36). In almost all cases, today's eye proportions are much smaller than those attributed to the gods. With rare exceptions, we will make the eyes appear larger and further apart.

Finally, measure the width of your lips (Fig. 37). By extending the measure from the corner of the lip to the eye, the line should bisect the center of the pupil. Again, in most instances, mouths are smaller than those in Greek sculpture, so expect to extend the size of the mouth.

It is still too soon to explain exactly how you alter irregularities in your face. Once you have followed the demonstrations in this chapter, the makeup techniques involved in changing the face will make more sense to you. Therefore, I conclude this chapter with four face variations—round, lean, square, and diamond—showing in diagrammatic line drawings how to use the makeup techniques to transform these to the oval ideal. Perhaps yours is one of those shapes. For the time being, try to digest some of the principles discussed, and we will return to them again when we actually apply the makeup.

GRECIAN BASE

In all makeups, the base color is selected on the basis of the part, the lighting effects, and the size of the theater. For practice purposes, we will use a base color that you may find most frequently practical. We use a base grease paint to which we add rouge in order to give the base color the lively, vibrant color that youth evokes. In actuality, this base—with the addition of rouge—gives you an enormous range of healthy, youthful skin colors to choose from.

In this demonstration, we will practice using soft grease paint. Men will use dark tan soft grease (see chart on page 18); women will use olive soft grease.

Cleanse the face in the approved manner. Put about ½" of the soft paint in the palm of your hand. Muddle it with a fingertip and, with the same fingertip, touch light spots of the paint all over the face. Then, with a gentle moving touch, spread the paint evenly over the face, covering all areas you wish to make up. Make sure the base is spread evenly.

Cleanse the fingers and, touching the finger to the moist rouge, put light spots of color all over the base. Blend this rouge evenly into the base. Does the skin begin to have a healthy glow? Repeat the process. Add more rouge to the base in the same manner and blend again. You should be getting a healthy look. Do the same thing a third time. Now you should have a robust, ruddy color.

There is a specific reason for your adding the rouge in stages. First, it shows you graphically how the base color can be changed. And, by adding the rouge in

successive amounts, you avoid applying more than you need. Finally, you are learning how to control the development of your base color.

When you have obtained an extremely ruddy, florid skin tone, stop adding the rouge. Remove the paint from your fingers and wet both hands with water. Pat the base with your wet hands to remove the excess grease. If necessary, cleanse your hands and repeat the process until you achieve an even skin color, smooth, without heavy grease areas. Check around the eyes, nostrils, and mouth and, if you are satisfied, proceed with the next step.

SHADING THE JAW FOR OVAL EFFECT

We use rouge around the jaw to create the oval effect of the face. The rouge acts as a shadow. (We use red here for shading because it accentuates the youthful color at the same time.) The shading will alter the face to bring it closer to the oval. How much shading and where it is placed will, of course, depend on the actual contour of your face. You bring the shadow up to the point where the oval shape occurs.

With a small amount of the rouge on your brush, outline the inner point of the oval shape as it relates to your face. Apply the rouge lightly in a dotted line fashion. This is simply to show you the inner limit of the shading we will do next.

Now use the same rouge color to shade the jaw. In order to get a mental picture of what we intend to do next, examine the optical illusion illustrated in Fig. 7. Imagine the face as a round ball or as a tube. To create the effect of roundness, the shading should be darkest at the outside rim and blend in towards the center. We use the rouge in exactly the same manner. The rouge is darkest at the outside (the jaw) and then blended into the cheeks.

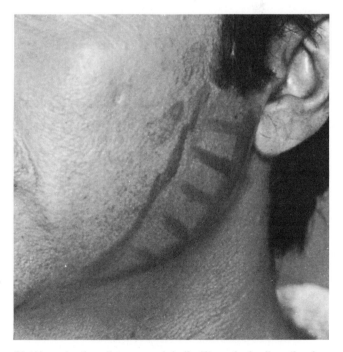

38. Here is the diagrammed indication of shading the jaw for the oval effect. The direction of blending always goes from the heaviest application towards the lightest.

39. In this illusion, two rectangles of the same size seem unequal because the border of the one on the right is darker.

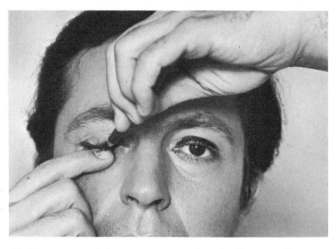

40. If you cannot keep your eyes closed with muscular control, then hold down the lid with your fingertip on the lashes as you draw with your pencil.

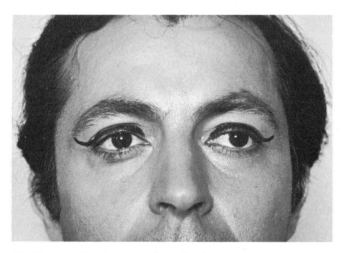

41. The eye line is drawn from the inner corner to the outer corner of the eye and then continued up toward the eyebrow for a good upward lift.

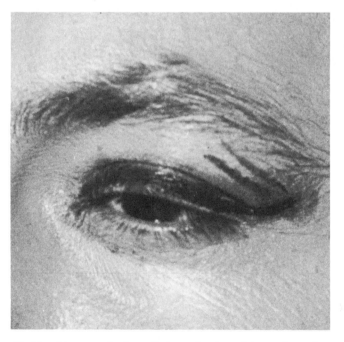

42. For the eye shadow, first apply the mixture along the black eye line, then up toward the eyebrow.

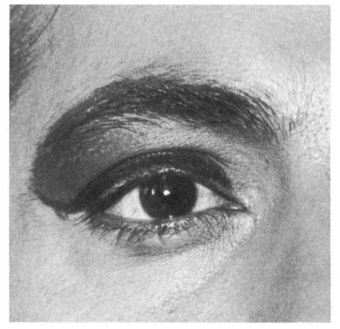

43. Here is the eye shadow blended.

With a fingertip, start by patting an application of rouge from the hairline to the jaw. (See Fig. 38.)

This application is the darkest tone of the rouge application. Using the fingertip, gradually blend this color up to the line you painted to create the oval shape. At this point, the rouge is to blend into the base color and disappears. We must not see a line. The rouge must graduate in tone from its darkest point, gradually diminishing until it blends and disappears into the base.

The dotted line itself blends and disappears into the base. The entire effect is designed to round and shade the face: the rouge grades from its darkest color, gradually lightening, until it blends into and disappears where the dotted lines were.

GREEK EYE

Now we are ready to paint the eyes so that they will appear larger and further apart. The eye will appear larger if its rim is darkened. Notice, for example, what happens to a rectangle when its edges are darker (Fig. 39).

As you work on the eye, keep it closed, with the muscular control of your eyelid. If you find this too difficult, keep the eye closed by holding your fingertip on the lashes (Fig. 40). Take the black eye lining pencil. Starting at the inside corner of the eye, draw a black line along the lashes (actually touching the lashes) and carry this line to the outer corner of the eye. Then open the eye and continue the line from the outer corner, out toward the ear, and up toward the eyebrow about ½" (Fig. 41). This line will actually be the most intense part of the shadow—which we apply in the next step. Be sure not to *continue* the line with your eye closed, because this will create an undesirable, sharp V at the corner of the eye.

Now that the line has been drawn, apply the eye shadow. The shadow helps create the illusion we are seeking: to enlargen each eye and to separate them from each other. For a natural shadow line, mix one part maroon to two parts brown lining color. Starting at the lash line, continuing beyond the eye and up, we will apply the shadow. First, with the fingertip, gently apply the shadow mixture along the black eye line. Clean the fingertip and then blend this shadow up toward the eyebrow. (See Figs. 42 and 43.)

You may encounter difficulty in this shading technique because you must blend the shadow in two directions at the same time: you blend up from the eyeline toward the eyebrow and you blend in toward the nose from its furthest point (close to the hairline). Painting this shape to the eye structure is the most difficult part of this work and requires practice.

PAINTING THE NOSE

The Greek nose is straight with an even bridge and with the sides of the bridge running parallel to each other down the nose.

At this point, evaluate your nose. Does it need lengthening? Then the shadows should be closer together. Should it be shortened? Then the bridge could

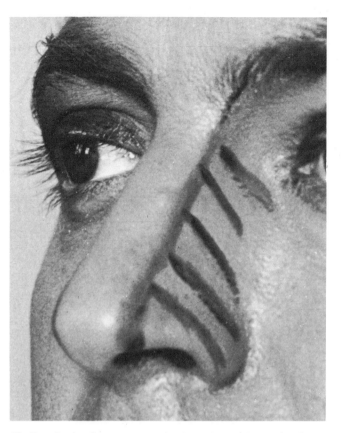

44. To shade the nose, apply the mixture from the inner corner of the eyebrow straight down the side of the nose.

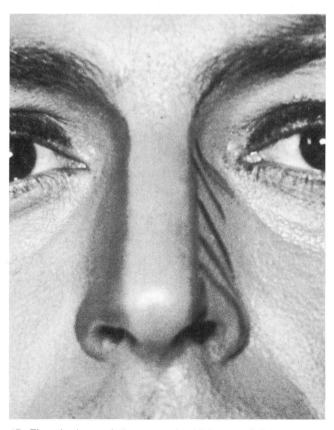

45. The shadows of the nose should be parallel to one another so that the nose appears straight and conforms in proportion to the classic Greek standard.

be a bit wider. (An average width for the nose is about ½″. Make it narrower or wider in proportion to the face.)

With shadow mixture on your fingertip, carry the shadow application from the inner corner of the eyebrow, or inner corner of the eye socket straight down the side of the nose (as in Fig. 44). Then blend this paint down the side of the nose, diminishing the intensity of the paint and making the paint disappear at the point where the nose joins the face.

After you have painted both sides of the nose, use a brush or ruler and hold it up along the nose to check whether your shadows are parallel to each other and to the center of the face (Fig. 45).

Noses are frequently uneven in shape and to various degrees off-center in relation to the face. You must alter this reality by painting the shadows straight down the center of the face, even if your nose is crooked.

EYEBROWS

The ultimate shape you choose for the eyebrow will depend on what altering effect you want to accomplish. For example, if you wish to lengthen the nose or diminish the forehead area, you will carry the nose above its own line and into the forehead, and raise the line of the eyebrows as well. If you want to lengthen that part of the face, draw a strong arching eyebrow. If you want to widen the face, moderate the curve to as horizontal a line as possible. (Refer to Chapter 2 for eyebrow variations and practice the gentle feathering strokes with your pencil.)

Use more than one color pencil to create the color tone you want. Always sketch in the directions of the hair growth, adding the pencil strokes first for the transparency of hairs and then for those parts you feel should be thicker, until the proper density is achieved. (See Fig. 46.)

UNDER THE EYE

To help define and project the total eye, frame the eye softly with a stroke of the eyebrow pencil at the lower lash line. Use a light or dark brown pencil if your base tones are light, and fair and a dark brown or black pencil for darker skin tone. Carry this toning to the outer corner of the eye and softly blend the edge to avoid the harsh effects of the line.

PAINTING THE CHEEK ROUGE

By shading the jaw we accentuated the over-all oval effect of the face. By applying cheek rouge, we tie the planes of the face together and continue toward the desired shaping. The blending technique for the cheek rouge is the reverse of that of the jaw rouge. In the latter, we blended from the furthest point toward the center. Here we blend from the center outwards.

The accurate placement of the cheek rouge is vital to reconstituting the new face. The exact placement of the rouge will vary with the shape of the face and the degree of alteration we are seeking. The final area covered will, in most cases, be oval shaped; in others, the shape may be as round as a ball. (See Fig. 47.)

As you recall, when we shaded the jaw for the oval effect, we shaded the application darkest at the outside, blending lighter toward the center. In shading the cheek rouge, however, we shade in the reverse, as illustrated earlier in Fig. 9. Our application of rouge is darkest in the center, gradually lightening and blending out until the color disappears into the base color.

Remember that while the rouge ties into the jaw shading and into the base, it must be strong enough so that its shape and color exist separately. Particularly avoid the danger of blending the cheek rouge and the jaw rouge into one homogeneous vast area of red. Each shading is separate but part of the whole.

46. The eyebrow, outlined here, is extended.

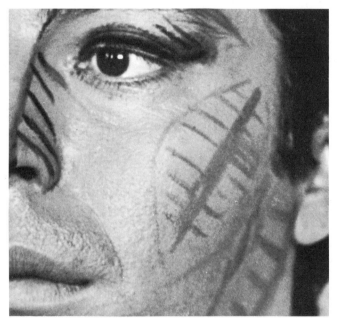

47. This is the area to be covered by cheek rouge. Note the direction of the heaviest application and the limits to which the rouge is to blend into the base.

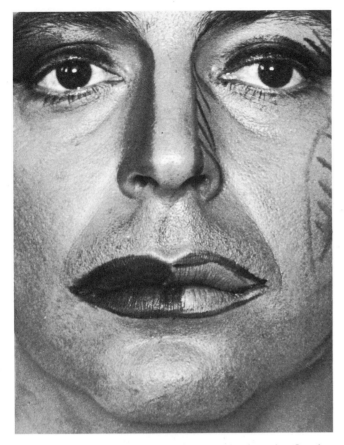 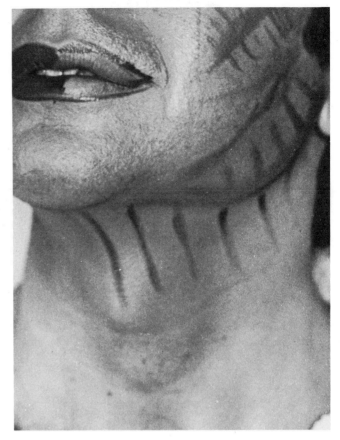

48. The mouth must be widened to conform to the Grecian standard. As you widen the mouth, you must also enlarge the size of the upper and lower lips.

49. The maroon shading under the jaw separates the face from the neck and removes a great deal of flesh from that area.

PAINTING THE MOUTH

In most cases, the mouth will have to be enlarged to conform to the size of the Grecian; that is, so the edges of the lips will be in line with the pupils of the eye. When you extend the shape of the mouth to the size appropriate to the Grecian makeup, the effect probably will startle and displease you at first. It takes time to get used to its greater size. Remember, the purpose of this makeup technique is to learn basic ways of altering the shape and size of the entire face. The mouth is an important part of the face for projecting expressions, and the ability to change its size and shape is most important for many roles. Actually, none of these effects need be used at their full size or strength, but understanding their full potential is the heart of this technique.

Keep in mind that when you widen the mouth, you must also increase the height of the upper and lower lips proportionately. (See Fig. 48.)

Enlarging the size of the mouth is particularly helpful when you want to diminish the size of the area from the base of the nose to the upper lip and from the lower lip to the chin. In other words, this technique can balance off disproportionate areas around the mouth.

Use the shadow mixture for the upper lip and the maroon liner for the lower lip. The reason for this is obvious: the upper lip is almost always undercut and therefore casts its own shadow. The lower lip always

projects into the light and is brighter in color. Use your brush to paint the lips. For the moment, don't concern yourself with shaping the inner areas of the lips. We will go into that in detail later on. Do not be afraid to paint over your own lip lines whenever necessary.

PAINTING BELOW THE CHIN

The area beneath the chin is frequently ignored by actors, yet it is extremely important in finishing off this makeup technique. It is, incidentally, also very easy to do. The shading has double value to anyone with a tendency toward jowls or overweight, since it removes a great deal of flesh from beneath the chin. Those who are slim will also benefit because this shading creates a separation of the face from the neck and strengthens the over-all look.

With the fingertip, apply the maroon paint at that point under the jawbone where your rouge started. Begin at the lobe of one ear and carry the maroon across the jaw to the other ear lobe. Blend this paint down onto the neck in sufficient color to create a frame for the face and then blend it to disappear into the base. (See Fig. 49.)

This now completes the application techniques. (See Fig. 50.) Powder the face to set the makeup and add appropriate wig and costume (Fig. 51).

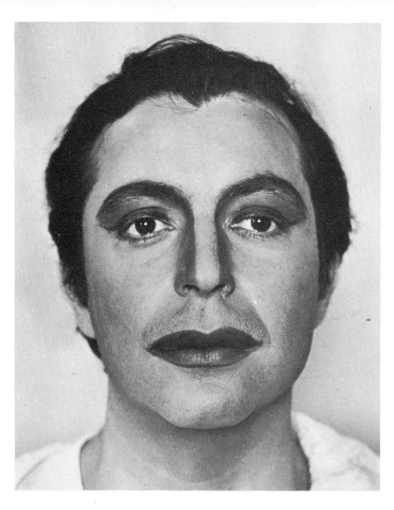

50. Here the painting of the Greek is complete.

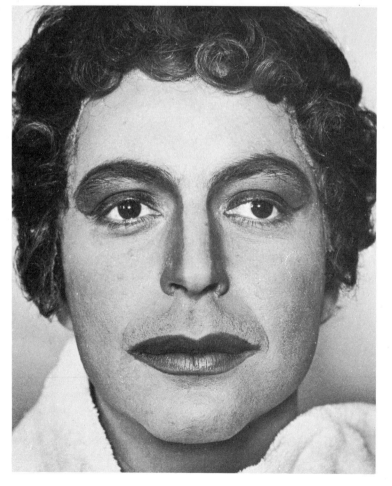

51. The wig is added for a new hairline.

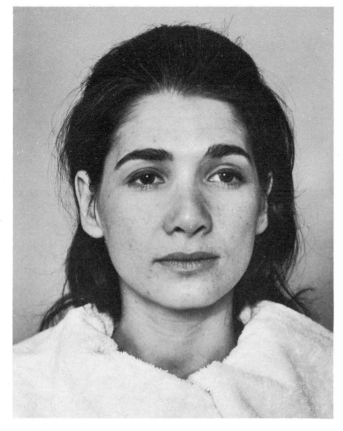

52. We will modify a classic Greek makeup for this model.

THE FEMALE PERFORMER

Although the steps here have been shown on a male actor, the stages are no different for the female performer (Figs. 52, 53, and 54). The makeup here has been modified slightly, false eyelashes have been added, but the stages are identical. (See also the color page in this chapter.)

False eyelashes have become part of the modern woman's wardrobe, and although I personally consider them rather unnecessary for the stage, I am willing to bow to the inevitable. To apply false lashes, spread a thin film of adhesive to the rim of the lash (Fig. 55 and 56). Hold the eye closed and place the lash along the eye line. Press gently into place. Open the eye, make sure the adhesive does not glue the corners together, then apply mascara to join the natural and the false eyelashes together.

The ultimate illusions may be softened and modified even more than is illustrated here. With practice, the most subtle effects can be obtained.

53. The same stages have taken place as with the male performer. Only false eyelashes have been added.

54. Notice that the shading is very subtle and the work is clean.

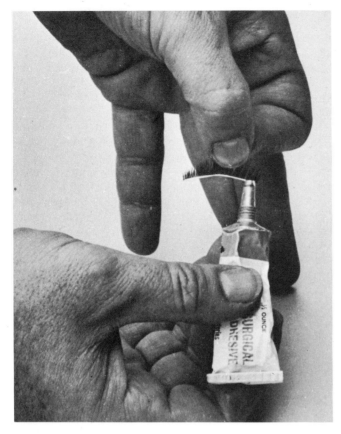

55. For false eyelashes, apply a thin layer of adhesive to the edge of the piece.

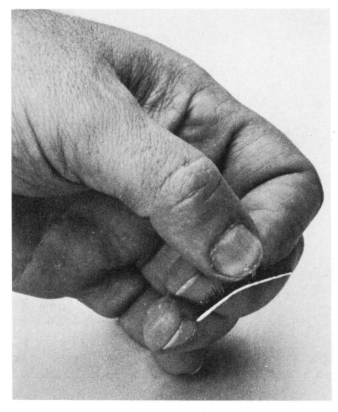

56. The application of adhesive must be thin, yet enough to enable the eyelash to adhere. Avoid too much adhesive or the eyelid will stick.

VARIATIONS IN HEAD SHAPE

Not all heads are as oval as those in the demonstrations in this chapter. If your face happens to vary in shape—being round, lean, square, or diamond shaped, for example—there are corrective measures you can take to alter the shape, to make it conform to the oval. The following line diagrams (Figs. 57 to 66) are designed to give you some direction in how to approach these variations.

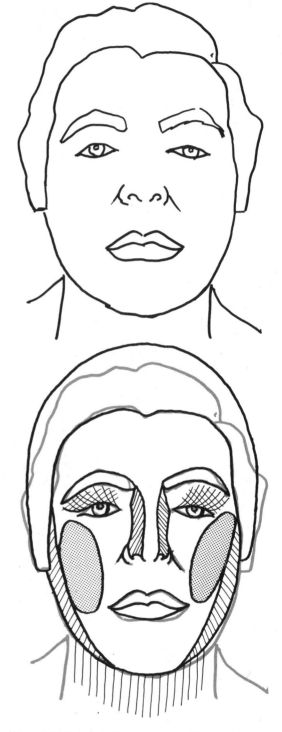

57. (Above) This is a fairly oval face, similar to the one used for the demonstration. **58.** (Below) This is the shading used in the demonstration; there are no extreme alterations necessary.

ROUND FACE

In this round face (Fig. 59), the mouth and nose areas are equal, but the forehead is larger than the other two areas.

Jaw Shading: To make the face more slender, the jaw shading should cover a large area of the face, from a point level with the eyebrow, extending down to a point directly below the corner of the mouth. This is blended to bring the face into the oval shape.

Eye Makeup: The eyebrows should be arched and lifted a bit into the ample forehead space. The eye shadow extends to the new brow, lifting up slightly.

Nose Shading: The nose should be carried up to the junction of the eyebrows, lengthening the nose.

Cheek Rouge: The cheek rouge should start below the outer corner of the eye and, running parallel to the oval shape, extend to below the corner of the mouth.

Mouth Painting: The mouth should arch roundly, using up some of the extra space available in the upper lip and chin areas.

Neck Shading: To separate the neck from the face, heavy shading is required, down and to include most of the visible neck area.

Hairline: The hairline equalizes the area of the mouth and nose areas. A new toupee or wig hairline should be used, giving as much height as possible to the face.

LEAN FACE

In this lean face (Fig. 61), the forehead and chin are larger than the nose area. You need to carry the nose up into the forehead and enlarge the mouth.

Jaw Shading: This face can take no jaw shading. Any shading will only diminish further whatever oval effect you already have.

Eye Makeup: The eyebrow should be arched in a strong horizontal direction, yet carried a bit into the forehead area. The eye shadow should extend to the new brow and should also be stronger horizontally.

Nose Shading: The nose shadow should carry up to the new eyebrow.

Cheek Rouge: The shading at the cheek should be completely horizontal, carrying from a point below the inner corner of the eye and extending almost to the ear.

Mouth Painting: The mouth should be full, with the upper lip arching up into the area above the mouth, yet dominated by a horizontal arch. The same is true of the lower lip extending down into the chin.

Hairline: Bangs should be used on the forehead, again horizontally, and the hair should fill out on each side of the head, especially filling in the jaw area. Dress the top of the head in a flat style, to diminish the length of the head.

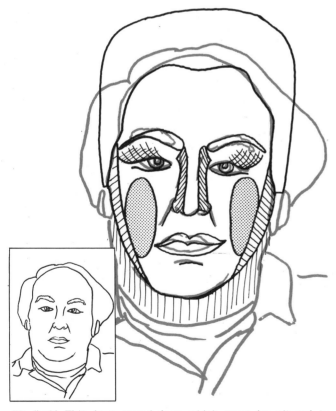

59. (Left) This is a round face which must be altered to conform to the oval shape. **60.** (Right) In the round face, the toupee, jaw shading, cheek rouge, neck shading, eyebrow line, eye shadow, nose, and mouth tend to lengthen and slim the face.

61. (Left) Here is a lean face. **62.** (Right) In the lean face, the shading and hairline emphasize the horizontal line so that the shape will approximate the oval.

DIAMOND FACE

In this diamond face (Fig. 63), the forehead and chin areas are larger than the nose area, so that it is necessary to lift the nose up a bit into the forehead and to diminish the chin area slightly.

Jaw Shading: The jaw shading involves only that small area from a point level with the eyebrow to a point just above the corner of the mouth. Shade this into the face to the point that creates the oval.

Nose Shading: Shadow the nose up to the eyebrow, then arch a new eyebrow from that point, lifting up a bit, then arching down gently.

Eye Makeup: Shadow the eye up to the new eyebrow.

Cheek Rouge: Carry the cheek rouge from the corner of the eye down vertically to a point level with the corner of the mouth.

Mouth Painting: Paint the mouth extending up into the lip area and below into the chin.

Hairline: Slight bangs will diminish the top of the hairline. Height is added to the hair, keeping it close to the ears, and filling in under the jaw.

SQUARE FACE

In this square face (Fig. 65), the three areas of the face are about equal. Your work should be directed to overcome the strong jaw.

Jaw Shading: The jaw shading should start at a point level with the corner of the eye and carry down the jaw to a point just below the outer corner of the eye. This shades up to the oval point on the face.

Nose Shading: The nose carries up to the eyebrow and a new brow starts and arches a bit into the brow, lifting at the outer corner.

Eye Makeup: The eye shadow carries to the new brow, also lifting at the outer corner.

Cheek Rouge: The cheek rouge starts level with the corner of the eye and runs parallel to the oval shape, to a point level with the corner of the mouth.

Mouth Painting: The mouth is full, arching roundly, and using up some of the jaw space.

Hairline: The hair style should lift high on top. Keep the line close to the sides, and, if possible, comb the hair to cover as much jaw as possible.

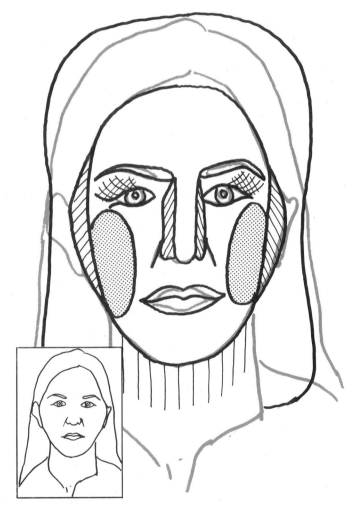

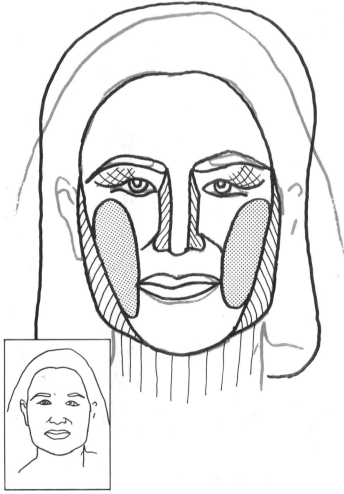

63. (Left) In the diamond shaped face, the forehead and chin areas are larger than the nose area. **64.** (Right) The shading enlarges the nose area and slims the chin and forehead areas.

65. (Left) In the square face, the jaw is too strong. **66.** (Right) The shading and hairline diminish the jaw and strengthen the forehead.

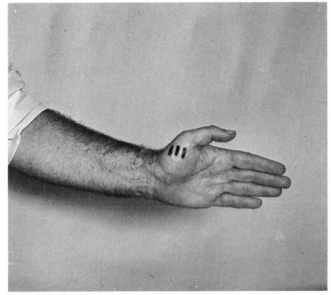

Shadow mixture for classic Greek: one part maroon to two parts brown.

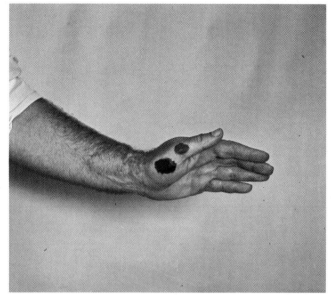

Shadow now mixed and rouge for jaw blending is placed on the palette.

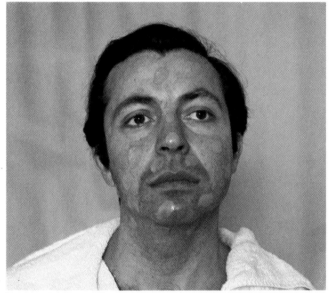

Base color is spotted onto the face before it is worked into the skin.

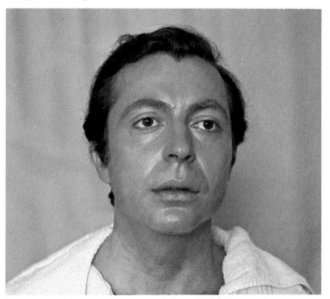

The base color is evenly spread on the face.

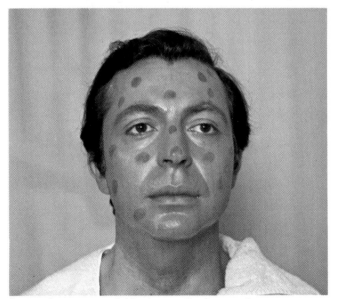

Spots of rouge are dabbed over the base color.

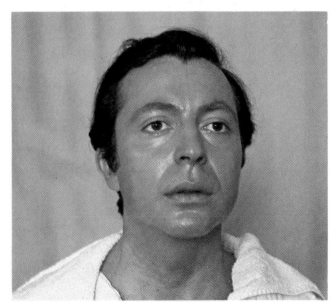

The rouge is blended into the base to redden the color.

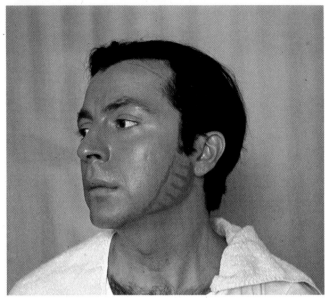

The area of jaw shading is defined and the direction of shading indicated.

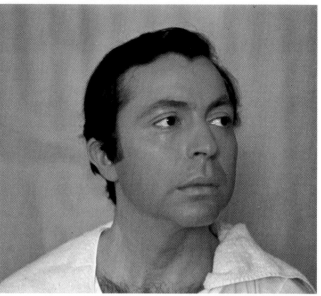

The jaw is shaded and properly blended to disappear into the base.

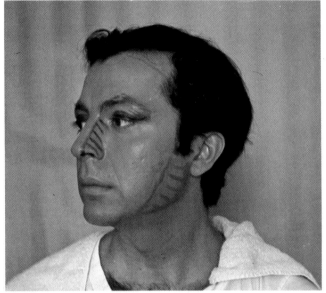

The nose and eye shadow placement is shown, with direction of blending indicated.

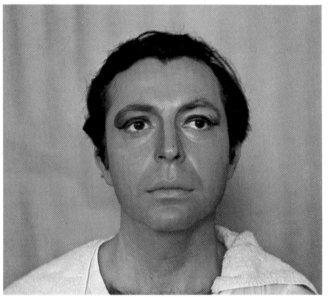

The nose and eye shadow are blended.

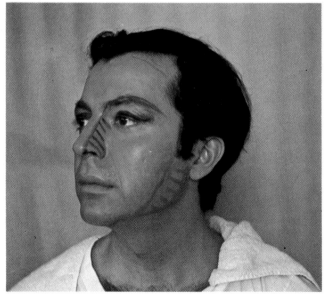

The placement of the eyebrow is shown and painted.

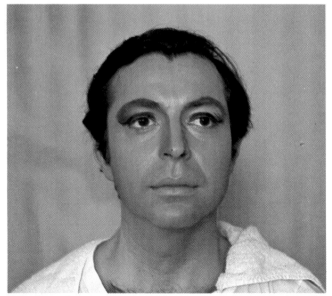

Note how the new eyebrow is above and longer than the original.

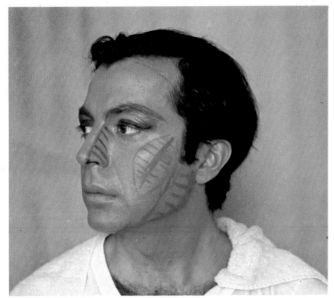

The placement of the cheek rouge, and its direction of blending is shown.

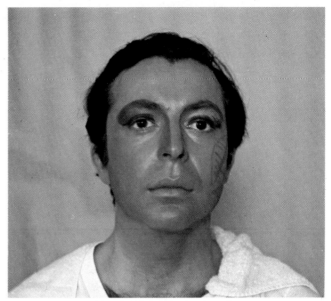

Cheek rouge is blended into the base color.

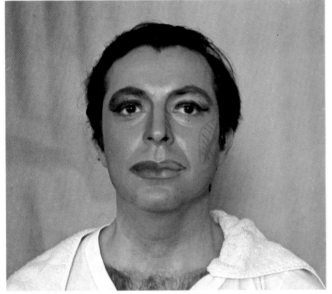

The outline and painting of the new mouth.

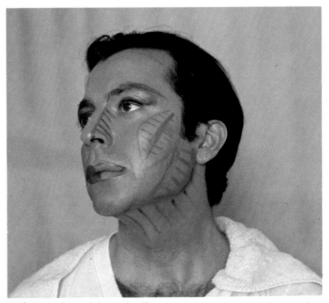

Under neck and jaw shading, showing extent and direction of blending.

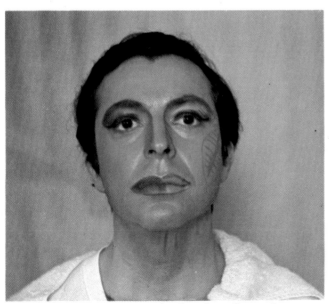

The neck shading separates the face from the neck.

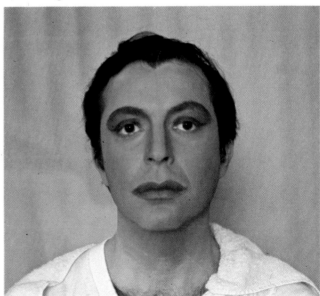

Blending is complete and makeup is powdered.

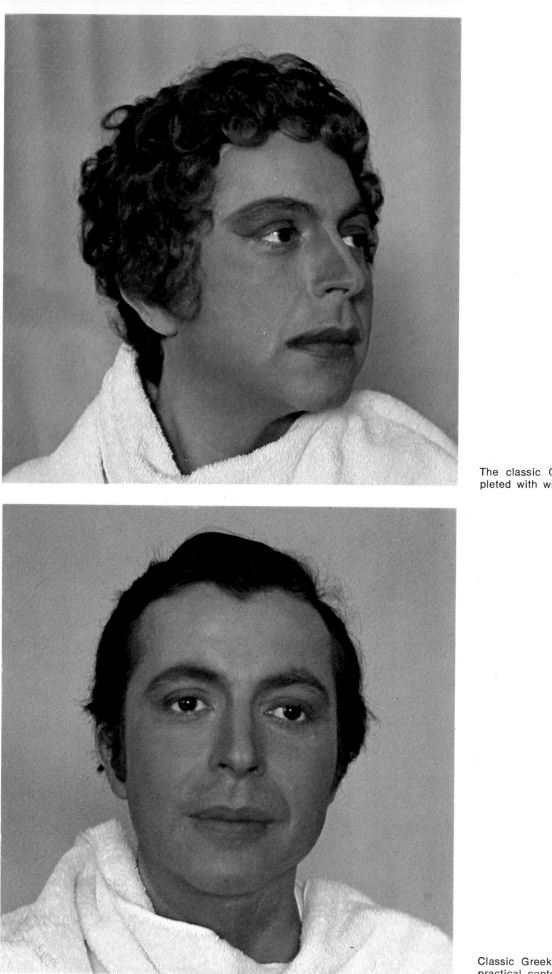

The classic Greek is now completed with wig.

Classic Greek, modified to more practical contemporary usage.

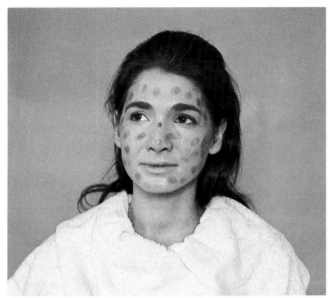

The base has been applied and the rouge spots added to redden base.

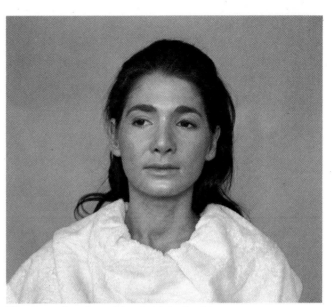

The rouge has been blended into the base.

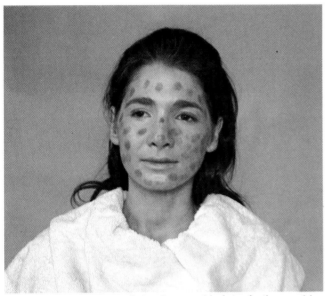

Additional rouge spots have been added to further redden the base.

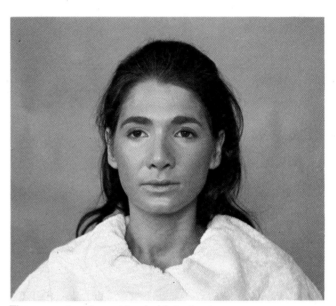

The rouge has been blended into the base.

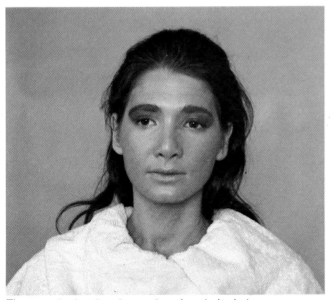

The eye shadow has been placed and shaded.

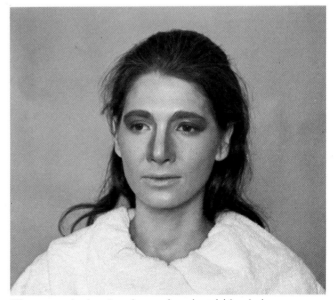

The nose shadow has been placed and blended.

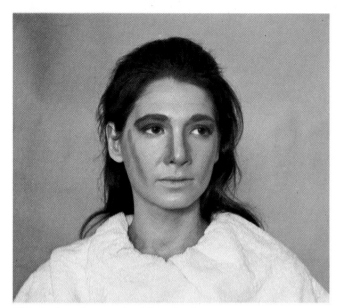

This is the placement of the cheek rouge.

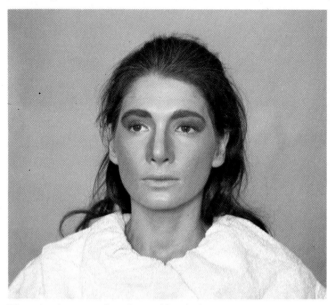

The cheek rouge has been blended.

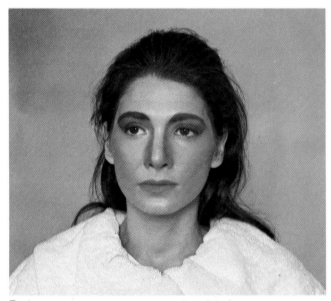

Eyebrows are penciled and mouth painted.

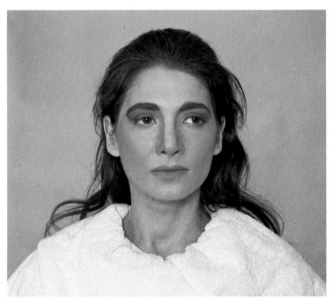

The neck shading has been added and makeup powdered.

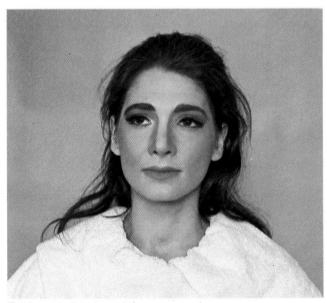

Falsh eyelashes have been added.

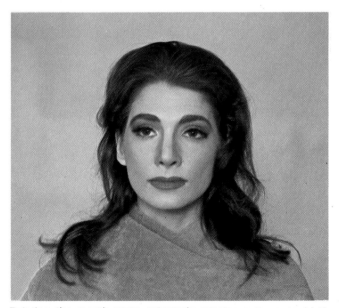

Painting the mouth more extremely creates a more sophisticated character.

Lifting the hair adds length to the face.

The makeup is complete. Note the soft blending of all paint.

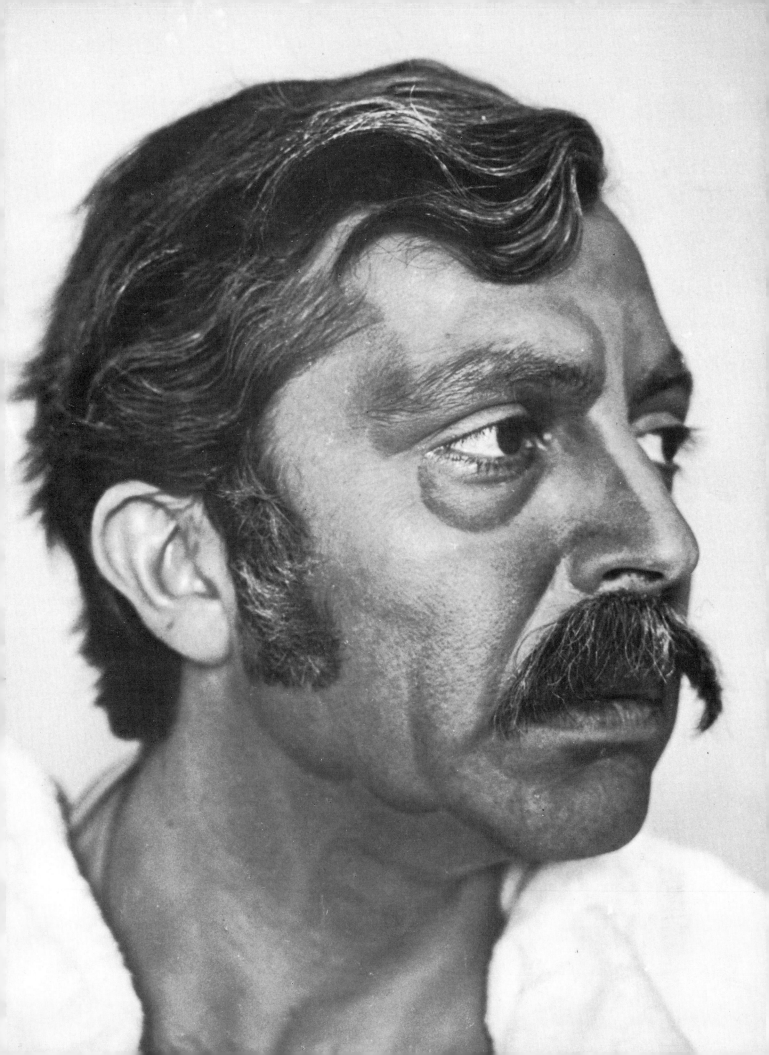

CHAPTER FOUR

AGING

The body at maturity is generally at its finest and healthiest. The muscles are strong and resilient, and the skin is firm and taut. Aging begins after the individual achieves full mature growth. It is a slow, progressive process and requires a good number of years to effect an appreciable change. The muscles become softer, more flaccid, less elastic, and the skin slowly stretches. This stretched skin still covers the same bone and muscle frame as in the younger years so that the excess skin begins to fall into the bony crevices of the face to form hollows. Where the bone is prominent, the skin sags into folds of flesh, forming what we call wrinkles, bags, pouches, or jowls.

As the performer, you must determine what phase of the aging process relates to your role, and adapt the appropriate makeup techniques to convey the age of your part.

The first signs of "aging" become evident in the late twenties. We consider the late twenties to about forty years the start of the aging process, forty to sixty years as the developed aging process, and sixty years and over as extreme old age.

UNDER FORTY YEARS OLD

The early stage of aging is the most difficult to convey through makeup. It demands a very slight indication of the aging process. There may be a beginning of the sinking process in the temple and cheek area, and a beginning of the aging around the eyes, plus a slight nose wrinkle.

All too frequently when actors attempt to communicate the start of age in the character they are playing, they fall into a ridiculous stereotype and apply gray to the temples, lines across the forehead, crow's feet at the corner of the eyes, and call that a makeup job! Although it is possible for an individual forty years or younger to have gray hair, no one of that age has yet developed absurd wrinkles across the forehead.

You must learn to recognize the slight, almost imperceptible differences that occur in the human face over the years and use makeup technique judiciously. Observe older people around you and look for sagging corners around the mouth, loss of teeth, thinning hair, and flabby flesh from gaining weight.

MAKEUP BASE FOR AGE

There is no specific makeup base for a category as broad as age. An aging person may have skin color in any range of human skin tones. Select your color according to the total demands of the part, the size of the theater, and the effect of the lights.

In order to demonstrate the application of age makeup, use a dark tan hard stick (see chart on page 18). It is a good color to show the contrast of your shadow and highlight work, and it will give you practice in handling hard stick, but don't get into the habit of always associating this color or this type base with age. It is fine if the part you are playing calls for a ruddy, robust, dark tan color, but only if you think it is appropriate on those terms.

Get in the habit of using a variety of colors for your skin tone in age and adjust your shadow highlight colors accordingly.

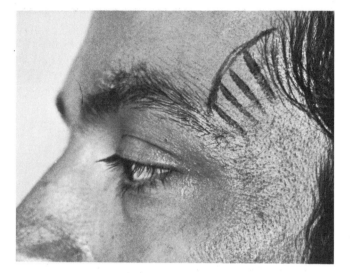

67. Place the line of the shadow at the temple bone: from the crest of the brow bone into the hairline.

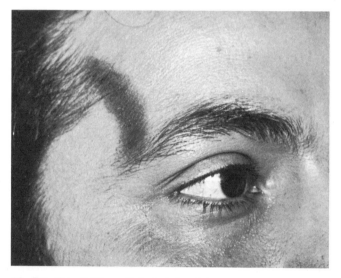

68. Pat the shadow mixture into place.

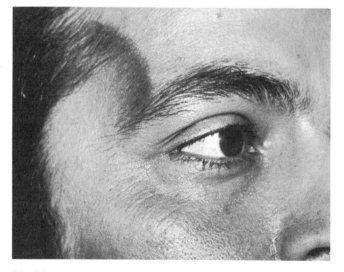

69. After cleaning your finger, gently blend the shadow towards the hairline.

SHADOWS

There are many possible shadow mixtures which you can properly use for the aging process. For practice purposes, we will use a mixture of one part maroon soft liner to two parts brown soft liner. This shadow mixture works well for many stage makeups. Don't hesitate to alter it even if you feel that it's too brown, too red, or too dark. You must learn to adjust all of these colors to your needs.

HIGHLIGHTS

As in shadows, highlights come in a great range of colors. For practice purposes, I suggest you use a hard stick whitish yellow. You will find it appropriate for a good range of highlight purposes and you can always mix it with other colors to adjust to your needs. And, again, it will give you practice in handling a hard stick highlight.

APPLYING THE BASE

Cleanse the face with cream to remove any soot, grime, or cosmetic. Remove the cream gently, and take off even the faintest film on the skin. The skin must feel clean, smooth, but without any trace of grease.

First, remove the hard grease paint stick from its cardboard container. Then remove the cellophane paper cover from the top half of the stick. Using the blunt, front end of the stick, apply a wide streak of paint across the top of the forehead, another across the center of the forehead, and a third above the eyebrow. Apply a streak down the nose, across each of the cheekbones, across the upper lip, across the chin, the line of the jaws, and a few streaks down the neck. Now, with the fingertips, gently spread this color so that it covers all surfaces of the face evenly and is also lightly carried into the hairline. Once it is spread evenly, the color will have no light, dry splotchy areas, or darker, excessively greasy areas.

Now cleanse your fingertips with tissues and then dampen the fingers and palms of your hand with water. Without rubbing, gently pat the face, until all of the excess grease is removed from the face and is on the palms of your hands. If you have applied too much base, cleanse your hands and repeat this process.

After the excess grease is removed, the skin should have the color you desire and a natural skin tone as well. There should be enough of the paint on the skin to make it easier to work on. Too *little* base will show as an uneven skin tone, and too *much* will smear.

SINKING THE TEMPLE

With your fingertip, feel the edge of the temple bone and follow its path as it goes from the corner of the eye up into the hairline. Become familiar with its placement. With your fingertips, gently pat the shadow into place, following the bottom edge of the temple bone (Figs. 67 and 68). Cleanse your finger and, with a gentle patting, blend the shadow back towards, but not *into* the hairline (Fig. 69).

SINKING THE CHEEK

With the fingertip, feel out the depression between the cheekline and the jawbone. It is not a sharp, sudden sinking—like the temple—but a gradual sinking from the height of the cheekbone into the hole (occupied by the back teeth), and then out onto the jaw. Since this area is covered by flesh, the sinking is actually not so dramatic. It will be about 1″ to 1½″ in length between the cheek and jaw and, when fully blended, will be less than 1″ in width. (See Fig. 70.)

With the fingertip, apply shadow to this area (Fig. 71). Clean your finger, then blend the top half up and off into the base, and the bottom half down and off into the base. (See Fig. 72.)

70. Locate the sinking of the cheek, a gradual depression from the height of the cheekbone, into the hole, and out onto the jaw.

71. Apply shadow to the sinking area of the cheek.

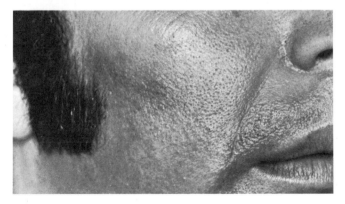

72. Blend in the shadow by gently patting the mixture, blending it into the base.

PAINTING THE NOSE WRINKLE

The nose wrinkle has a width of varying size. It begins at the edge of the nostril line, gradually widens to its widest point about level with the bottom of the nostril, and then gradually tapers down to a point near the lip.

With a flat sable brush, pick up a small quantity of the appropriate shadow mixture and apply it with the edge of the brush, starting at the inside of the nostril and extending down to below the mouth (Fig. 73). Clean the brush. Use the flat side of the brush to carry the paint in the wrinkle line up towards the nose and up towards the cheek.

Blend this paint with your fingertips so that it is darkest along the original line and gradually becomes lighter until it disappears into the base. (See Fig. 74.)

With your fingertips, apply the high paint highlight at the crest of the wrinkle and follow its shape for the full length. This highlight is blended both towards and away from the wrinkle until it disappears into the base, remaining strongest at its original point of application. The width of this highlight at its widest point is no more than ½″.

With the flat side of the brush, apply the contrast highlight, just below the dark line of the nose wrinkle, touching the darkest point of the shadow for its full length. Blend this paint towards the mouth first with the brush and then with a finger. Finally, check the wrinkle at its end point, and if it ends abruptly or is too conspicuous, blend it so that the end disappears into the base. (See Figs. 75 and 76.)

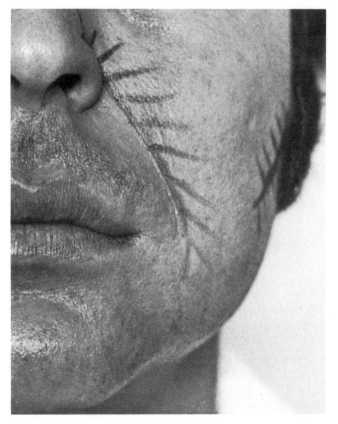

73. The nose wrinkle begins at the edge of the nostril line and continues down to about the line of the lips. Notice how the shadow seems to fan out.

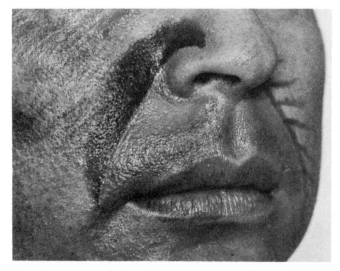

74. Blend the shadow mixture so that the line is darkest at the original line and disappears into the base.

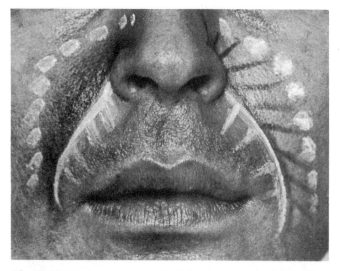

75. Highlights are now applied to the nose wrinkle: first, at the crest of the wrinkle, well onto the cheek, and secondly below the wrinkle.

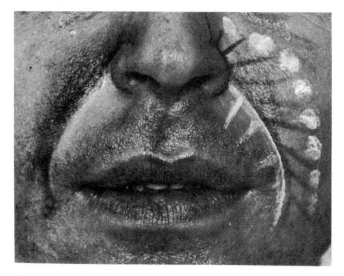

76. The highlights on the cheek are blended towards and away from the wrinkle, no wider than ½" at the widest point. The contrasting highlight is blended towards the mouth.

PAINTING THE CHEEK-CHIN WRINKLE

To locate this wrinkle accurately, pull your chin into your neck and grin widely (Fig. 77). Although the fold you see running from the cheek to the chin is the wrinkle you wish to paint, you cannot do so in the grinning position. Since your flesh is stretched, if you paint it and then relax your face, you will find that the wrinkle is incorrectly placed. So determine its position and then relax the face before applying the makeup.

With the flat side of the sable brush, pick up a small quantity of the shadow and—starting on one side of the face at a point close to the depth of the cheek hollow—apply the paint with the edge of the brush. Carry the paint down the face under the chin, and up the other side of the face. Clean the brush. With the flat side of the brush, blend the paint towards the mouth. Start at the top point, gradually widen to the widest point under the chin, and gradually diminish up to the other side. Blend this paint with a fingertip so that it graduates in intensity from its darkest hue at the point of application to the point where it disappears into the base. (See Fig 78.)

Apply a high point highlight to its crest. Blend this highlight both towards the wrinkle and towards the mouth so that it disappears into the base, varying from ⅛" to ½" at its widest. Apply the contrast highlight. Touching the darkest point of the shadow, blend this away from the direction of the wrinkle. Make sure that the beginning and end of the wrinkle disappear into the face. Always check for splotches in the grading of both shadow and highlight. (See Fig. 79.)

PAINTING THE TOP HALF OF EYE

In order to understand the variety of ways to paint the area above the eye, you must consider the three separate parts of that structure: (1) the eyeball and its socket; (2) the prominent bone above the eye; (3) the hollow next to the nose.

First sink the eyeball. With your brush, pick up a small quantity of the appropriate shadow. You will use the edge of the brush to paint the deepest point of the shadow. Start at one corner of the eye, continue along the top part of the eyeball until you reach the edge of the bone at the eye socket. (Fig. 80.)

Clean the brush. With the flat side of the brush, blend the paint towards the eyeball and then blend with the fingertip until it disappears into the base. Apply the high point highlight along the lid, and blend this into the base. Powder this area very lightly so that this work will not blur while you paint the rest of the eye.

Now follow the same area, this time blending in the opposite direction.

With your brush, apply the shadow mixture along the top part of the eyeball, as you have just done. Follow the shape of the eye bone up towards the brow and then around and down into the eye socket area and then around and up the eye bone towards the outer edge of the eye. Blend the shadow towards the corner of the eye and up towards the brow, exactly the opposite direction you blended earlier. With your fingertip, blend the paint to shape the roundness of

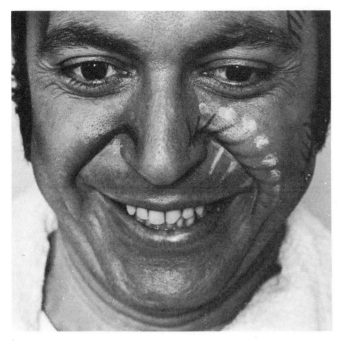

77. To locate the cheek-chin wrinkle, pull in your chin and grin widely.

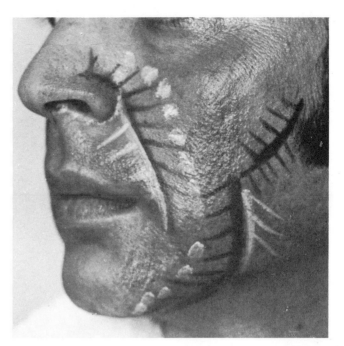

78. Starting at the origin of the cheek-chin wrinkle, apply shadow down the face under the chin. Apply both high point and contrasting highlights.

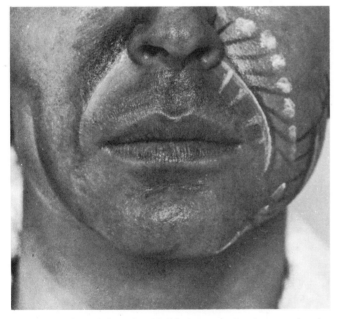

79. Blend the high point highlight towards the mouth; the contrasting highlight away from the wrinkle.

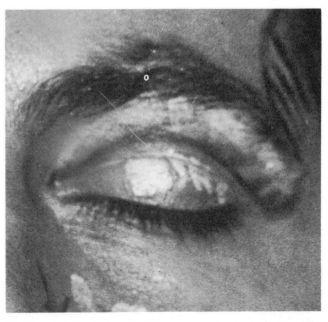

80. To paint the top part of the eye, apply shadow along the top part of the lid and highlight along the lid.

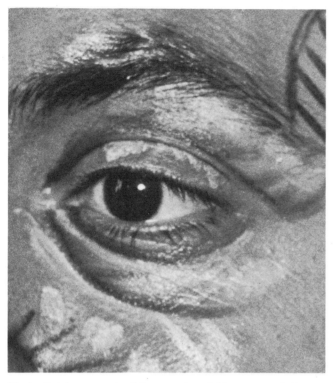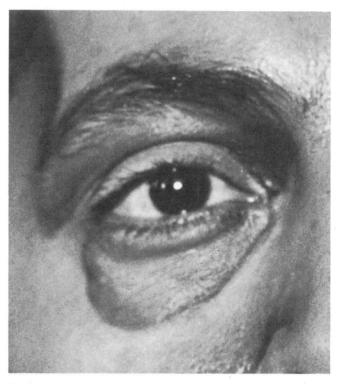

81. In the lower part of the eye two folds are created: one just under the eyeball and a pouch below that.

82. Here the lower and upper part of the eye are blended.

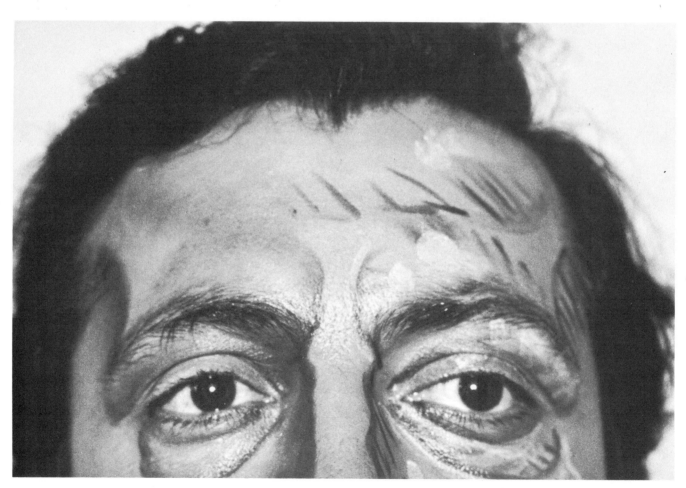

83. The frown wrinkle is created first on the forehead, and the rest of the forehead is shaped with shadow and highlights, giving the impression of greater bone prominences.

the bone. Put a high point highlight on the bone. Blend this into the base. Finally, apply shadow to the deepest point of the eye hollow in the corner of the nose and blend the shadow out to meet the other areas of shadow application. Powder the entire eye before proceeding further.

PAINTING BELOW THE EYE

In aging, the lower part of the eye also involves more than a single structure. Just as we did in the area above the eye, first we will consider the lower part of the eyeball and its socket.

With your brush, apply the appropriate shadow just below the eye, following the shape of the eyeball just under the lower lid (Fig. 81). This paint is then blended up towards the eyeball into the base. The high point highlight is applied at the eyelid, just below the eyeball, and blended into the base.

In the lower eyeball area, use a contrast highlight and apply it next to the shadow, blending it down from the eye and into the base.

Next, we form the eye pouch or eye bag. This hanging fold of flesh may be varied, according to your preference, to extend from the inner corner of the eye, halfway to the outer corner, or it can extend three quarters of the way, or it may extend all the way to the outer corner of the eye as shown here.

To create this lower fold, apply shadow with the brush, starting from the inner corner of the eye, and extend it down as far as you wish the bag to go (Fig. 81). The shadow is then blended up towards the eyeball with the brush, and is blended into the base. The contrast highlight applied underneath the eyeball structure will be sufficient for a high point highlight in this structure. The lower fold requires a contrast highlight below, which blends down and away from the fold. (See the completed eye in Fig. 82.)

FROWN WRINKLES

The small folds in the forehead—the frown wrinkles—ought to be accurate. They are more pronounced in the aging face than in the youthful one. Make the depressions as the role demands: they can be light in tone, or dark and intense, depending on the effect you wish. They should *not* be symmetrical or equal.

With a small amount of paint on the brush, shape the fold at the frown line. This can be found by frowning strongly and by then relaxing the forehead. Carry the line into the deep sinking of the eye. Blend it up and around into the base. Give the wrinkles a light high point highlight and a light contrast highlight. These small wrinkles act as a starting point for shaping the prominent eyebrow bone sinking to follow.

Age also affects the forehead itself. The flesh, as it sags, reveals the bones in the forehead. This should be conveyed in the makeup as well. With a small amount of the appropriate shadow color on your fingertip, lightly pat a continuation of each frown wrinkle around the deepest point of the prominent bone above each of the eyes. Carry this bit of shading all the way around the eye to where the depression joins the

temple sinking. Gently blend this shading down and in towards the eye and accentuate it with a high point highlight above the eyebrow. Do the same with the massive round bone prominences in the center of the forehead.

Now move to the upper part of the forehead. Start with the fingertip at one side of the head where the bone emerges from the hairline. Shape it down, across the forehead, and across the other side. Blend this shading in towards the center and add a prominent high point highlight. The forehead should be shaded in the manner shown in Fig. 83.

Notice that those areas of the forehead not shaped by the shadow become more obvious and conspicuous, since they are of a lighter base color. It's necessary to subdue and minimize these areas by gently shading them so that they give the illusion of sinking to a point below the prominences.

The common practice of just painting lines across the forehead is false and unreal. Remember, it is only at an advanced stage of old age that the skin of the forehead stretches sufficiently to create wrinkles of its own *while the forehead is in repose.* In less elderly faces, the wrinkles are formed only when the eyebrows are lifted.

NOSE

The shape of the nose can be altered considerably with paint alone. It may be made to appear slimmer, wider, larger, or shorter. For our purposes, in this natural development of age, I suggest we simply follow the natural shape of the nose. To do so, apply the appropriate shadow with your fingertip lightly along the natural edge of the nose bridge. Avoid a sharp edge. Then, blend this shadow down the side of the nose and over the nostril to that point where the nose joins the face, at which point the shadow disappears and blends into the base. (See Fig. 84.)

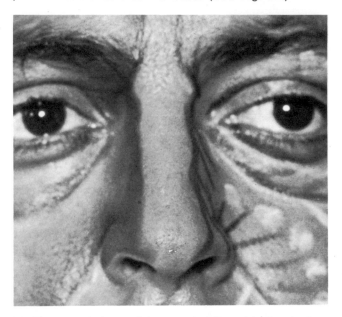

84. The natural shape of the nose is followed in the shading. The shadow disappears into the base where the nose joins the face.

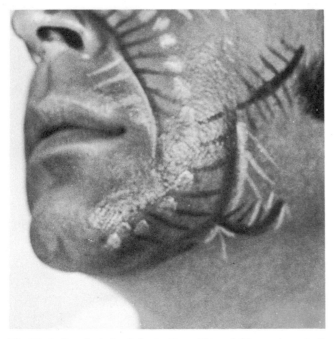

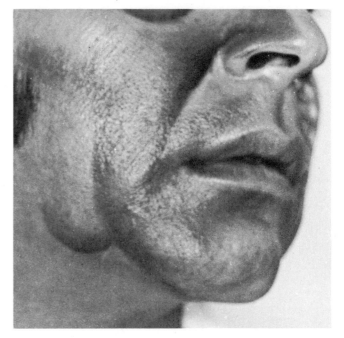

85. Start the first jowl from the chin wrinkle and arch it around toward the cheek. Apply high point highlight on the jowl, and contrast highlight in the triangle where the jowl joins the chin wrinkle.

86. Here is the first jowl blended. Note that the edges are not too sharp.

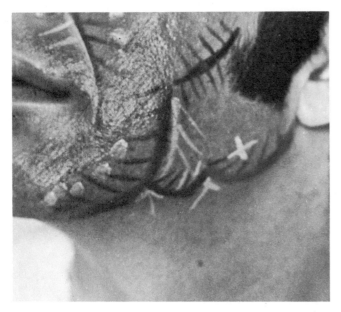

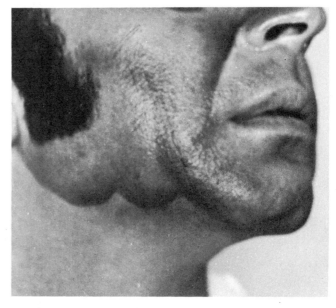

87. The second jowl is larger and runs to behind the ear. Apply highlights in the same manner as in the first jowl.

88. Blended carefully, the jowls are like two hanging sacks.

PAINTING THE FIRST JOWLS

The jowls are more difficult to understand than they are to paint. One of the most common errors is to paint them like scallops, but they are actually hanging folds of flesh, which frequently hang from and over the jawbone, like sacks. Positioning these folds is difficult and requires practice and observation.

Working with a hand mirror in addition to the regular mirror will help you in painting jowls, so that you can see the painted effect in full profile. This way, you can be sure of its success.

Put the shadow on your brush. Start the first jowl, touching the chin wrinkle from ¼" to ⅜" up from the jaw. Carry the paint down the jaw, shape a sag, and arch it around on the jaw, and up towards the cheek, again lifting it no more than from ¼" or ⅜" above the jawbone. Blend the paint up into the base with your fingertip, the heaviest application towards the front. Apply the high point highlight and blend it into the base.

The contrast highlight is applied only in the little triangles where the jowls join the wrinkles and where it joins the next large jowl to be painted. Don't carry the contrast highlight along the full length of the jowl. Instead, soften the sharp edge of the mid-jowl so that it doesn't appear too sharp and destroy the effect you desire. (See Figs. 85 and 86.)

SECOND JOWLS

The second and larger jowl starts in the same manner as the first. This one runs down along the jawbone all the way up to and behind the ear. Blend this jowl in the same way you did the first. Since it is larger, the area to be painted is larger. However, don't be tempted to use any darker or greater intensity of paint. (See Figs. 87 and 88.)

Paint the two sides of the face as mirror opposites. Learn to observe carefully. The jowl is deceptively difficult to paint and must be used with discretion. It is usually a sign of more advanced age or is evident in middle aged people who tend toward stoutness. Don't over-use the jowls, but introduce them whenever the role seems to call for these characteristics.

NECK

You would be amazed at the vast number of actors whose aging process stops at the jawbone. Although it may not be a very expressive part of the face, the neck ages just like all the other parts of the body.

First, shadow both sides of the windpipe and blend again toward the center and highlight the center (Fig. 89). Next create a few folds down the length of the windpipe and blend these up into the base and highlight (Fig. 90). Next shade both top and bottom of the large neck muscle cords (Fig. 91). Blend these shadows toward the center and highlight in the middle. The two large triangle shaped areas between the neck cords and the windpipe must be subdued and sunken in the same manner and for the same reason as the empty areas of the forehead were.

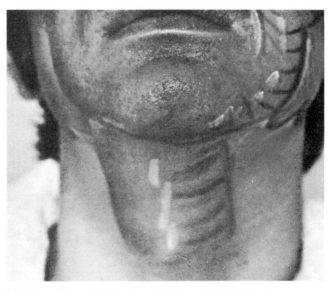

89. Here the windpipe is shaded and highlighted.

90. Add a few folds down the length of the throat pipe.

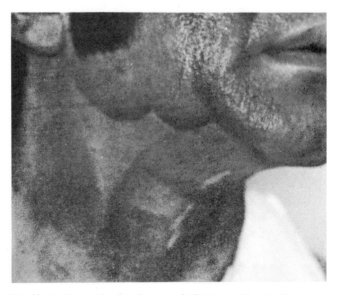

91. Next the neck muscles are indicated with shading.

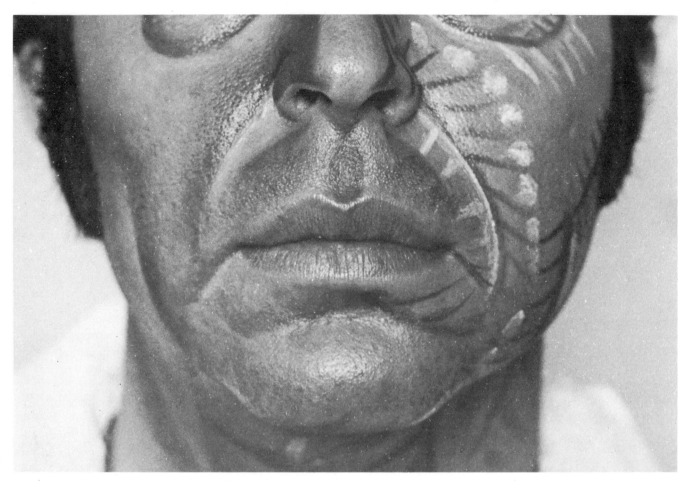

92. The area around the mouth is aged. A fold is created below the mouth, folds at the corners of the mouth, a wrinkle under the chin, and the cleft over the upper lip.

PAINTING THE CHIN AREA

The aging in and around the chin is softer and more subtle than those areas with more prominent folds. Folds tend to occur in areas where there is a dominant bone structure. Sagging flesh falls from these bony prominences. The area under the mouth is one such structure: a bony mass of chinbone and the teeth. The flesh covering this bony mass is what we work on to create our aging effect.

With a brush, apply appropriate shadow mixture under the center of the mouth and shape it down and around the fold of flesh under the lower lip. With a gentle patting technique, blend with your fingertip, lightly following the shape of the fold. Diminish the intensity of the paint as you reach the point outside the mouth. Blend this shadow up towards the lip and out towards the outer corners of the mouth. Apply a light high point highlight to the highest point of the mouth and blend this into the base.

At the corners of the mouth you may create a small sagging fold of flesh using the wrinkle technique. Here, however, you are working in a much smaller area than you've done previously, and you will be creating a much smaller fold of flesh. Therefore, use a less intense amount of shadow than you did in the major wrinkles. (See Fig. 92.)

PAINTING AREA ABOVE THE LIP

The area below the nose and above the upper lip presents a definite problem in making up the aging character. The area is comparatively firm—which means there are no major wrinkles—yet it cannot be ignored. The cleft below the nose and above the upper lip is a most difficult area to recreate. It is a natural hollow and its appearance is constantly changing because of the light that casts its own natural shadow on the cleft. In creating the cleft, we can only show the shadow as it is cast from one side. With a brush, apply a small amount of shadow along one ridge of the cleft, starting at a point beneath the nose and shaping around and down towards the top of the upper lip. Blend this paint in towards the center of the upper lip where it will disappear into the base. Soften the outer edge so that it does not present too soft or too harsh a line.

With your fingertip, lightly shape the appropriate shadow on the portion of the upper lip that forms the *movable part* of the mouth. Blend this down towards the mouth, making sure the shadow has no evidence of an edge. Then give it a soft high point highlight. (See Fig. 92.)

The painted effect is now complete. Powder the face and take a good look (Figs. 93 and 94).

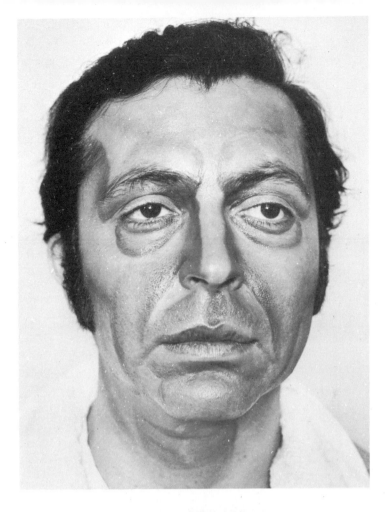

93. The completed painted effect of aging.

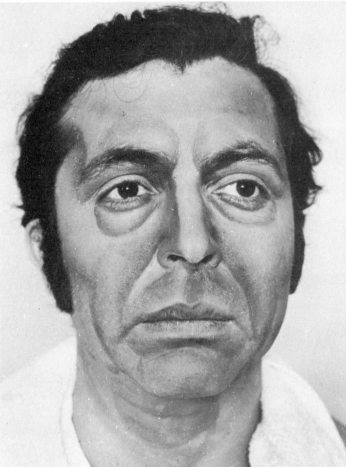

94. The face has been powdered to set the makeup.

GRAYING THE HAIR

Another area of makeup that too readily lends itself to theatrical caricature is the graying of hair. When graying the hair, make an effort to avoid the cliché (that distinguished look!) of white temples and a silver streak up front.

Graying the hair requires no great skill or ability. Using the technique intelligently does. Graying is a slow, gradual process throughout the entire head of hair. Moreover, most men lose their hair simultaneously, which means that partial baldness communicates the aging process most effectively in combination with graying.

Obviously, you're not going to remove your hair for an acting part, but you can give the illusion of greater age and loss of hair by changing the direction you comb your hair. For example, make a part far over on one side and then comb the hair as flat as possible over to the other side. This simulates what many men do when they are actually losing their hair. Some gray added judiciously to this hairdo can create a very good illusion.

Applying the gray is essentially the same whether the material is white liquid, cream, grease, or pancake. (Avoid using powder for graying. It sheds.) Pick up a small quantity of the material on a toothbrush. Using the tip of the brush, apply the gray lightly on the hair, following the direction it is lying (Fig. 95). Use a comb to break up any excess amounts (Fig. 96). Try first for a salt and pepper effect and then build it up to the intensity of gray you need. Don't be in a hurry. Do it slowly and do it right. (See Fig. 97.)

If you choose, you may use a touch of the graying material on the eyebrows. If your role is of an old enough person, you may even add a touch of gray to the eyelashes. Facial hair, which has been grayed, is also another means of indicating age (Fig. 98).

Experiment with all of these for the time being and be critical of your efforts.

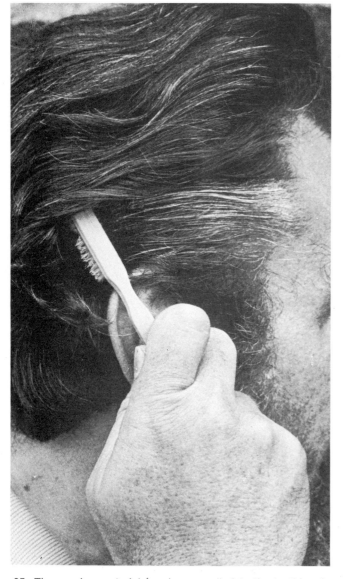

95. The graying material has been applied to the toothbrush and the brush is run through the hair.

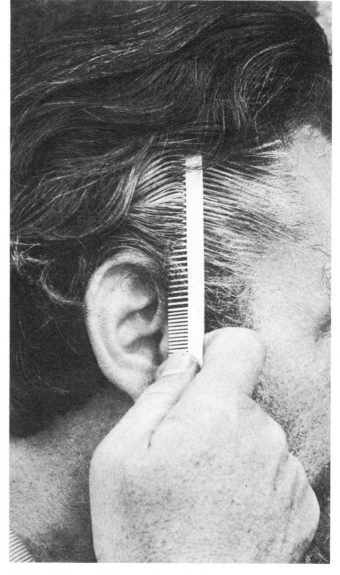

96. Next the comb is run through the hair to distribute the graying material more evenly.

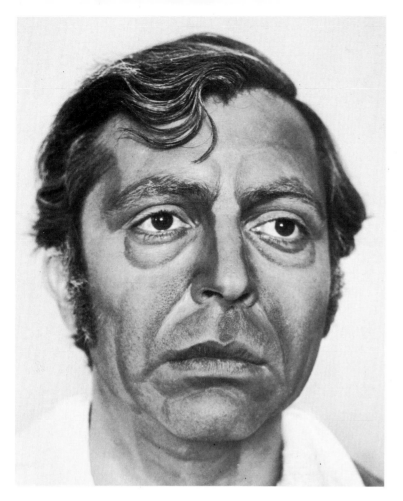

97. The hair has been combed in a way that makes the character appear to be balding. Gray has been worked evenly through the hair and eyebrows.

98. A grayed mustache has been applied.

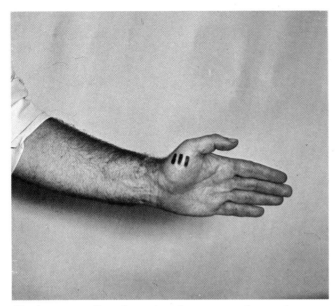

Shadow proportions for aging: two maroon to one brown.

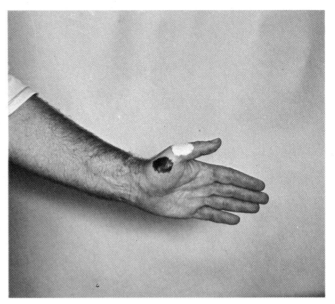

Shadow proportions mixed and highlight color added to the palette.

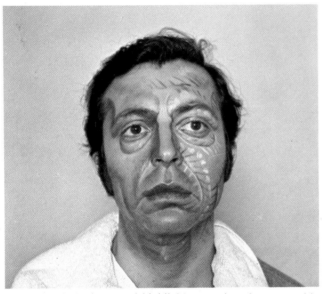

Direction of shadows and highlights are placed on one side, blended on the other.

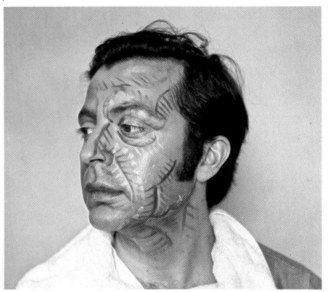

The profile shows shadow and highlight placement for neck and jowls.

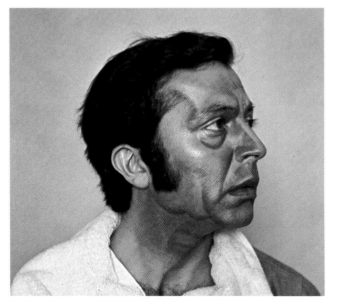

Profile showing all shading and highlights blended, including jowls.

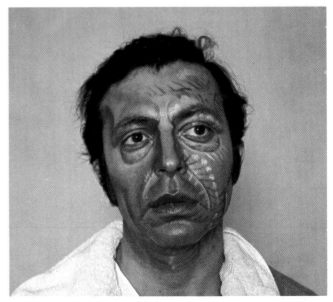

Beard tone has been added.

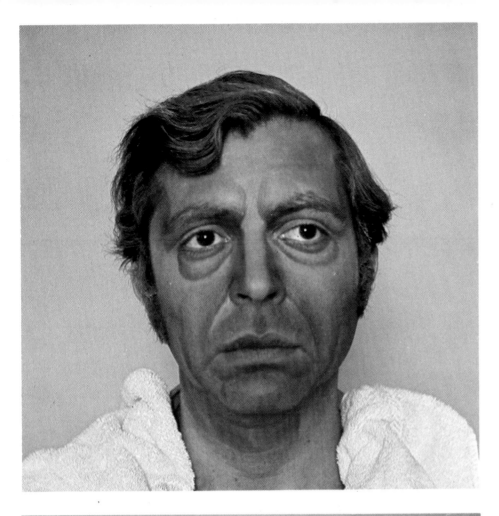

Age makeup has been blended and powdered with gray added to the hair.

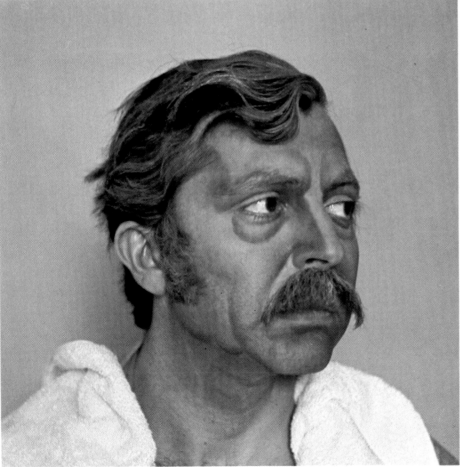

A mustache is added to complete makeup for age.

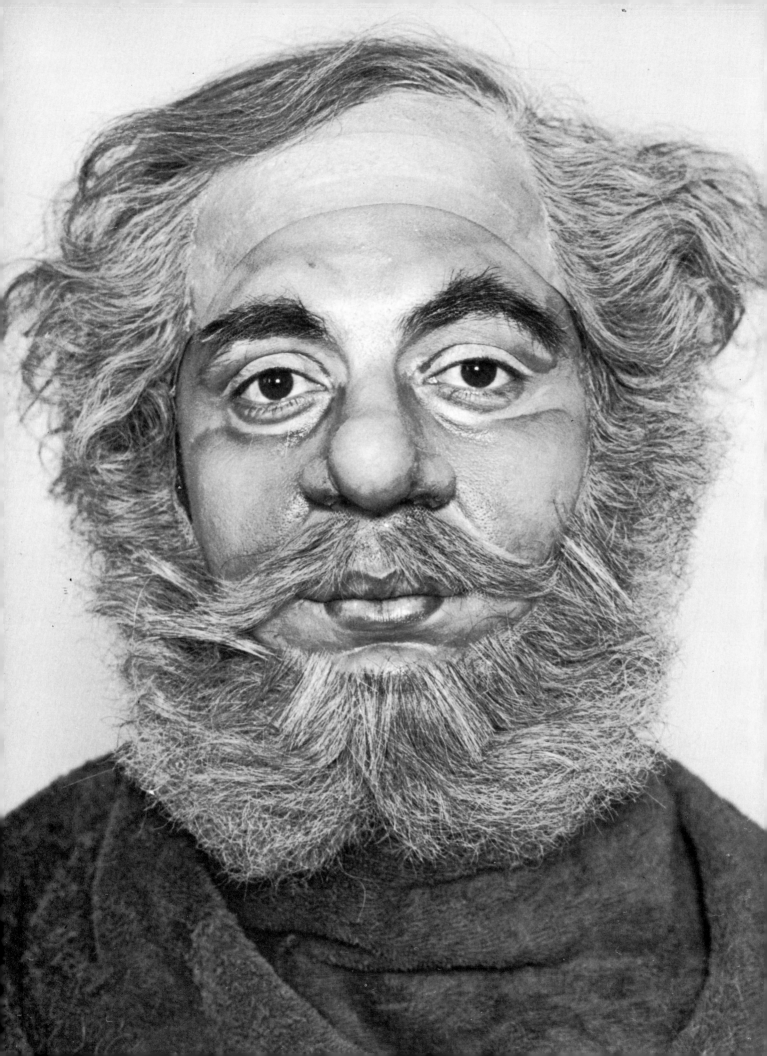

CHAPTER FIVE

EXTREME STOUT

Only after you completely conquer the techniques of making up an *extreme* stout can you freely use its effects on a limited level. The experience of learning to paint some of the exaggerated aspects of the extreme stout—creating these illusions with paint alone—will be of great practical use to you: the technique will demand a high degree of advanced painting skill. This form of practice will be of enormous value to you in the future. If the total effect is grotesque, unreal, and difficult to achieve at this stage, don't despair. Once you have acquired these skills, you will be much the stronger in your ability to pick and choose the effects you want with greater selectivity and assurance.

There are two major illusions which need to be created in the extreme stout technique: (1) All wrinkles and folds of flesh will be shaped as horizontally as possible to make the face seem wider. This will apply also to the use of wig, mustache, and beard. (2) We will create the illusion that the face is larger than it actually is by making many features appear smaller than they actually are. Therefore, carrying the facial lines horizontally, making the features smaller, plus creating specific optical illusions of roundness, will contribute to the extreme stout effect we seek.

EXTREME STOUT BASE

The extreme stout is frequently ruddy in color, so we will start with that base color. A robust, ruddy complexion can be achieved by starting with any of the tan base colors and adding rouge until we arrive at the robust quality needed.

Find a ruddy, healthy skin color in soft grease and apply this the way it has been shown in the Grecian technique. Add rouge to the base and blend it in, repeating this process as many times as necessary to achieve a ruddy skin tone. The result should look like a face with a case of sunburn.

Remove the excess grease from the face with water on your hands, patting until the skin tone looks even and clear. Clean the grease from your hands and prepare the shadow mixture and the highlights.

EXTREME STOUT SHADOW

For the extreme stout, the most effective shadow mixture should be a reversal of the amounts of color we have used previously. Blend two parts of maroon liner to one part of brown liner. For an approximate highlight, mix about four parts of white liner to one part red moist rouge. Remember, these colors are only approximations and may have to be modified according to the demands of your theater, lighting, or director.

PAINTING THE NOSE

We begin by putting our first principle into effect: the face can be made larger by making some of the features appear smaller. We make the nose smaller by creating a new bridge which is shorter and wider. Starting at the inner corner of one eye, carry the shadow in a gentle arc towards the nose with a brush. Round this arc as you reach the bridge of the nose and carry it around and down towards the nostril. Blend this shadow down to where the nose joins the

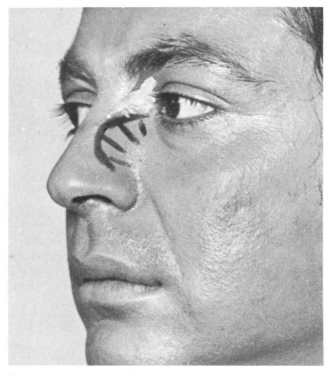

99. To make the bridge of the nose shorter and wider, carry the shadow from the corner of the eye onto the bridge in an arc, moving down to the nostril. Apply a strong highlight in the corner of the eye.

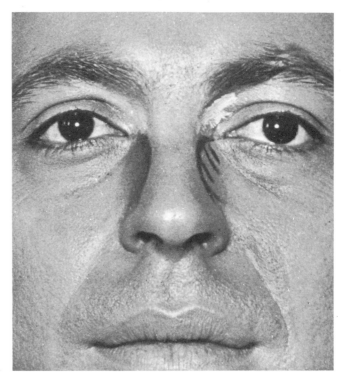

100. Blend the shadow and highlight.

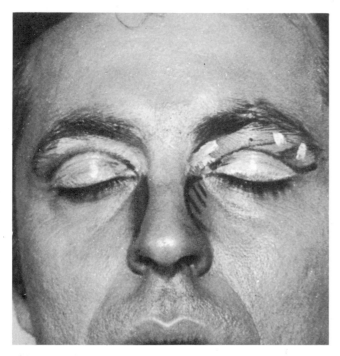

101. The shadow mixture is applied and blended in the upper eye. The high point highlight is applied to the lash and prominent bone structure above the eye.

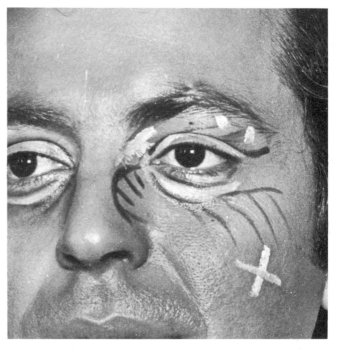

102. Place the shadow mixture and high point highlight to create the illusion of a pouch just under the eye and to indicate the upper part of the cheek.

cheek, at which point it will blend into the base.

Apply a strong highlight in the corner of one eye and carry it across the bridge of the nose to an equally strong application in the corner of the other eye. This highlight minimizes and erases the normal nose bridge structure for the upper part of the nose. Carry this highlight onto the inside part of each eyebrow and try to minimize or obliterate the eyebrows. (See Figs. 99 and 100.)

ABOVE THE EYE

We want to make both the eye and the eye area appear both smaller and horizontal. With a brush, apply the shadow mixture to the deep point of the eye. Blend the shadow towards the eye, and apply a high point highlight at the lash. Next, go over the already sunken area with another application of shadow, extending this beyond the outer corner of the eye and shaping it around and up to form the bone structure above the eye. Blend this shadow out towards the outer corners and up to the brow. Blend this into the base. Then apply a high point highlight along the prominence of the bone structure above the eye, which also adds to the horizontal effect. (See Fig. 101.)

PAINTING THE LOWER CHEEK ROUNDNESS

The bulging cheek effect combines two optical illusions we have encountered already in Chapter 3. The first illusion we discovered when we shaded the Greek jaw (see Fig. 7). We use this illusion of shading darkest at its outer edge, graduating toward lighter at the center. This applies to the upper cheek bulge, just under the eye, and the nose wrinkle at the bottom of the cheek. We are, in effect, attempting to give a round, ball-like illusion in the cheek. The painted effect should be approximate to a ball.

The second illusion follows the pattern we saw when shading the jaw in Chapter 3 (Fig. 9). Here the shading is darkest at the center, gradually lightening towards the edges. This illusion ties the top and bottom of the cheek together by utilizing the principle of painting a ball. The prominent cheek we must create demands the use of both optical illusions.

With your shadow mixture on a brush, start at the top part of the cheek. First, however, sink the area of the bottom part of the eyeball, just under the lower lash. Blend this up towards the eye, applying a high point highlight in its center and a contrasting highlight under the pouch.

Then, start the shadow at the corner of the eye, as if you were shaping a second pouch. Carry it along the eye pouch, then arc it up and then around and down onto the cheek (Fig. 102). Blend this paint out towards the ear and down towards the cheek and have it blend and disappear into the base. Next, do the lower part of the cheek in a similar manner. With your shadow mixture on a brush, start at the nose wrinkle in the nostril, carrying the stroke down the cheek towards the mouth and then across and around the cheek and up a bit towards the ear. Blend this paint

up towards the eye and towards the center of the cheek and then blend, until it disappears into the base (Fig. 103).

Next, apply a contrasting highlight beneath the lower part of the bulge, and blend this down and into the base. Then apply a contrasting highlight above the upper half of the bulge, blending that up and into the base. Now apply your high point highlight strongly in the center of this structure and blend it out in each direction, to tie the top and bottom parts together. Then blend this highlight into the base.

You should now have painted an enormous, round, bulging cheek (Fig. 104).

PAINTING THE CHIN

There is one problem that is impossible to overcome with paint: an illusion on a face can create a satisfactory effect while the face is seen head on, but when the face turns to a profile, all the work is negated. For example, it is possible to create the illusion that a long, thin nose is a shorter, squat nose. However, as soon as that same nose is seen in profile, our painting is seen for what it is, a success from only one perspective.

This problem occurs frequently in the chin area. We can create the satisfactory illusion of a double chin, until that chin is seen in profile, when our deception is discovered. It is only possible to create a truly three dimensional effect when we work in putty, rubber, or plastic. (We will deal with these in a later chapter.) In spite of the limitations of paint, you can only profit by developing your skill in illusory painting. Therefore, whether the ultimate work will ever be of practical value or not, don't neglect this phase of work if your own facial structure happens to be slim and narrow.

The double chin is simple to paint. Starting about mid-way up the actual chin, using the appropriate shadow mixture, paint a cleft and a round, smaller chin directly in the chin area and carry these out to the jowls on each side of the face (Fig. 105). Pull the chin strongly into the neck and where you see the fold of the double chin from one side of the neck to the other. Let the shadow fade into the base on each side of the neck where the double chin starts and ends. Blend this paint up towards the first chin until it disappears into the base. Apply a strong highlight under the first chin, strongest under the chin proper, and blend this in all directions and into the base (Fig. 105).

Paint and blend the jowls in a manner similar to the way you would in the aging technique (Fig. 106).

PAINTING THE FOREHEAD AND EYEBROWS

In the stout, the temple sinking is subdued, more than a suggestion, but not at all a deep sinking. It will be arched in a rather quick curve and angled for as horizontal an effect as possible. Its appearance, however, should remain realistic.

The bone structure of the forehead is quite similar to that in aging, except that all the bones are modified horizontally. The lower part of the frown line does not

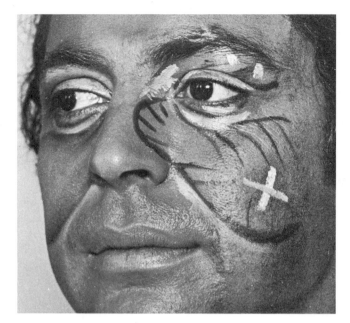

103. Paint in the lower part of the cheek.

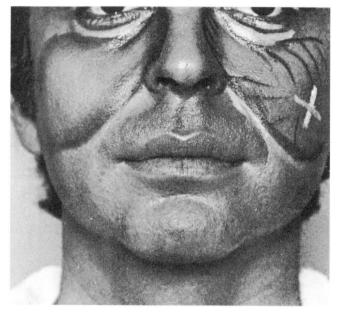

104. After applying a highlight below the bulge and in the upper half of the bulge, the cheek is blended.

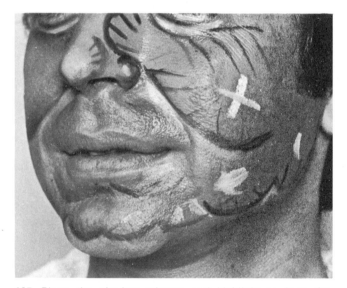

105. Place the shadow mixture and highlight to form the double chin and jowls.

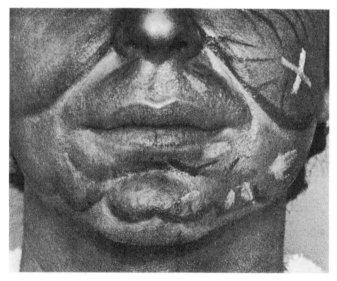

106. The jowls are painted and blended in a technique similar to that in aging.

carry into the hollow of the eye corner. It is only suggested, then stopped short of the inside of the eye (Fig. 107).

The eyebrows are much smaller in size and scope than they actually appear. This enlarges the total face even more. You can quickly see the effect of a short eyebrow and don't forget the effectiveness of the horizontal line. In Figs. 112 and 113 you will see how even large eyebrows, applied for their illusory effect, can help our ultimate purpose.

At this stage, paint a round ball at the end of the nose, using the natural shape of the nose bulb (Fig. 108). Don't carry the painting across the center or high part of the nose bridge. Blend this shadow towards the center of the bulb and blend it into the base. Apply a high point highlight in the center of the bulb and blend it out to and into the base. Using the same technique, do the same for each nostril and highlight it in the same manner. Does the nose seem bulbous?

PAINTING THE MOUTH

The mouth is also made much smaller. Use the shadow mixture for the upper lip, and maroon soft liner for the lower lip.

For the extreme stout, paint the *entire* lip; that is, all the shapes of different parts of the lips are utilized to their greatest effect (Fig. 109).

First, carry each of the halves of the upper lip above the natural lip line and shorten the length of the lip by at least a third. Carry the point of the shadow mixture in towards the center from the top and bottom of the upper lip. Blend in towards the center and into the base, and apply a high point highlight.

The area above the mouth is treated very much as it is for aging, except that the accenting may be a bit stronger in the stout. First, one half of the cleft is painted and blended down towards the center to disappear into the base. The two prominences over the lip are accented with shadow and then highlighted. You can, and should, go a little larger and stronger on the little pouches at the corners of the mouth, being careful, at the same time, to hide the fact that the mouth has been shortened.

If possible (depending on how finely the lip is shaped), carry the lower lip below the natural lip line and up to the upper lip, shortening the length of the lip by about a third. Use the maroon liner for this painting and blend the paint towards the center. Paint the upper part of the lower lip and, if possible, create a cleft in its center. Blend this paint towards the center of each bulb you create. Highlight at the high point and blend into the shadow lining color. Make sure that the base color conceals the portion of the mouth not covered by the new lip painting.

Next, recreate the slight sinking found under the bottom lip and accent the folds under and on each side of the mouth for as much horizontal effect as possible.

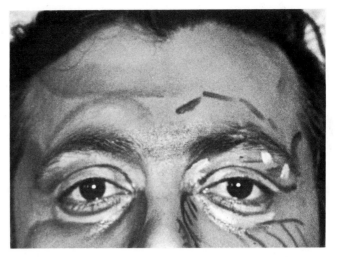

107. The forehead is suggested: a horizontal effect is desired.

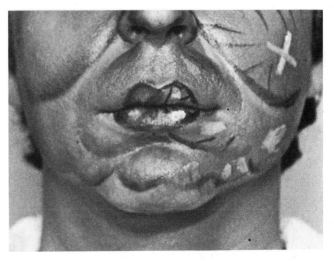

108. For the bulbous nose, paint a round ball at the tip and blend toward the center.

109. The entire shape of the lips is painted: the bulbous quality in the upper and lower lips, the areas above, below, and alongside the mouth appear pouchy. The lip line has been shortened considerably.

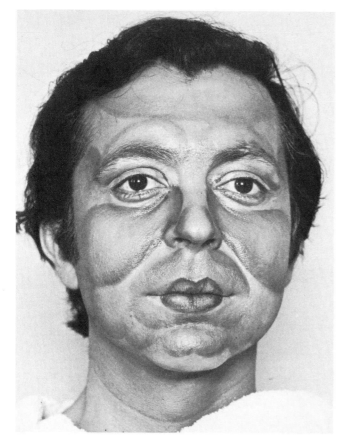

110. The extreme stout has now been totally blended.

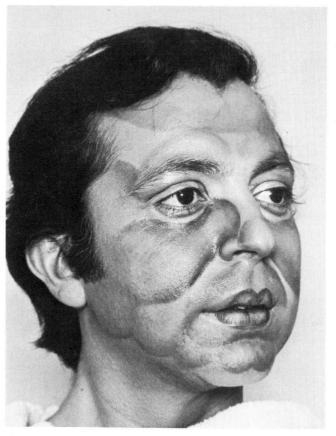

111. Three-quarter view of extreme stout painting.

112. By adding nose, wig, eyebrows, mustache, and beard to the extreme stout, we create a Falstaff.

113. Notice how the hairpieces accentuate the horizontal effect so desirable in the extreme stout. Compare this to the hairpieces used in Chapter 6 on Don Quixote.

POWDERING

Now powder carefully and, after removing the excess powder with water, examine your work critically (Figs. 110 and 111).

Has the work gotten too liney? Does the face have an unnaturally puffy and swollen look? If it does, you have essentially been successful.

Now, use your imagination and try to visualize the circumstances in which you can utilize some of the effects created here. You will soon realize how useful they can be. By adding nose, wig, beard, and mustache, the extreme stout can be used for many character roles. (See Figs. 112 and 113.) Adding these details will be discussed fully in later chapters.

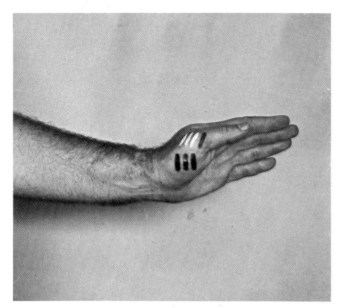

Shadow mixture for stout: two maroon to one brown; high-light: four white to one rouge.

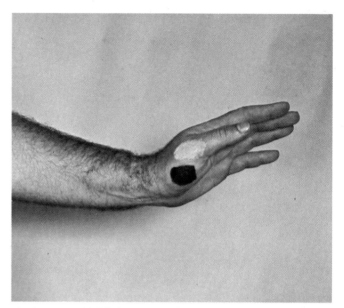

Shadow and highlight proportions have been mixed on the palette.

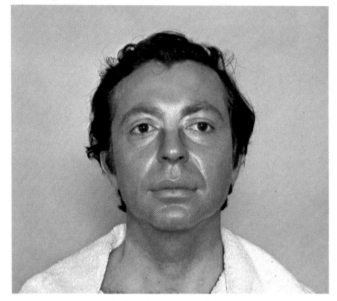

Ruddy base is applied and nose shadow indicated.

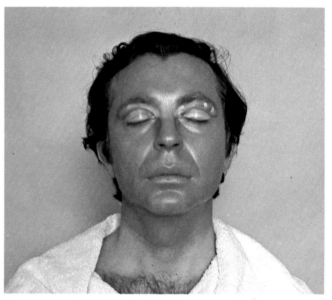

Upper eye shadow and highlights have been placed and blended.

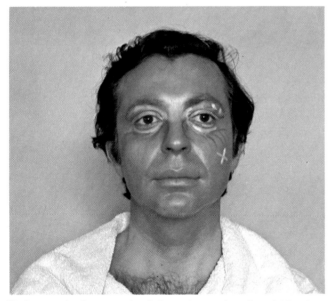

Under eye and upper cheek have been placed and blended.

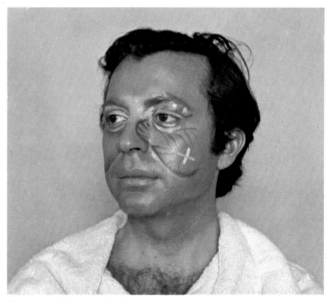

Upper and lower cheek painting is shown here.

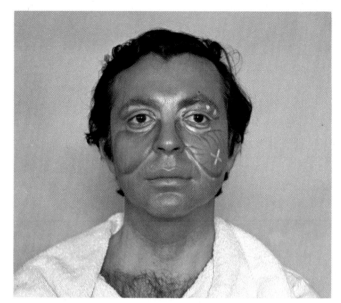

The cheek has been blended on one side.

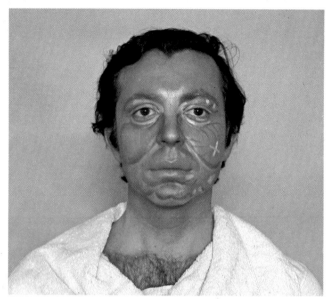

The chin, jaw, and area around the mouth have been painted.

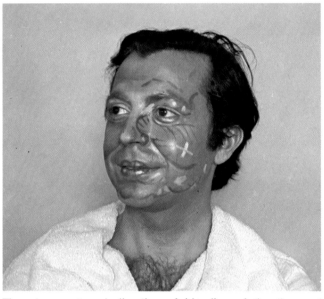

The placement and direction of blending of the lips and forehead are shown here.

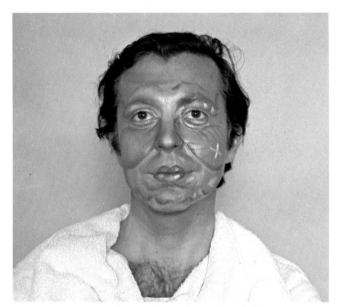

Half the lips and forehead have been blended.

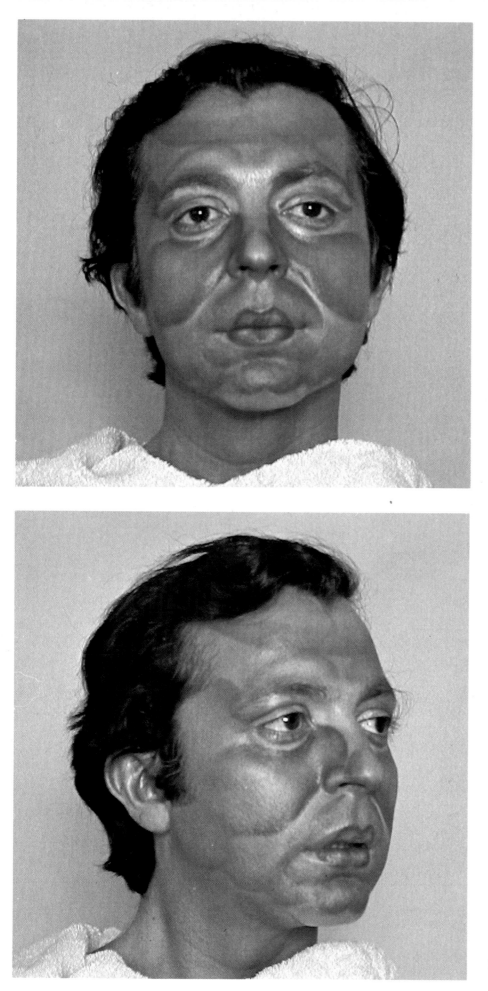

The makeup has been totally blended and powdered.

Note illusions of puffiness painted in the stout.

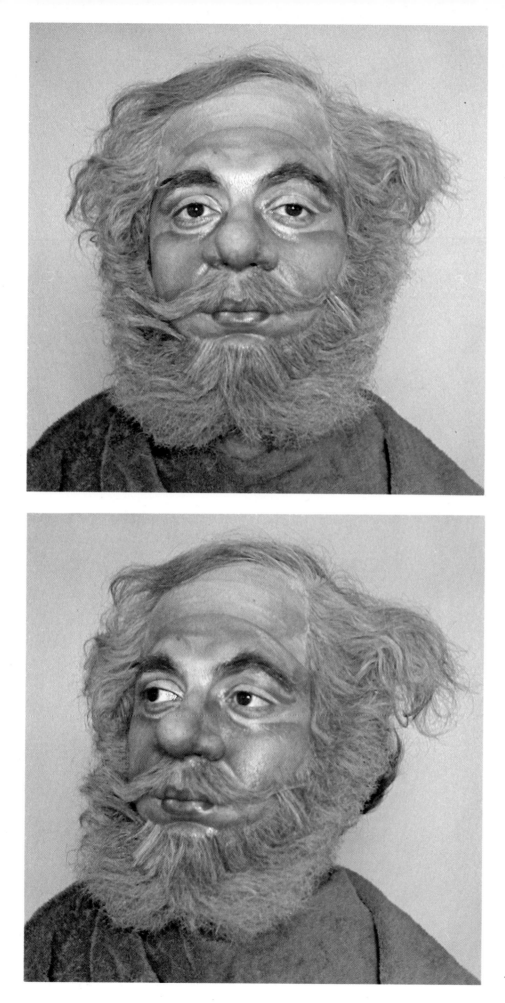

A wig, beard, mustache, eyebrows, and putty nose complete this stout character.

Three quarter view of Falstaff.

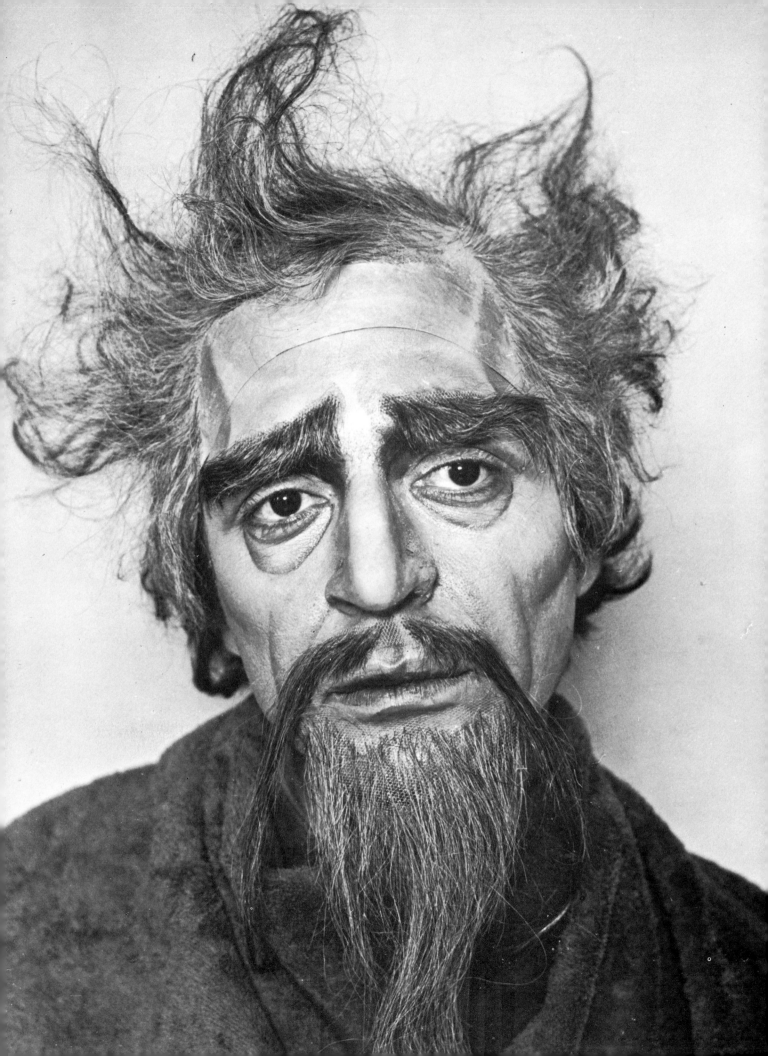

CHAPTER SIX

EXTREME LEAN

Here we want the exact opposite of the extreme stout just concluded in the last chapter. Just as we worked in the extreme stout for a horizontal effect, here we will utilize the illusions that create vertical, elongated effects. The face will be very sallow in color, elongated, and thin to the point of emaciation. The prototype character for this makeup is Don Quixote. Therefore, in addition to creating a long, lean face, we shall also use the vertical lines to add *sadness*. In this way, we can project a physical visualization of "the knight of the woeful countenance."

As with the extreme stout, this makeup is not complete until wig, mustache-beard, and artificial nose can be added. These stages will be added here just for effect. In later chapters we will describe specifically how these are applied.

BASE FOR LEAN FACE

Use either soft or hard, very pale and sallow base colors. Blend these until you arrive at an unhealthy skin tone. Then, remove the excess grease with water on the hands in the usual manner and continue to the painting.

Never forget that many manufacturers' products in a vast array of colors are available for your use. Certainly, you can, and should, feel free to mix and utilize any products you choose. Never feel constrained about a cosmetic number or name and remember that the proportions have merit only in their ability to give you the base color that suits you and your purpose. This attitude toward your materials will give you latitude.

SHADOW MIXTURE

For your shadow color, I suggest gray lining color. Add some maroon to this or add some black liner. Your choice depends on how sick a tone you want or how dark you want the shadows to be.

HIGHLIGHTS

For highlighting color, I suggest the same gray lining color. To this add some white liner in the proportion of one of gray to two or three white.

TEMPLE SINKING

The first area of the face that can be appreciably lengthened is the temple part of the forehead. If you have a low hairline, or lack ample forehead area, you can correct this with a high hairline wig.

In the lean face, the temple sinking is carried much further into the temple area than is normal and you minimize the normal curving back towards the hairline and ear. This creates a vertical line that lengthens the face, yet still allows for a "real" look.

Using the fingertips, apply a small amount of the appropriate shadow mixture to the temple bone area, with a light patting stroke, creating a slight, gentle curve. Avoid the effect of a straight painted line. Shadow should be darkest at the initial placement of the bone sinking and gradually blend back towards the hairline until it blends and disappears into the base. Be careful about spots and pay particular attention as you blend: a soft, gradual diminishing of tone.

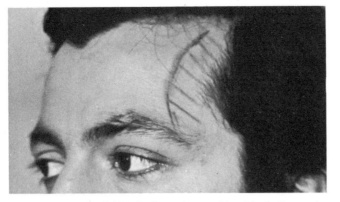

114. The temple sinking is brought considerably further onto the forehead than usual, and is given a more vertical line.

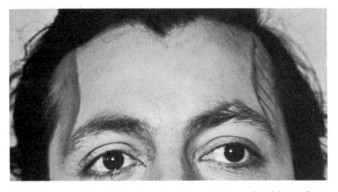

115. As you blend the temple, the shadow should gradate from darkest at the sinking, diminishing into the base towards the hairline.

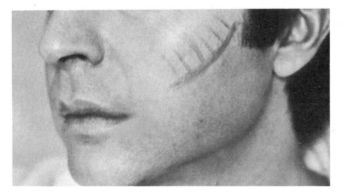

116. The cheekbone sinking is carried higher than usual and onto the cheekbone itself. The bottom part of the sinking is stronger and sharper.

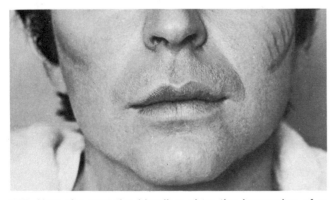

117. Note the way the blending gives the impression of a bony prominence in the cheekbone.

Too often, painting this area fails because the blending is too uniform in tone and intensity, rather than being darkest at the sinking and gradually grading in tone, effects which accent the sinking. (See Figs. 114 and 115.)

PAINTING THE CHEEKBONE

Painting the cheekbone seemingly contradicts all that has been described for this makeup. In order to create an intense gauntness, it will be necessary to sink the cheek quite deeply. That in itself is not a contradiction. However, to sink the cheek deeply, we must follow the line of the cheekbone structure which is much more horizontal than it is vertical. To counteract this, we must minimize the horizontal as much as possible to favor the vertical.

Before you begin to paint, run your fingertips along the contour at the bottom of the cheekbone. Feel the depth of the bone structure and how far it comes up to the base of the nose. We cannot effectively carry the paint to this point without interfering with the nose area wrinkles.

With some of the appropriate shadow mixture on your finger, begin applying the depth of the cheek hollow. Start where the cheekbone begins, near the ear, and carry it forward until it is even with the center of the eye pupil. Blend this shadow up onto the cheekbone so that it too disappears into the base and creates a strong rounding of the cheekbone. Apply a strong high point highlight along the crest of the cheekbone. Blend the bottom part of the cheek, sinking only enough to remove the sharp edge. (See Figs. 116 and 117.)

TOP OF EYE

Now we sink the inner corner of the eye and, at the same time, shape the character of the face. This effect sinks the eyes into their sockets. With the brush, apply the appropriate shadow mixture to the inner corner of the eye, carrying it up towards and into the brow and onto the nose. Since we are trying to sink the bridge of the nose which is a prominent area, it is necessary to apply the shadow more heavily at this particular point. In addition to sinking the bridge, we also use the eye shadow to create a definite downward shaping in the eye (Figs. 118 and 119).

To accomplish this, first apply the paint to sink the top of the eyeball. Blend down to the lid, and then a high point highlight at the lash. Apply the shadow heavily at the inside of the eye and up onto the bridge of the nose and brow. Carry the line above the eye heavily down at an angle into the deep point of the eye socket and down past the eye a bit onto the cheek. Blend this shadow up towards the brow and around the bottom part a bit, and come up to create a little fold. At that point, on the bridge of the nose, carry the shadow down the full length of the nose. Blend this shadow down the bridge of the nose into the base at the point where the nose joins the face. Make this bridge a bit narrower and sharper than you usually would, so that you create a thin, elongated nose and, at the same time, you get a woeful, downward line in the eye.

BOTTOM PART OF EYE

The bottom part of the eye is a pouch which lengthens the face and also saddens it. First create the sinking around the bottom of the eyeball. Blend this paint up towards the eye and place a highlight at the lash. Then, below this sinking, paint a full eye pouch, letting it sag more to the outside of the center to accentuate the elongation. Apply high point and contrasting highlights. (See Figs. 120 and 121.)

If you want an extremely bony cheekbone, you paint the bottom part of the eye in reverse. (See the two illustrations of Mephisto, Figs. 134 and 135.) Paint the first pouch under the eye as we have just described. Apply both high point and contrasting highlights. Reverse the second pouch, in a way similar to shading the large cheek in the extreme stout.

Start the paint in the inner corner of the eye. Follow the line of the eye socket and the edge of the cheekbone, then arch it up towards the bottom part of the upper eye structure. Blend this paint down and out towards the cheekbone. Accent the area by applying a strong cheekbone highlight. The result is an intense bony prominence which accentuates the lean face.

NOSE WRINKLE AND CHIN

In comparison to what you have completed so far, the nose wrinkle is simple. Paint it as you usually do, except that you elongate it a bit, making it slightly more vertical, if possible. (See Figs. 122 and 123.)

Start the second or chin wrinkle up higher than usual and accent it more strongly. Blend it towards the mouth. Apply a strong high point and contrasting highlight. (See Figs. 122 and 123.)

Shaping the chin is quite simple. Carry the outside corners of the mouth downward with a vertical fold from the corner of the mouth. Just below this fold, start the chin and carry it down to the edge of the chin, under, and up the other side (Fig. 124).

This shape of the chin can vary for effect. In order to achieve the most length, the chin can be narrower at the bottom. Blend this paint in towards the center and add a high point highlight at the lower part of the chin.

The center of the lip sinking can be carried up onto the lip if your own lip does not have a very definite edge. Carry the highlight on the mouth sags up onto the lip. Each lip is painted as thin as is reasonable and shaped to have the outer corners sag downwards. The cleft of the upper lip is straightened and carried down to the new lip line. Shape the prominences above the lip in order to accent the vertical (Fig. 124).

JOWLS

The jowls and neck areas are handled very much the same way as they are for old age. You can elongate

118. The sinking above the eye extends from the nose at the eyebrow down and beyond the corner of the eye. The diagonal line lengthens and saddens the eye.

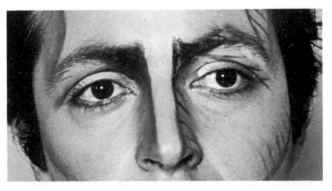

119. The bridge of the nose is carried up into the brow. This adds length to the nose. The bridge is narrow for additional length.

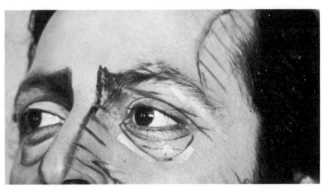

120. The bags beneath the eye sag most heavily at the outer corners of the eye. Notice the two pouches that have been delineated.

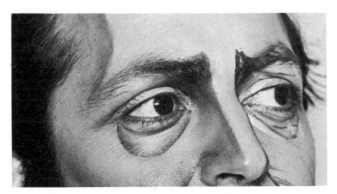

121. The bottom part of the eye has been blended. This structure helps elongate this feature.

the jowls a bit and create heavier, stronger neck muscles and detail the windpipe more so than usual (Figs. 125 and 126).

You may have noticed that through this makeup technique I have stressed a number of times that certain applications should be strong or dark. This reminder is necessary because the shadow mixture for lean (unless you have added black to it) does not have a deep color and tends, when blended, to soften, diminishing its effects. Be certain that your work is clean. If some of your results do not project as well as they should, add a touch of black liner to the shadow mixture.

FOREHEAD

In the extreme stout, we shaped the lines of the forehead in such a way that the horizontal effect was accentuated. Here we must also alter the shape of the forehead to help create the length needed for this extreme lean. Carry a frown line from the inner corner of the eye up onto the forehead. Blend this and highlight. Then, with paint on your finger, gently arch this wrinkle around and then down to the end of the eye structure for maximum elongation. The center bone of the forehead will also be elongated, and will therefore be carried down almost to join the eyebrow bones. Subdue the empty triangular area of the forehead with shadow. (See Figs. 127 and 128.)

The eyebrows will require some patience and practice. The hairs are sketched as if they were growing down and almost straight. Emphasize the transparency and unevenness of the eyebrow in order to get an effect of reality. (See Fig. 129.)

This now completes the painted stage of the lean makeup. In itself, this is extremely useful. The total extreme effect is completed only when nose, wig, beard, and mustache are added, as illustrated in Figs. 130 to 135. These stages will be dealt with in detail in later chapters.

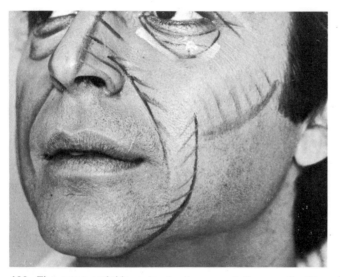

122. The nose wrinkle extends down past the mouth. The chin wrinkle starts higher than usual.

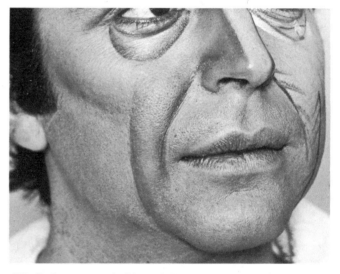

123. Both nose and chin wrinkles are blended.

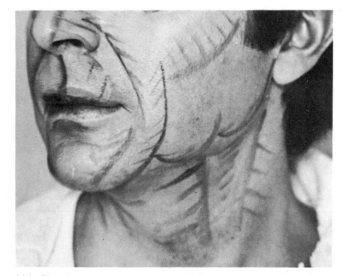

124. The lips sag downward and the chin is carried down just below the sagging mouth. The lips are painted thin and the cleft is carried into the new lip line.

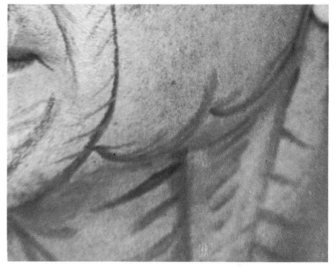

125. The jowls sag slightly more than they do in old age. Otherwise, they are created in the same manner.

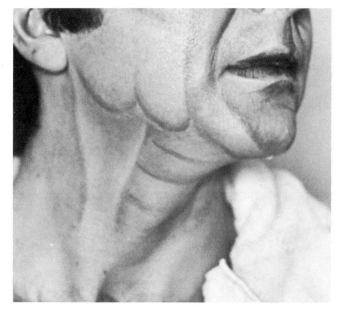

126. The jowls are blended.

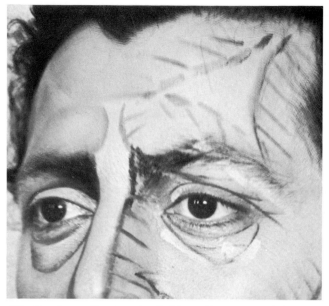

127. The frown line is extended from the corner of the eye, then arched around to the end of the eye. The forehead bone is carried almost down to the eyebrow bones.

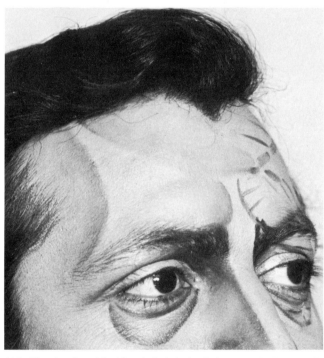

128. The forehead is blended: it is both bony and elongated.

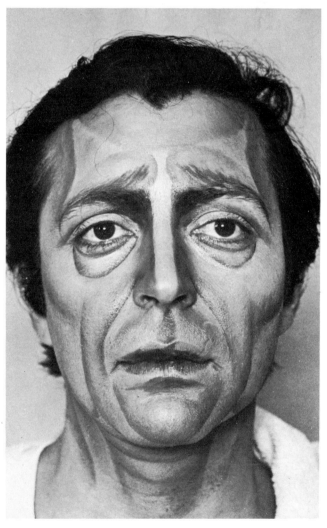

129. Here is the complete painted face for the extreme lean. Notice the placement of the eyebrows.

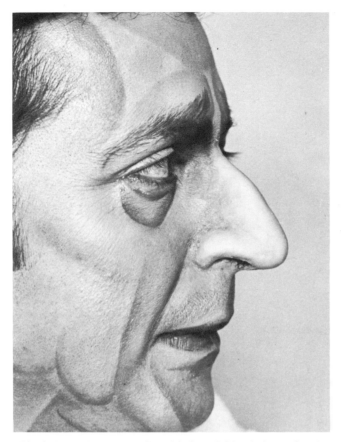

130. A long, lean nose is added and blended so that its edges disappear into the face. (See the chapter on putty for further details.)

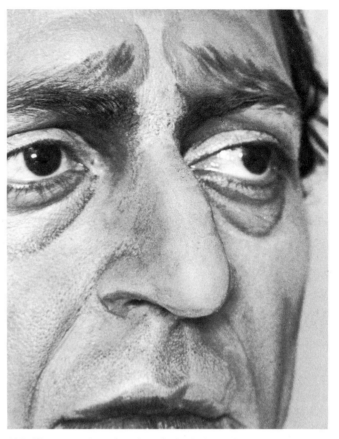

131. The nose is painted and shaded so that it blends into the face properly.

132. Wig, beard, and eyebrows are added to complete the Don Quixote character. Note that these details enhance the long vertical quality of the face. Notice the woeful quality.

133. Notice that the line of the wig is visible in this black and white photograph. Color and distance help it to fade into the base properly.

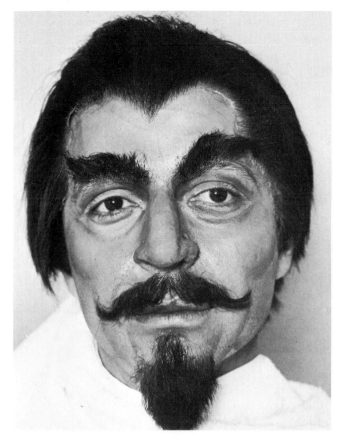 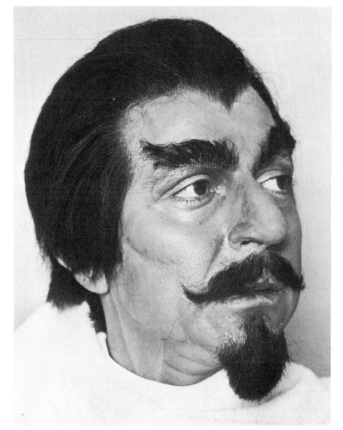

134. A darker base, different wig, eyebrow, mustache, and beard, and Quixote becomes Mephisto.

135. The only change in structure from the Quixote is in removing the long pouches from beneath the eye and creating a stronger cheek line by reversing the shading to blend down onto the cheekbone.

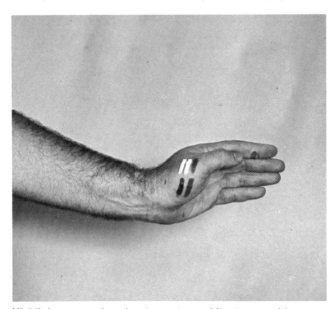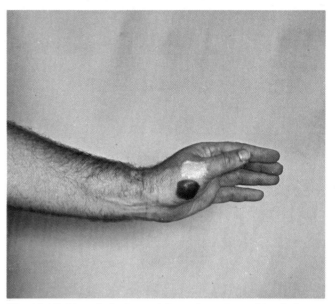

Highlight proportion for lean: two white to one blue-gray; shadow mixture: one maroon to one blue-gray.

The highlight and shadow mixtures have been blended.

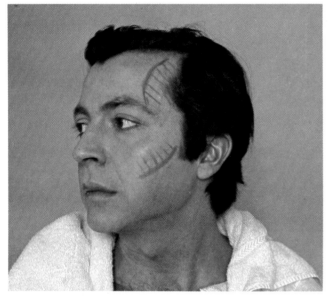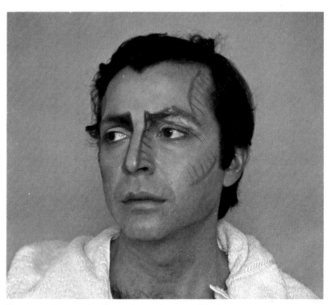

Note placement and direction of temple and cheek shadow.

Nose and eye shadows have been added.

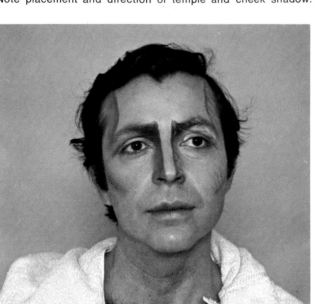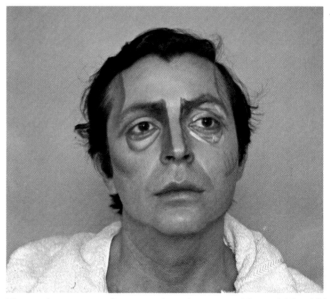

The temple, cheek, eye, and nose shadows have been blended on one side.

The under eye pouches are placed on one side and blended on the other.

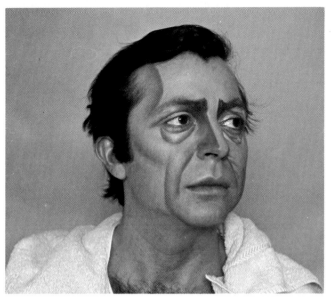

The cheek wrinkles have been blended.

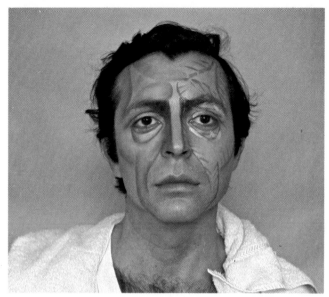

The forehead is placed and blended on one side.

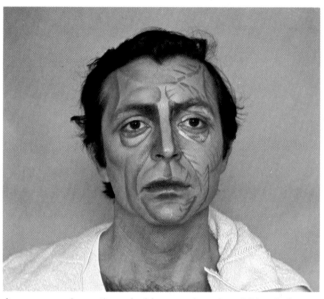

Areas around mouth and chin are placed and blended.

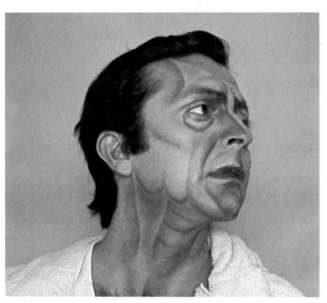

The neck shading and jowls are blended.

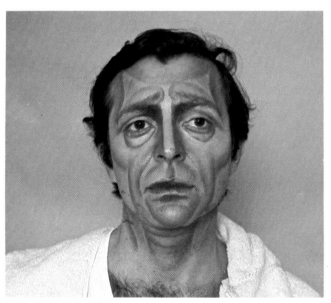

Eyebrows added, the lean face is fully painted and powdered.

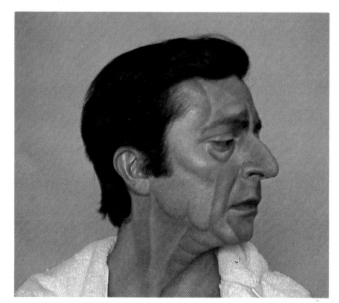

A putty nose has been added and painted.

To the lean makeup, wig, eyebrows, beard, and mustache have
been added.

Don Quixote shown in profile.

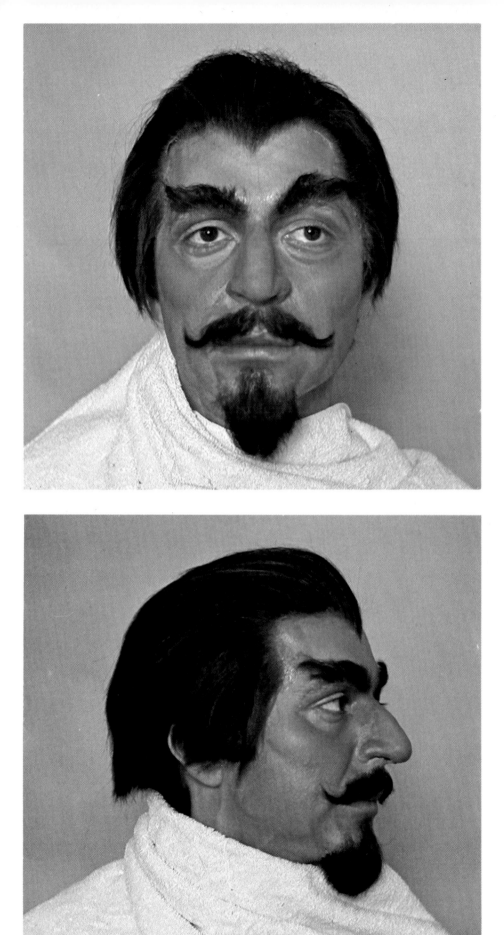

The lean has been adapted with new face pieces to create Mephisto.

Note that the cheekbone blending is the reverse of that shown earlier in the lean.

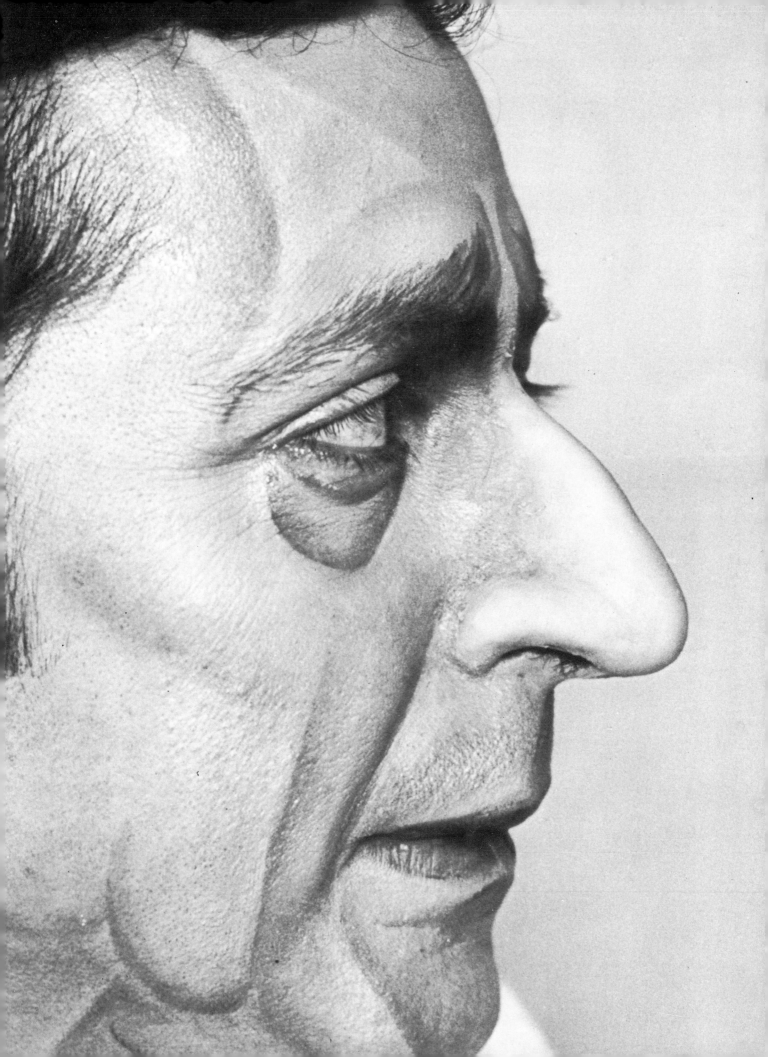

CHAPTER SEVEN

BUILDING UP THE FEATURES WITH PUTTY

There will be many occasions when your facial features simply do not suit the role you are playing and will need to be built up. Although there are times when other features may need to be built up—such as cheeks, chin, etc.—the nose is the feature most commonly altered. Building up the nose is what we will demonstrate here. By reshaping the nose, you can dramatize an effect enormously, as we have already seen in the last two chapters.

To build up a facial feature to a larger size, use nose putty (which is quite hard) or a combination of putty and mortician's wax, to soften the material. These structures are temporary, useful only for a single performance. Removing the putty after its use misshapes it so badly that it is necessary to entirely reshape it for its next use. This material is useful to you when you have a single performance or too few performances to warrant making a prosthetic piece (see Chapter 10). Nose putty is available from many manufacturers, and all are essentially the same. The putty comes as a stick or as a length of pinkish, malleable material.

KNEADING THE PUTTY

Pick up half the quantity of the putty in the container. Slowly begin to knead it with your fingers (Fig. 136). The kneading, plus the body heat of your fingers, will soften it, making the putty pliable. To prevent the putty from sticking to your fingers when it gets tacky, moisten your fingers with a touch of cold cream. Avoid doing this too often or using too much cream: the putty will absorb the cream, which will soften it too

greatly and the cream tends to grease the putty too much, minimizing its adhesive qualities.

To hasten the time needed to get the putty to a working consistency, you can mix some mortician's wax with the putty and blend them together. The putty must be malleable so that it will shape to the pressure of the fingertips, yet not so soft that a mere touch will alter the shape.

After you have achieved what seems a proper consistency, shape the putty into approximately the shape you're after (Figs. 137 and 138). (For this work you must have an additional mirror so that you can see both the profile and the front view.) Check the amount of putty on the nose (Figs. 139 and 140), and estimate how close this is to the way you envision the finished product. If your segment is too large, remove some of the excess. Likewise, if your build-up is too small, add some more. Try to get the rough model close to the size that suits you. Now add nostrils and check in the same manner (Fig. 141).

ATTACHING THE NOSE

The experienced performer will first apply his makeup base, then attach a putty nose and blend the base color onto the nose. For practice purposes, however, we will apply the putty nose directly to the bare face and apply makeup base at a later stage.

First, cleanse and dry your face, then apply a layer of spirit gum on your nose, with a brush, so that the putty will adhere better. During practice, you can overlook the spirit gum, but for an actual performance it's advisable to use it. With the putty shaped as close to

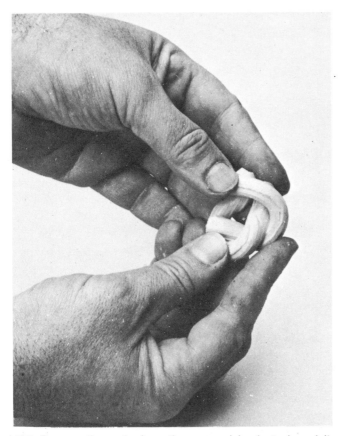

136. Remove the putty from the can and begin to knead it in your fingers.

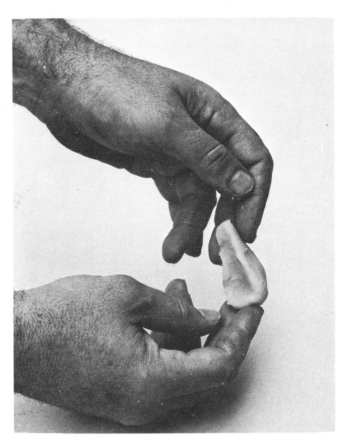

137. As you knead the putty, you will be able to rough out a nose shape. Work in all the lumps so that the texture of the material is smooth.

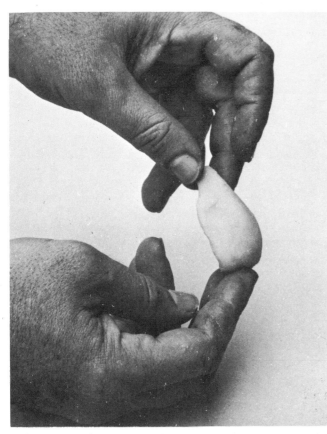

138. Approximate the nose shape.

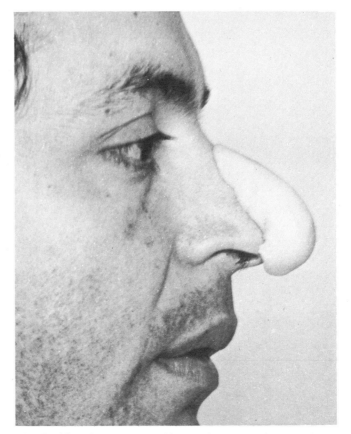

139. Position the putty roughly on the nose.

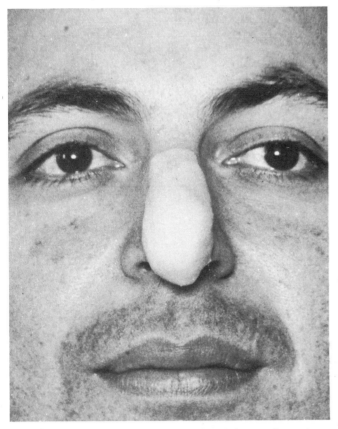

140. Check the front view to see if the shape conforms to a real nose bridge and if the proportions are structurally possible.

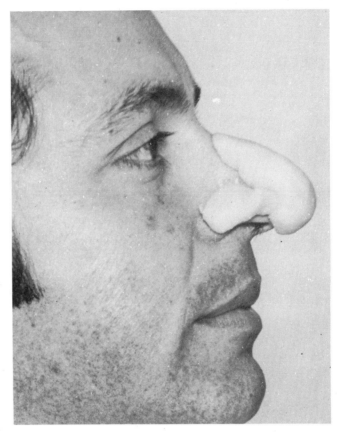

141. Add rough nostrils.

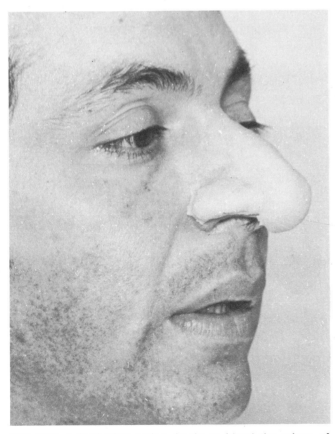

142. With a feathering action, begin to blend the edges of the nose onto the skin.

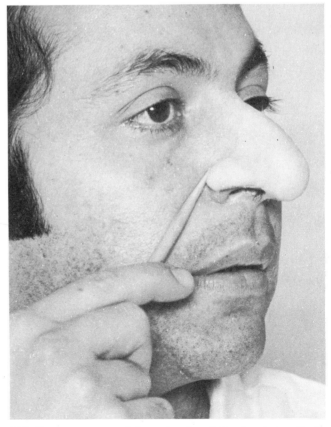

143. Use an orange stick or the tip of the brush handle to work the edge into a tight area.

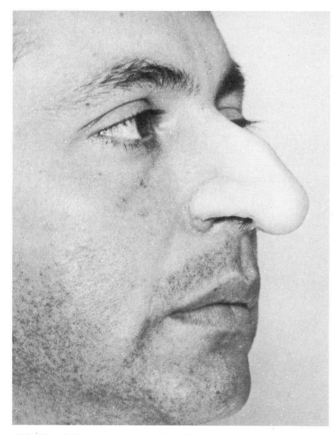

144. Blend the putty onto the skin without spreading it all over the face.

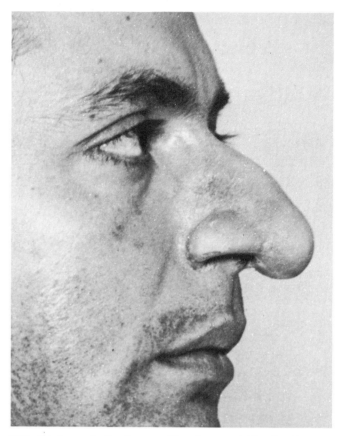

145. Gently apply the base, patting it on and blending it onto the face.

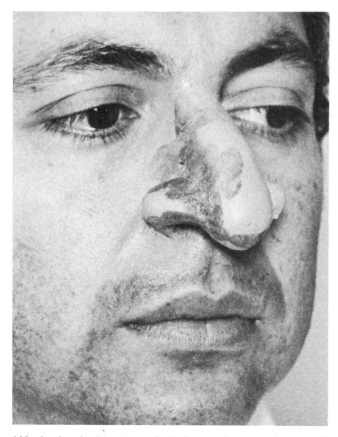

146. Apply shadow to project the newly shaped nose. It must be shaded as any other feature. Apply the shadow gently with a tapping motion of the fingertip.

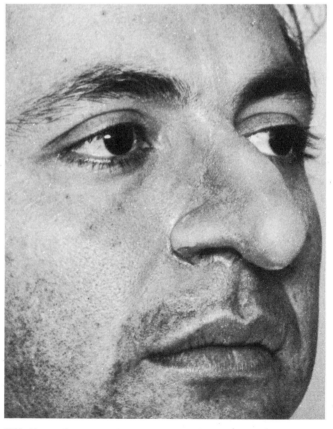

147. Here the nose has been shaded and blended. The feature now looks like a natural addition to the face.

the feature as possible, position it on the nose. While holding it in place with the finger of one hand, begin to slowly feather the edges onto the nose in all directions with your fingertip. Spread the edges of the putty onto the clean skin until all the edges are smoothed onto the skin. This feathering action is a major factor in making the work appear natural and realistic, and, at the same time, it helps make the nose more adhesive. (See Fig. 142.) For the tight areas, push in the putty with an orange stick (Fig. 143).

The most common error in building up a feature is that the performer tends to spread the edges further and further onto the face until the putty seems to cover the face. Practice allows you to feather the edges just enough to shape the feature and have it look real. (See Fig. 144.)

NOSE SHAPES

The actual shape of the feature and its relation to your own features is of vital importance. The initial temptation is to use too much putty and, frequently, instead of creating a nose, a monstrosity emerges! The overall size of the nose is determined by the over-all size of the face and the makeup intended for that face. Noses have certain lines and proportions and nostrils have a specific relationship to the total nose.

In all cases, the added piece must take its shape from the actual feature in a natural manner. Bear in mind that large noses are not false bulbs attached to a small structure; there are no sudden, sharp changes in shape. In particular, observe the angles of the nose and how to add to the nose without distorting the actual forms. Even when the required nose is huge, out of proportion to the rest of the face, it is only believable if its shaping is that of a real nose. The

cartilage of the bridge, the fleshy bulb, and the nostrils must all be proportioned to the total nose.

PAINTING THE NOSE

Putty work is not complete until it is covered with the base and then shadowed and highlighted with the rest of the face. Painting the built-up feature is more difficult than any painting you have done so far. The putty cannot be manhandled; it is soft and becomes tacky easily. Too much pressure quickly distorts or alters its shape.

Blend a quantity of the base color in the palm of one hand, mixing the proper colors until the base is as close as possible to the necessary color. With a fingertip, gently apply this base to the putty. Try to apply it and spread it in the same motion, spreading the color as quickly and as smoothly as possible. Avoid excess handling and do not apply too much base. Carry the base down the putty and blend it into the base on the rest of the face (Fig. 145).

Clean your hand of excess base and mix the shadow mixture to its proper color. Do the same for the highlights. You cannot use a brush for applying the shadow or highlights as you normally would because the brush would misshape the putty. Gently, with the fingertips, apply the shadow with a tapping motion to the putty nose. A different amount of pressure is needed to apply the paint to the putty than you used directly on the face. Do all your blending with this light patting touch (Fig. 146). The entire nose—the bridge and the nostrils—must be highlighted and shaded.

After the painting is complete, powder the nose, but don't touch the puff to the putty. Dust some powder lightly on the paint and very carefully remove the powder with a damp silk sponge. (See Fig. 147.)

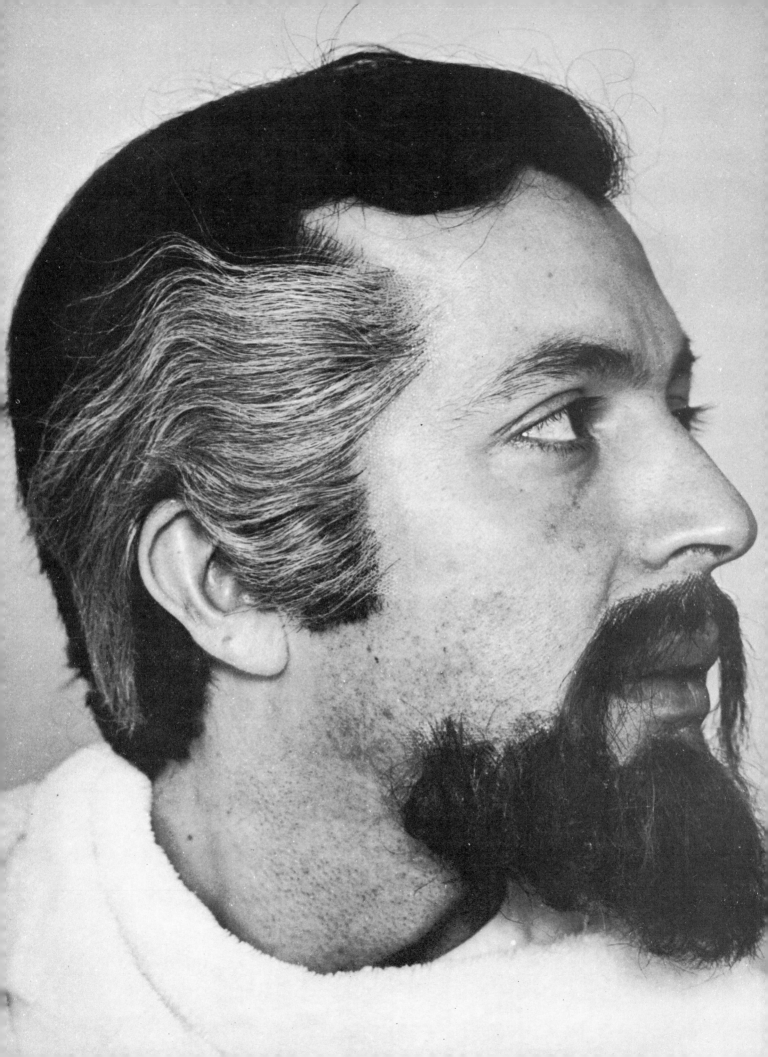

CHAPTER EIGHT

BEARDS

Facial hair is usually the final touch in completing a makeup job. Hair can be applied loosely to the face or a ready-made facial hairpiece may be applied. First let's consider loose facial hair, then the hairpiece.

There are many types of hair available for facial hair, and this variety allows for a wide range of quality, depending on the techniques used in application and the amount of time you allow for the work. Crepe wool can be applied in a matter of a few minutes, and the final result is often excellent. The use of straightened crepe wool, yak, or human hair will take much longer but, when applied properly, will achieve superb, lifelike results. You must ultimately judge which material and technique will best suit your purpose. In order to select with authority, learn to use each material skillfully; practice is mandatory.

DIRECTION OF HAIR GROWTH

Before dealing with the actual application, let's examine some of the problems of facial hair. Even though the various materials can be applied in different ways, success always depends on understanding hair growth.

Hair must be applied to the face so that the direction of the growth seems vertical. Facial hair grows down in a vertical direction. When false hair is applied, it is frequently (and mistakenly) applied at an acute angle to the face. This error is so common that I must emphasize it!

Facial hair must be trimmed beforehand so that its angle of application will cause it to lie on the face in a real and natural manner, and run vertically from

the face. In these illustrations, the hair is laid against the face (a dummy is used here) to show how the hair must be trimmed so that when it is applied it will hang vertically from the face. The angle at which the hair is trimmed will allow the hair to fall vertically. To cut the hair in the correct angles, follow Figs. 148 to 153.

By trimming the hair as shown here, you will lay on the hair and it will hang in a vertical direction. For specific illusions, some beards may have to give the *appearance* of horizontal growth. (Falstaff, for example, appears fatter because his beard appears horizontal.) This illusion must be achieved by applying the hair correctly (in a vertical direction) and then by cutting and dressing it for the desired horizontal line.

The same principle of pre-cutting the angle of the hair before applying it to the face applies to all kinds of loose beards, whether you are using yak or human hair, or crepe wool, straightened, or as it comes from the hank. Bearing the principle in mind, let's examine the methods of putting on loose hair beards from these materials.

PREPARING CREPE WOOL FOR BEARDS

The least expensive beard and the fastest to apply is the crepe wool beard. Crepe wool is a soft, wool-like fiber that comes braided in solid colors, usually black, brown, tan, gray, and white. In preparing crepe wool for the beard, you must unravel the braid so that you can cut the sections of wool which will form the beard. Laying out the hank on your lap or any flat surface, first open the string which ties and holds the braid together (Fig. 154). Loosen or cut this string

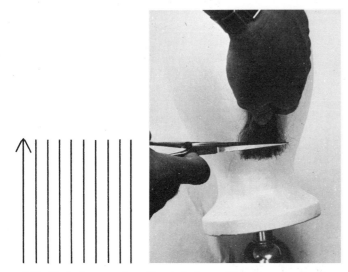

148. Underjaw, center: The hair is positioned under the jaw and is trimmed horizontally or straight across.

149. Above jaw, center: The hair is positioned above the chin in the center of the face and is trimmed horizontally.

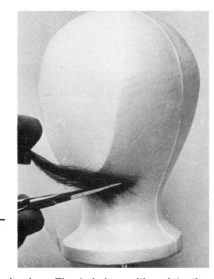

150. Side of face, under jaw: The hair is positioned to the underside of the jaw and is trimmed at a slight angle to the line of the jaw.

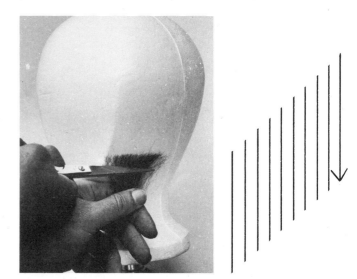

151. Side of face, top jaw: The hair is positioned above the chin and on the side of the cheek and is trimmed at a similar angle to the jaw.

152. For the mustache, the hair is positioned above the lips and is cut at a slight angle, so that the hair grows away from the center of the face.

153. A different angle is used for the other side of the mustache.

about half-way down the braid and pull the braid free (Fig. 155). Then separate about half the length of wool. In its braided form, the wool is curly and compacted and this braid must be opened. With the fingers, spread the wool and open it up so that it is somewhat transparent (Fig. 156).

With the wool opened and separated, it becomes possible to remove a segment. Put the spread open wool on your thigh and hold down firmly the open part of the segment with the palm of your hand (Fig. 157). Try not to cover or hold more than ½" or 1" of the spread. The wool will stretch and open considerably. Gently pull the braided part of the hank (Fig. 158) until a segment is separated from the braid (Fig. 159). Now go back to the rest of the braid and pull more segments. Pull as many segments from the braid as you will need. (For example, you will need two segments for a Van Dyke beard, and six segments for a full beard.) Try on each piece for the area of the face you intend to cover, then pre-cut the edges to conform to the shape of that part of the face. Cut the segments and put them aside until you are ready to apply the beard. (See Figs. 160 to 163.)

APPLYING CREPE WOOL BEARD AND MUSTACHE

Now you have a basic idea of how to make the segments and how many you may need for a Van Dyke beard, which we will apply first. Then we will add the additional sections to transform this into a full beard. Let's put the beard on the face. To apply the crepe wool beard you will need crepe wool spirit gum, barber's shears, and a clean section of cloth about the size of a man's handkerchief, which should be clean and lintless, either silk, rayon, or nylon.

After you have pulled two segments and have trimmed them to the appropriate angle, fit them roughly onto your face to check that their size is correct for the space you intend to fill.

Before you actually adhere the beard, check that the beard area of your face is free of any makeup. Now take the spirit gum brush and apply the gum to the center of the bottom of the jaw. When the gum has been applied, give it a moment to dry.

Take the first segment of hair and position it under the jaw, the trimmed edge touching the windpipe and the uncut edge projecting forward past the chin (Fig. 164). Press the segment into place with the fingers, holding it for a minute until you can feel that the wool has adhered slightly. Hold one end of the cloth in each hand and, using the center portion of the cloth to apply pressure, press it against the adhered edge of the beard. The cloth holds the hair in place while the gum dries and you can pull away the cloth without removing particles of hair at the same time. Remove the cloth, make sure the wool does not stick to it, and check the segment for adhesion and placement. In turn, follow the same procedure for the upper segment. When you have these in place, move to the top of the chin.

Apply spirit gum to the upper part of the chin. Slowly and carefully, using the same approach, press

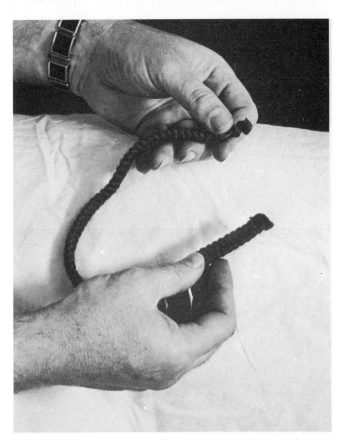

154. Place the hank of wool braid on your knee and open the string that ties the braid together.

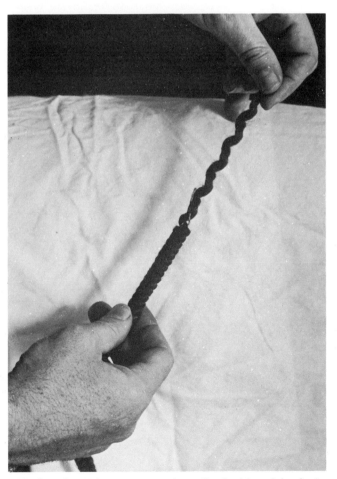

155. Cut the string part way down the braid and begin to loosen the hank.

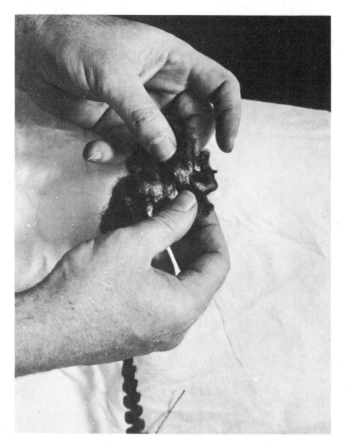

156. Separate the crepe wool, to midway down the braid.

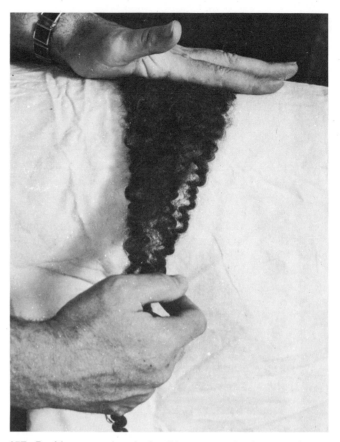

157. Position your hands in this way to begin to pull out a section.

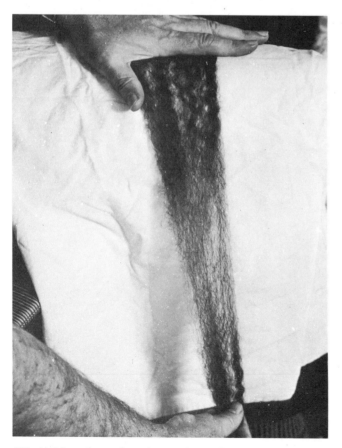

158. Holding the palm of your hand firmly on your thigh, gently pull out a section with the other hand.

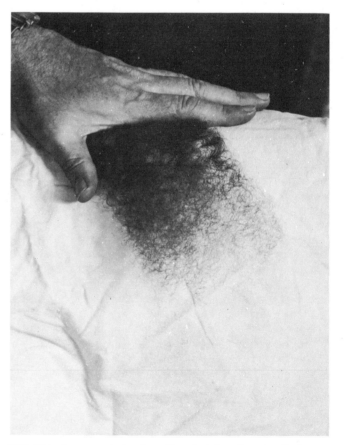

159. This is a good sized section that has been pulled.

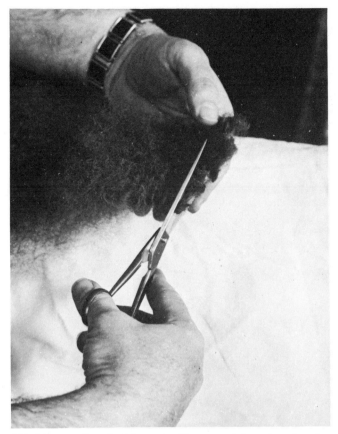

160. The section is trimmed with a straight edge for the bottom section of the beard.

161. The bottom section is now ready to use.

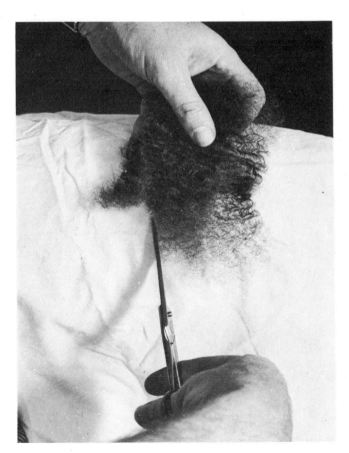

162. Here the top part of the beard is being trimmed.

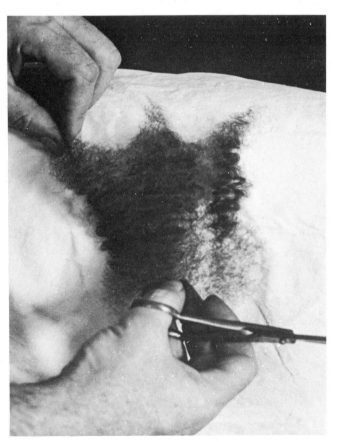

163. The top section of the beard is now ready to use.

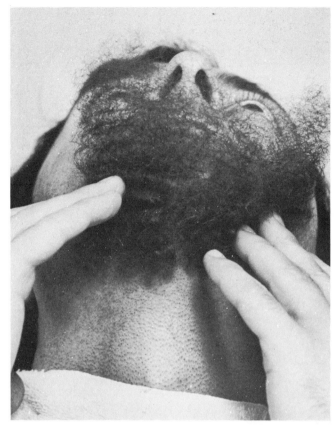

164. Position the first section of the beard to the lower part of the jaw as shown here. Cradle the chin in a cloth, holding the cloth to adhere the wool to the spirit gum you have applied.

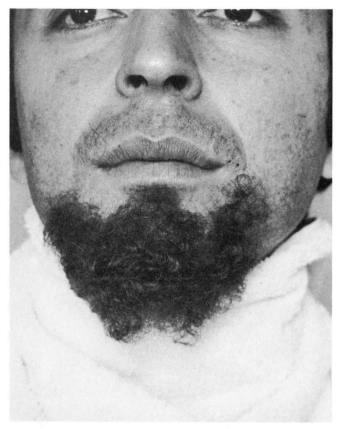

165. The upper section of the beard has been pressed into position with the fingers.

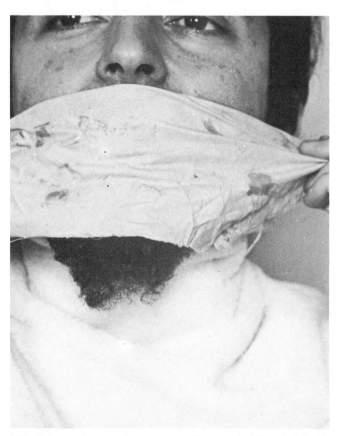

166. Using a downward pressure, with an end of the cloth held in each hand, adhere the upper part of the beard to the skin.

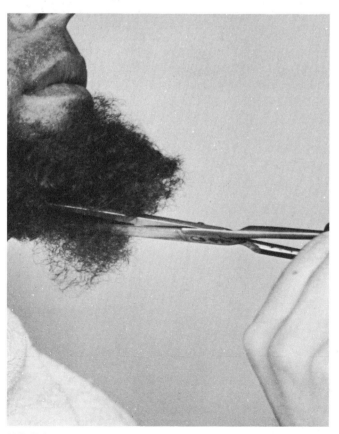

167. Trim excess wool from the beard with the scissors.

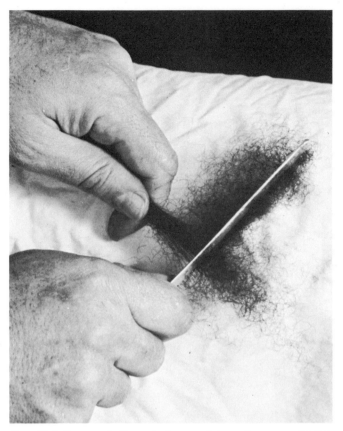

168. Pull the comb through the wool to gather a mustache section. Let the teeth of the comb catch the wool.

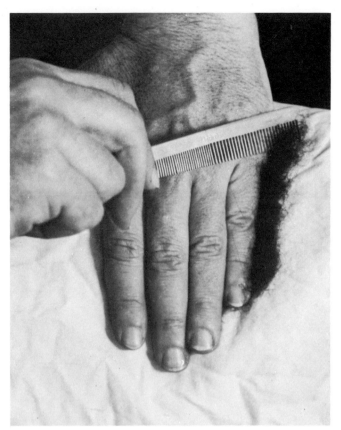

169. Hold the mustache section with the palm of one hand and lift out the comb.

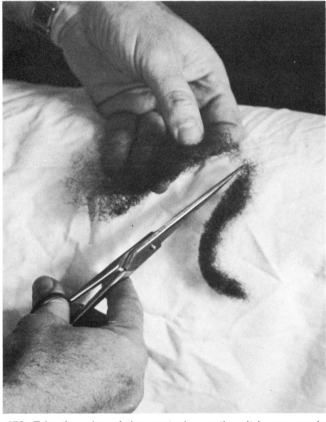

170. Trim the edge of the mustache section. It is now ready for use.

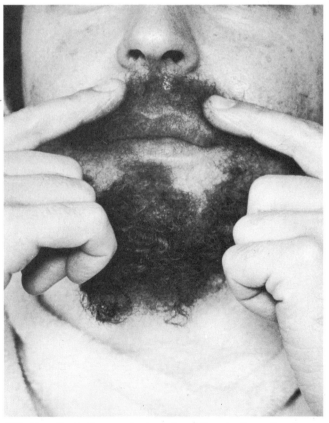

171. To attach the mustache, place the wool section in an area you have coated with spirit gum.

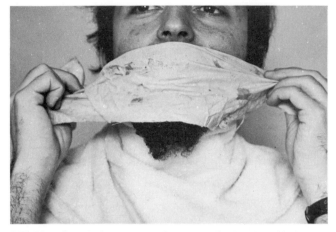

172. Use the cloth to press the mustache into position.

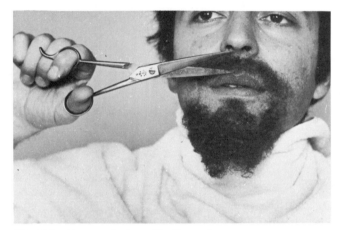

173. Trim the mustache with the scissors.

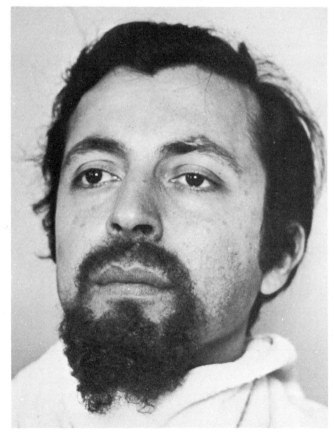

174. Here is the complete mustache and Van Dyke beard.

the second segment to the upper part of the chin (Fig. 165). Cover the segment with the cloth and use a downward pressure to adhere the wool (Fig. 166). Once the beard has adhered, you can trim it to the shape you desire, using the barber's scissors (Fig. 167).

Suppose you want to add a crepe wool mustache. First pull a section of wool from the hank and comb it through so that you catch a quantity of the wool in the teeth of the comb (Fig. 168). Hold down the combed section of wool with the palm of your hand as you lift the comb out of the section (Fig. 169). Then trim off the rough wool to make the lip section (Fig. 170). To apply the mustache, follow the same procedure as you did for the beard: apply spirit gum, press the wool into position (Fig. 171), use the cloth for final adhesion (Fig. 172), and trim the mustache (Fig. 173). You now have a complete Van Dyke beard (Fig. 174).

If you want to add sections up the sides of the face for a full beard, pull four more sections and again follow the same procedures. (See Figs. 175 to 177.)

MIXING COLORS FOR CREPE WOOL BEARD

The crepe wool used in the technique just demonstrated came directly from the braid in the braid's original solid color. For our second beard technique, we will mix different colors. No hair is composed of only one color, especially facial hair. We'll pre-mix those colors as we make the segments.

Prepare the braids as before. Open them on your lap and separate the wool. Select the colors that you feel will give you the end color you need. Remember, facial hair is often lighter in color than the hair of the scalp. Here we have used white to give the effect of a graying beard.

Hold the wool as before. This time, however, you hold down only the very tip of the opened wool, so that instead of pulling out the entire segment of the braid, you only pull out a very thin amount. (See Figs. 178 and 179.)

Proceed to build up the segment by pulling small amounts of wool and adding them to the segment. Hold the wool in place lightly with the hand and again pull the braid so that some more of the wool is added to the amount pulled out the first time. Repeat this process as many times as necessary to build up the segment to the size and density you desire. (Check the segments against the face to determine this.) During this process of building up the segment, you alternate the colors of wool so that successive use of different colors will create a segment of the desired mixed color. (See Figs. 180 to 182.) When the segment is properly mixed, pick it up, try it on the face, and trim the edge to make it fit (Fig. 183). Put it aside and continue making the mixed segments until you have enough to make the beard.

STRAIGHTENING CREPE WOOL

In applying segments of crepe wool we achieved a fast method of simulating a beard. However, for an even more natural looking beard, you might prefer to use straightened wool, yak, or human hair. The human hair is most expensive, yak less so, and wool the least expensive of all. The procedure for using these materials for a beard is more complex, but the results are worth the effort.

Because of the expense, I suggest you practice with straightened wool. As you know, crepe wool in the braid is very wiry and, for this procedure, will have to be straightened before it can be used. First remove the string around the braid. Wet the braid with water. Then, while it is still wet, stretch the braid to its normal length and fasten it in a fixed position until it is completely dry. You might lay it on or between some toweling to help hasten the drying process. If you are in a great hurry, you can apply a heated iron to the wool. In fact, today's steam irons permit you to straighten crepe wool without prior wetting. Place the wool on a board and run the steam iron back and forth over the braid until the wool is straight. (If you use an iron, keep a cloth between the iron and wool.) Wetting and stretching the wool overnight is usually sufficient time to allow for preparation. You may tack it to a board or tie one end and let it hang over a basin or tub so that the water dripping from the braid does no damage. Moisten and stretch enough colors to allow you to mix the shade you will need.

When the wool is dry and straight, open the wool from its tight braid. While holding it with one hand about 8" from the end, use the thumb and forefinger of the other hand and take a light hold on the edge of the wool. Gently pull at the wool until a small segment is loosened and then pull this away from the wool. Repeat this process and, as you do so, add the newly pulled wool to the first. Use this technique to mix your colors. These new segments should be no more than 1" to 2" in width and about 6" to 8" long.

These straightened segments will be applied to the face in a technique called *layering*. As the name implies, this technique means applying the hair in layers and duplicating actual hair growth on the face. It is far more difficult than the application of the larger segments and takes a great deal more time. However, it is very much worth the effort, because it gives a truly natural beard look.

LAYERING THE BEARD

Layering can be done with straightened crepe wool, yak, or human hair. The technique is the same. Your fingers will have to make adjustments to the varying textures and strength of the type of hair used, but the procedures described here are identical. As I have already said, because of the prohibitive cost of yak or human hair, I suggest you practice this technique with straightened crepe wool.

To layer the beard, small segments of straightened wool will be applied in layers so that each layer overlaps the preceding one. By this means, it will be possible to build up a beard, control its density, and lay the hair in precisely the correct direction of growth to create a remarkably natural beard.

To learn the physical coordination necessary in layering, practice without using the spirit gum to glue the

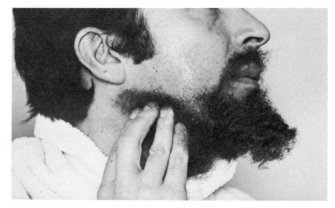

175. To fill out the beard on the sides of the face follow the same procedure. Press one section into position and adhere in the same manner.

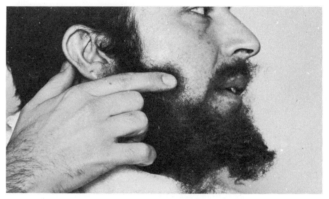

176. A second section is placed into position on the side of the face.

177. The beard has now been transformed into a full rugged beard.

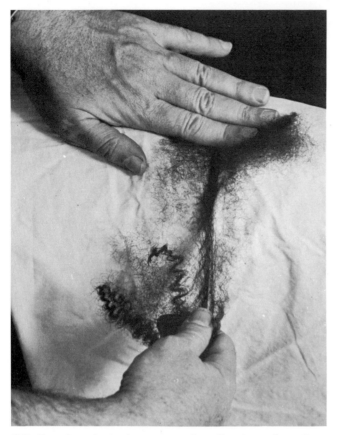

178. To mix colors of crepe wool, pull out small sections from the braid. Hold down only the tip of the opened wool.

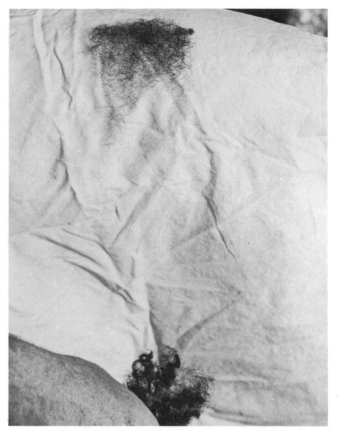

179. Pull a small section of wool, much smaller than when you made a beard of only one color.

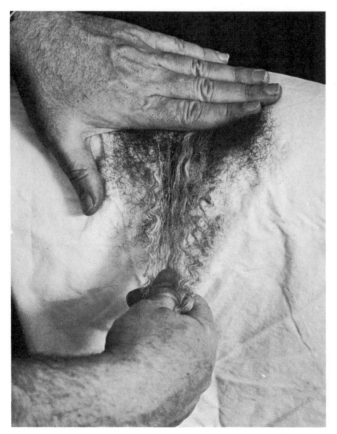

180. Add the color to the segment and pull another small section in the same way.

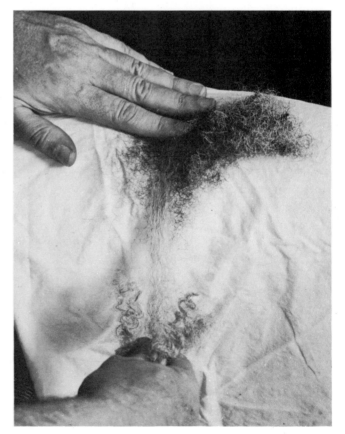

181. Build up the section to the desired thickness.

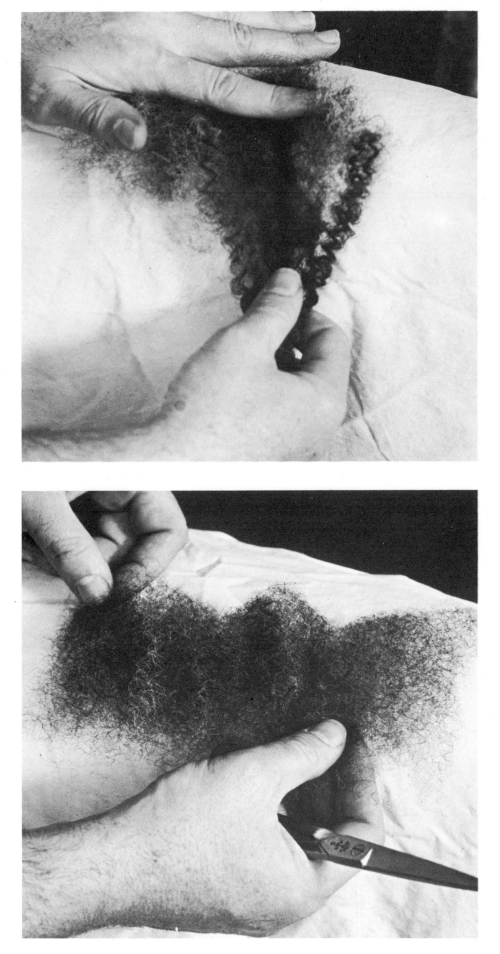

182. Alternate the mixture of colors as you pull the wool.

183. When you have achieved the thickness and color you want, trim the edges to make it fit on the face. This will be used for the upper chin section.

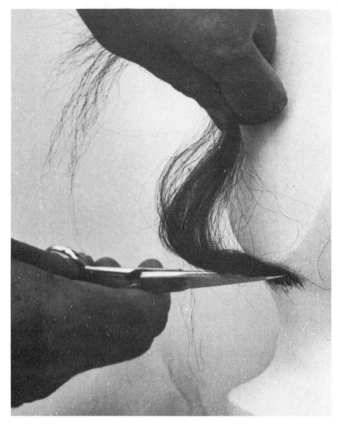

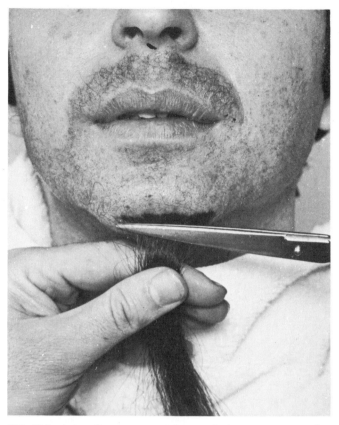

184. To layer the beard, trim the straightened wool or hair in the necessary angle, press the shears against the hairs and onto the desired area. A dummy is used here for clarity.

185. This shows the same operation as in the last photograph. Pressing the shears against the hairs will secure the adhesion.

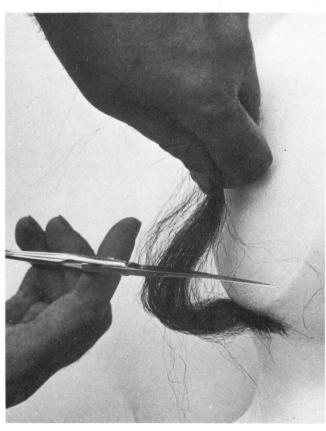

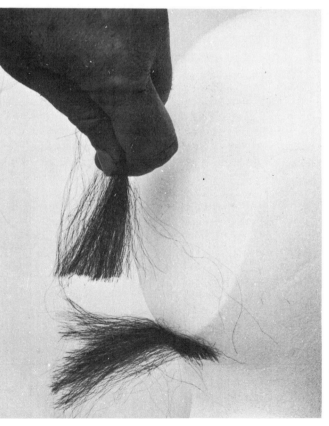

186. Slightly relax your hold on the hair, causing the hair to loop, then roll off the shears from the face and gently trim to the length you want for the final beard.

187. By bending the hair as shown, you avoid pulling the section off the face when it is cut.

wool or hair to the face. First, take a segment of the mixed straightened wool or hair in your left hand if you are right-handed (the reverse if you are left-handed). Hold the segment 1½″ to 2″ from the edge. Trim the edge in the proper manner—a horizontal cut for laying in the center of the face and a right angle or left angle cut for the respective sides of the face, as shown earlier in this chapter.

To attach the beard, first put aside at least a dozen segments before you begin application. (After you've used this supply make up another supply.) To adhere the hair, apply the spirit gum to the desired area. Carefully position and lay the hair or wool on the gummed area. Pick up the shears and, using the flat part of the closed blades, press the shears against the hairs to secure the adhesion (Figs. 184 and 185). Then, slightly relax your hold on the hair, roll the shears off the hair and gently, in order not to pull out any hairs, trim the length of the segment to approximately the length you want for the final beard (Figs. 186 and 187). Do not cut the hair too short, because you want to allow some hair for the final trimming.

If the flat of the shears is tacky or covered with spirit gum, clean it with a rag dipped in acetone and then go on to the other segments until all the hair has been applied to the face. When you complete the area below the jaw (Fig. 188), use your cloth for pressing the hair against the face for adhesion, as you would do with the large wool segments. Do the same for the upper center section of the face and for each of the sides (Fig. 189).

The layers should not be much more than ½″ apart. Placing them closer creates a beard that is too bulky and further apart leads to a thin, sparse, sketchy beard. As you did in the first beard technique, you should complete the under part of the chin first. Start ½″ in from the edge of the chin and add successive layers as far back as you intend the beard to go.

The greatest difficulty occurs on work done under the chin. Use any arrangement of mirrors that will help you to see under the chin. This, of course, creates its own problems because it takes time to adjust your sense of depth perception to the mirror's image; at first your hands and hair will always seem to get in each other's way. Try to be patient. It will take time, but given the time, you will master the technique and find continual use for it in your work.

TRIMMING THE BEARD

Trimming the beard is an art in itself. Using the shears properly demands practice, first in conceiving the mental image of the style you desire, and then in developing the skill to render that style effectively. For a variety of styles, refer to the gallery in Chapter 15. Think carefully about what you intend to do before you actually begin to trim. Remember, once you have trimmed the beard, you cannot make it larger without starting all over again. Use your hand mirror to view both sides of the face, and constantly clean the blades of your shears as you work.

When you have trimmed the beard completely (Fig. 190), spray it lightly with a hair set lacquer to keep

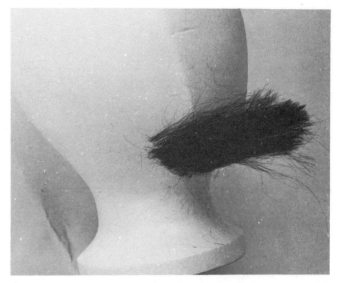

188. The bottom of the jaw has been layered, the hair angled in the proper direction of growth.

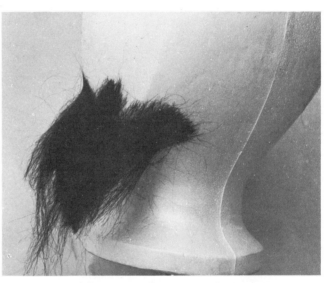

189. The top of the chin has been layered, also following the downward direction of hair growth.

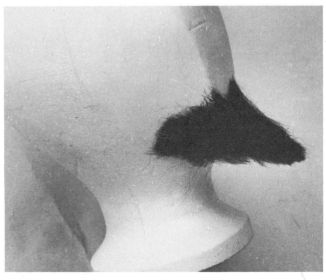

190. The beard has been neatly trimmed.

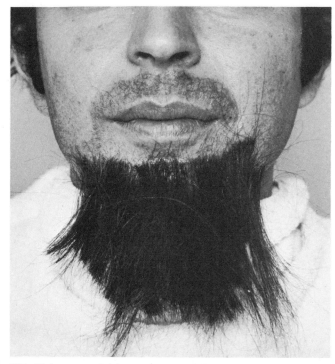

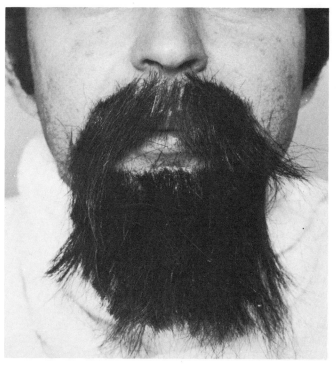

191. Using a model here, you can follow the stages of layering the beard and mustache in a more real example. Here the upper and lower parts of the chin have been layered.

192. The mustache has been added.

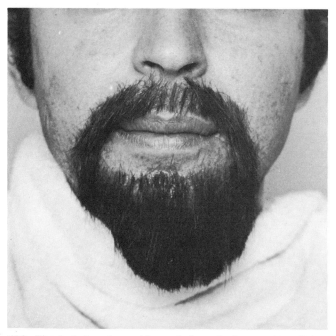

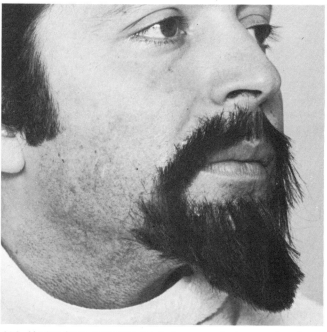

193. The hair has been trimmed down to form a Van Dyke beard.

194. Notice how naturally the hair seems to be growing from the face.

the shape for a longer period of time. Very gently remove the wool or hair that has not adhered to the spirit gum, using the large teeth of your comb. Remove these loose bits and pieces as soon as posssible in order to give you the time and opportunity to make any minor repairs, such as adding or patching up any spots where the adhesive is bad or the wool or hair has matted because of careless application. Study Figs. 191 to 194 for further details on layering the beard.

REMOVING THE LOOSE FACIAL HAIR

To remove the wool or hair from your face, simply pull the material away. The adhesive will not hold so tightly that it will pinch your skin. Wet a cloth with acetone and rub it over the part of the face where you had spread the spirit gum. Be careful, when using acetone, to avoid breathing the fumes. It is a strong solvent and should be used only in a well ventilated room. When most of the spirit gum has been removed, cleanse your face with cold cream and finish as usual.

FACIAL HAIRPIECES

There may be occasions where you will want to apply the same style beard for several performances and do not want to be bothered styling the same beard each time. In such a situation you may find use for the ready-made facial hairpieces, which you simply apply to your face in the same way you would a wig. Hairpieces are available sewn onto a cloth backing or tied onto a lace net. The net provides a transparency and therefore a more natural effect. The net is also less durable than the cloth, so it must be handled with extreme care. Facial hairpieces range in style and use from sparse mustaches to rakish sideburns to beards of all sizes and shapes.

To apply the facial hairpiece, first fit it onto your face for size. Then remove it and apply spirit gum to the area of the face the beard will be adhering to. Replace the piece on your face and gently press it into place. Use your cloth to press the piece against the face, adhering it firmly. Once the piece is set, you can gently comb through it.

Figs. 195 to 210 illustrate various kinds of beards, mustaches, and a temple piece, as they appear on and off the face.

REMOVING AND CLEANING THE FACIAL HAIRPIECE

To remove wig or mustache, peel the hair away from the face. It will come off without any pain or discomfort. Dip a cloth in acetone and rub this into the area where spirit gum had been applied. Rub until the gum is loose and dissolved to avoid hazardous fumes. Work in a well ventilated area. After the gum is off, cleanse face with cleansing cream as usual.

To clean the lace beard or mustache, lay the piece lace side up on a clean towel. Dip a brush in acetone and carefully brush the surface of the lace until the gum is removed (Fig. 211). Dry the piece by waving it in the air and put it away in a box large enough to hold the piece without crushing it.

195. This is a short, full lace beard.

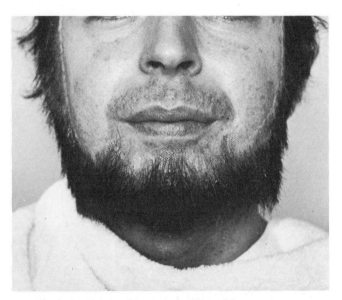

196. The beard is glued into place with spirit gum.

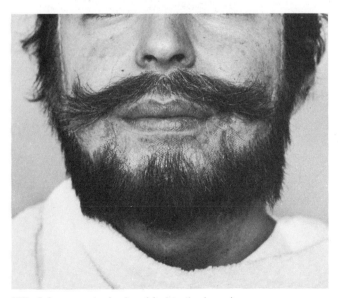

197. A lace mustache is added to the beard.

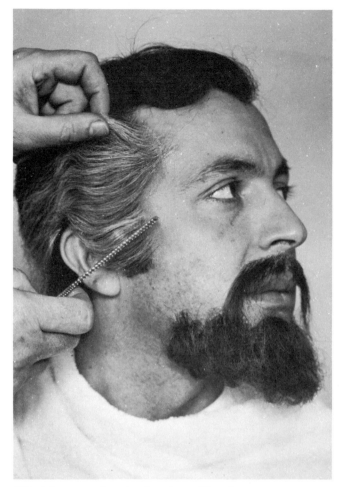

198. A lace gray temple piece is positioned.

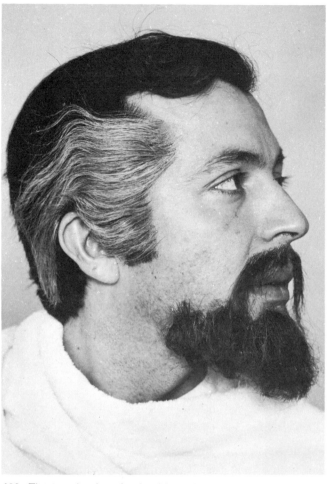

199. The temple piece is glued into place.

200. Here is a lace Van Dyke beard.

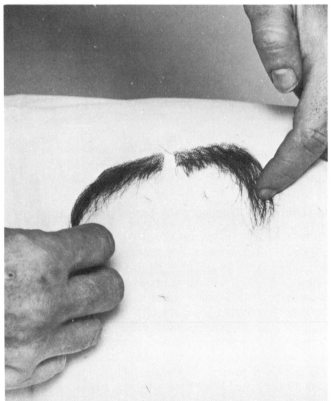

201. This mustache can be used separately or with a beard.

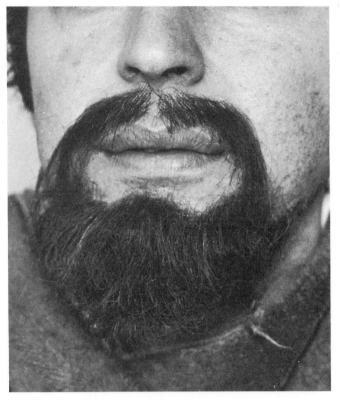

202. The Van Dyke beard and mustache are glued to the face.

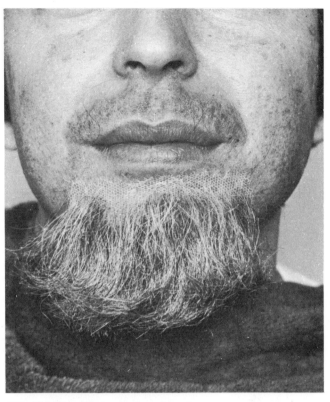

203. This is a short, gray lace beard.

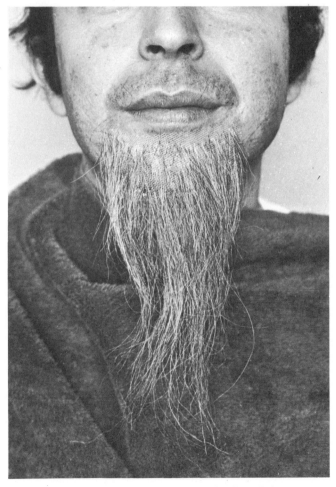

204. A long, gray lace beard is suitable for Don Quixote.

205. This is a trim, modern lace mustache.

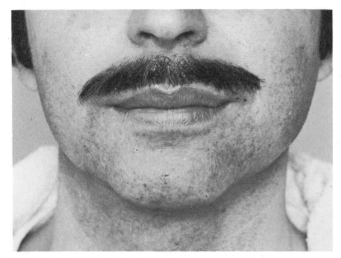

206. The lace mustache is applied.

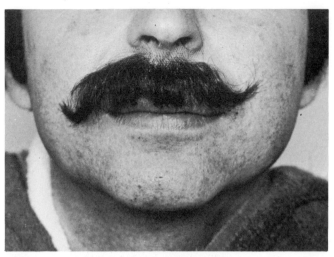

207. A large, black lace mustache is applied.

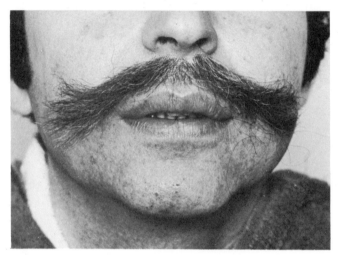

208. A grayed mustache, rather long, is applied.

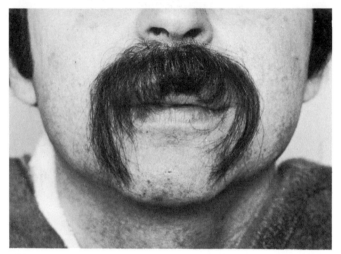

209. There is no end to the shapes available.

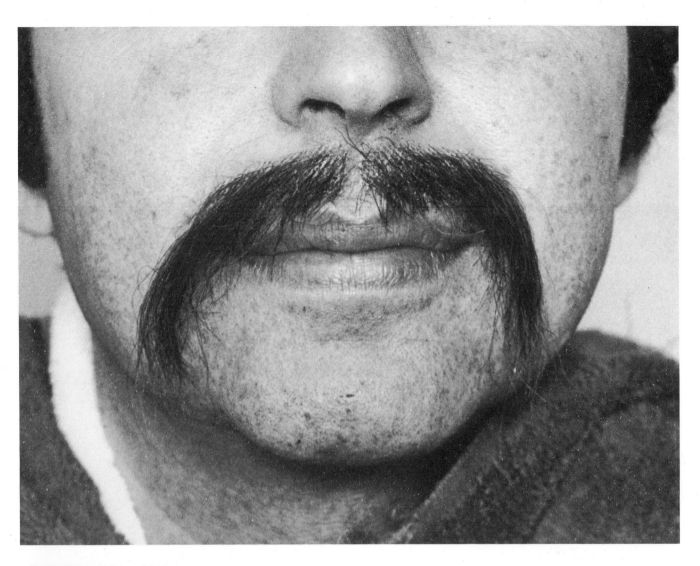

210. (Above) The mustache may be applied curling down or, turned in the other direction, may swirl upwards.

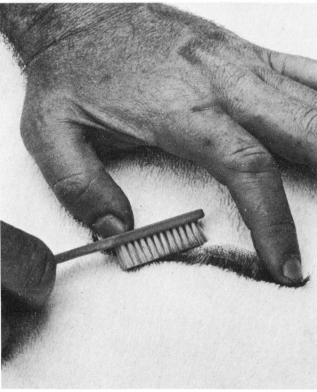

211. (Left) To clean a hairpiece, dip a brush in acetone, and brush the surface of the lace on a clean towel until you remove the spirit gum.

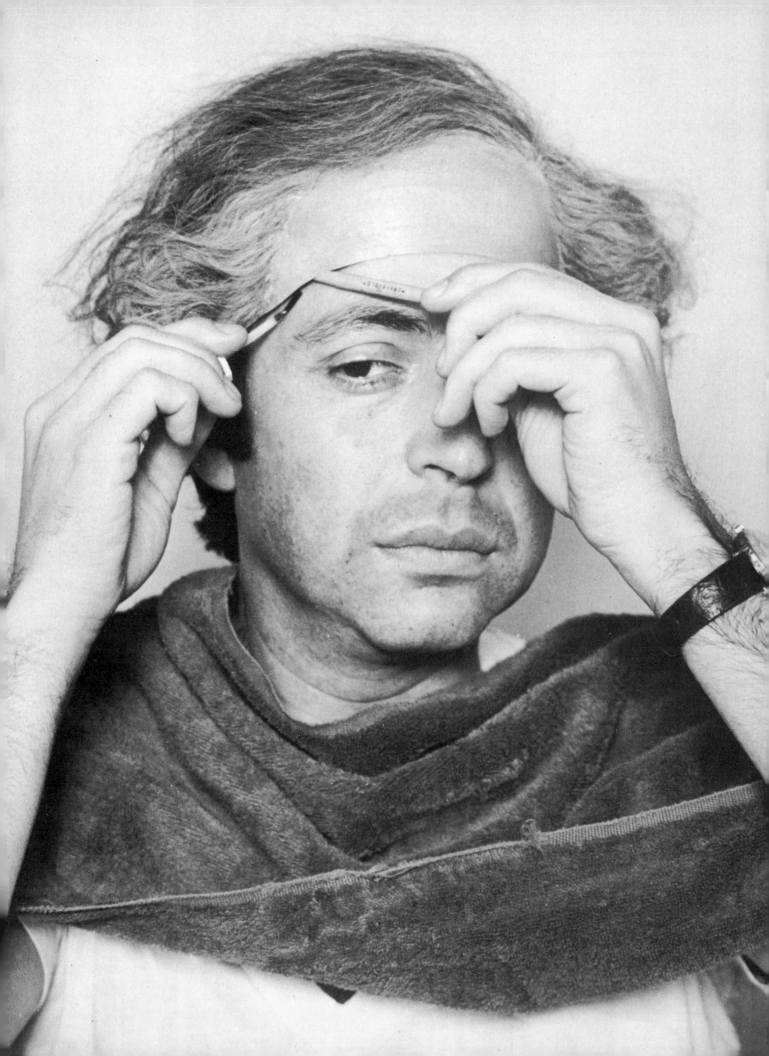

CHAPTER NINE

WIGS

The categories of makeup range greatly in variety. This is true of wigs as well. Not all wigs *add* hair to the head; they can range from totally bald caps, through bald fronts, to full heads of hair, to stylized formal law and court wigs. The simple thing wigs have in common is that the hair is attached to a base which is worn on the head. The base is made of a netting or of a silk material which is cut and sewn to conform to the shape of the head. The hair is attached to the base and either knotted in long strips—called *weft*—or knotted and tied on in very small clumps by hand, a process called *ventilating.*

Cloth front wigs (silk front being the best in this category) carry the fabric of the base onto the forehead, covering the performer's own hair in order to create the effect of baldness. Other wigs have a very fine transparent net front which simulates the hairline most naturally. The hairs attached to this net front are tied in one at a time, and resemble the natural hairline.

MEASURING FOR A WIG

To serve its purpose, the wig must fit properly. It must cover all existing hair without being too large (it may shift or not hold), nor too tight (it may cause discomfort). Before anything else, therefore, learn to measure your head so that you can order the correct size. (See Figs. 212 to 216.) There are four measurements that are necessary and these illustrations will show how they are evaluated.

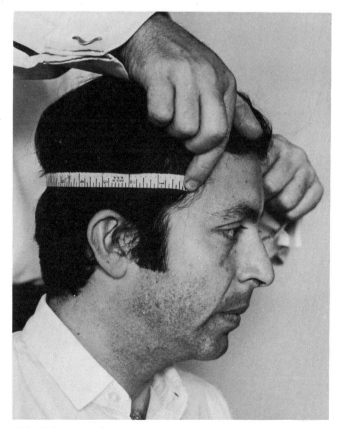

212. Using a cloth tape measure, first measure the area from the hairline at the temple around the back of the head to the temple on the other side. This is described, when ordering by mail, "from temple to temple."

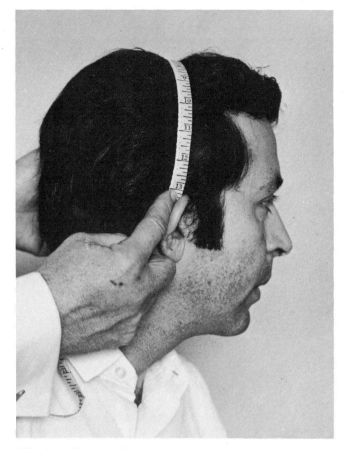

213. Start the tape from the point where the top of the ear joins the head. Measure up and across the top of the head to the same point at the other ear. This measurement is described as "from ear to ear over the head."

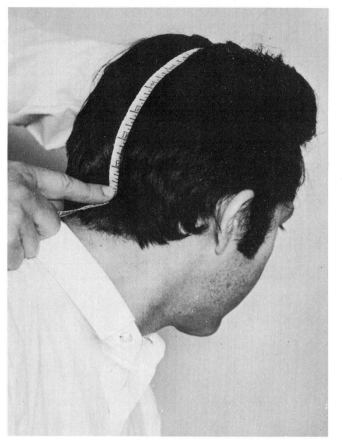

214. Start the tape at the hairline and carry it back over the head to the nape of the neck. Measurement is called "from hairline to nape of neck."

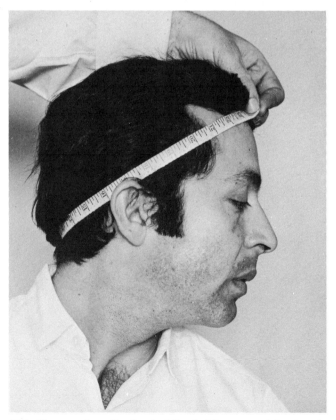

215. Measure from the front of the hairline around the temple and around the base of the head. Describe measurement as "around the head."

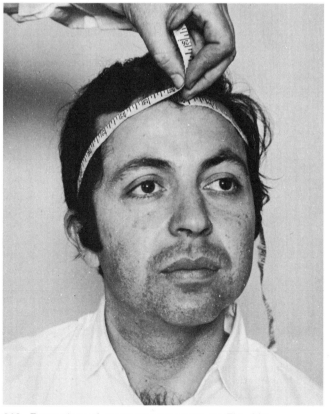

216. Front view of same measurement as Fig. 215.

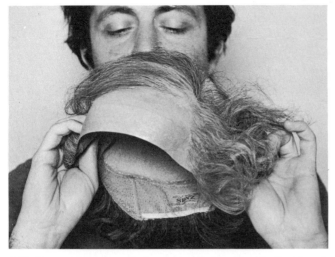

217. To position the silk front wig, first hold with the thumb and forefinger of each hand, the thumbs placed on the inside of the wig. Holding the wig as open as possible, lower the wig onto the head. Position the wig below the desired hairline point, slightly above the eyebrows.

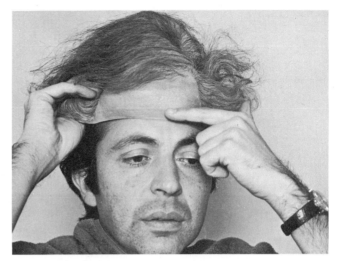

218. Holding the front carefully with a gentle but firm finger, make sure the wig is centered properly on the head.

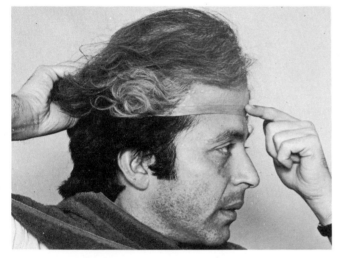

219. Holding firmly with the front finger on the forehead, ease the wig down by pulling gently at the back.

220. With the left hand, let the front slide up the front of the forehead, until it is firmly positioned on the head. Adjust the temples so that they cover the hairline.

221. Lift the edge of the wig gently with an orange stick or with the handle of a brush and apply spirit gum underneath the edge all along the front hairline.

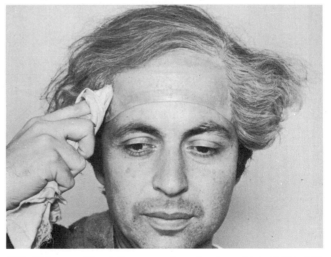

222. Using a silk cloth, press the glued portion of the wig firmly until the gum dries and the wig is solidly glued in place.

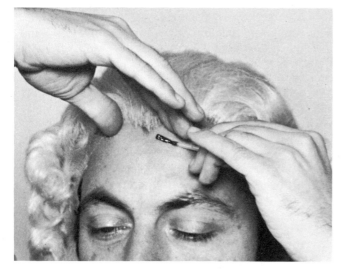

223. A lace or net front wig is positioned and fitted in the same manner as the silk or cloth front. Hold it in position between two fingers and apply the spirit gum over the lace in the space between the fingers.

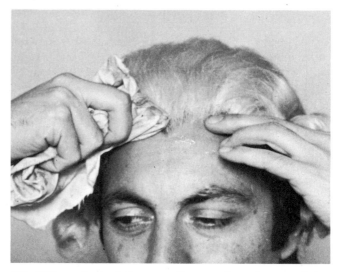

224. With a clean cloth, press the gum into place until the adhesive dries.

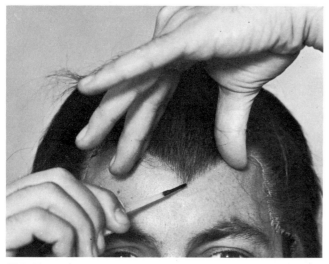

225. Here, the same process of positioning a different style of lace front wig is shown.

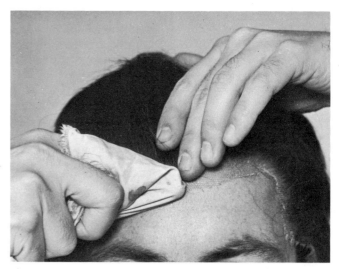

226. The gum is pressed until it adheres.

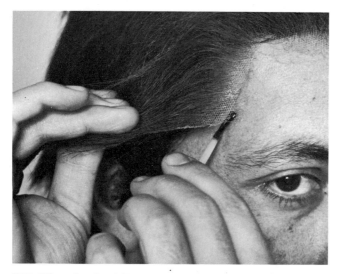

227. When the front is secure, apply glue under the lace at each side in turn and press dry with the silk cloth.

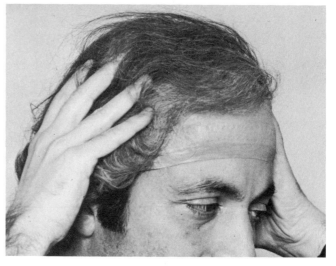

228. To remove the wig, first apply acetone to loosen the spirit gum. Hold the wig with both hands on each side of the head and gently lift the wig up and off the head.

POSITIONING THE CLOTH FRONT WIG

Not only must the wig fit well, it must also stay in place on the head. To fix it in position, the wig is usually glued to the scalp with the application of spirit gum. The most efficient place for gluing is on the portion of the forehead along the hairline. Glue both silk front and lace front wigs onto a clean forehead, free of makeup. Study Figs. 217 through 220 for placing the silk front wig onto the head. Study Figs. 221 and 222 for gluing the wig. Carefully lift the silk front and apply a layer of spirit gum to the forehead beneath the wig. Press the cloth front firmly with a clean cloth. Apply your base color on the cloth front, so that the same facial color is carried onto the forehead. Carry the style of your makeup onto the cloth front, treating it as an extension of the forehead.

POSITIONING LACE OR NET FRONT WIGS

Now let's study the method of placing the net front wig on the head. First, gently position the wig on the head. Check the net front for any loose, stray hairs and carefully comb them out of the way. Grip the net in place while you do this so that it does not move or shift. Hold the midsection of the forehead with two spread fingers of the left hand and apply spirit gum to the net area between the fingers. (See Figs. 223 and 225.) Blot and press the gum into the net with a piece of clean silk cloth until that area adheres and the gum is dry. (See Figs. 224 and 226.)

Now that the frontal part is adhered, carefully hold the net in place around one of the sideburns. Apply the spirit gum and blot. Press with clean silk cloth until dry. Do the same on the other side. (See Fig. 227.) Gently comb the hair into place. Carry the makeup onto the net.

REMOVING AND CLEANING THE WIG

Acetone is the most effective solvent to use in removing and cleaning wigs or hairpieces. This solvent is extremely inflammable and very harsh on the skin, so use it with care. Dip a clean cloth into a dish containing a small amount of acetone. Don't leave the bottle open any more than is necessary, and don't use a large dish or a large amount of solvent. The fumes are dangerous, especially in a small, confined room.

With the moistened cloth, dab the acetone onto the lace or silk front until the solvent softens and starts dissolving the spirit gum. Carefully loosen the net or silk from the skin. When all adhesion points have been freed, remove the wig by lifting it carefully away from the head (Fig. 228). With the cloth, dab some more of the acetone on that area of the forehead or temple until all the spirit gum has been removed. Apply a small amount of cold cream to the skin where the acetone was used and then continue to remove the makeup.

To clean the wig or hairpiece, take a small brush (eyebrow or soft toothbrush with wood or rubber handle. Acetone will dissolve plastic). Dip it into a shallow dish of acetone. With a gentle brushing motion, apply the brush to the part of the lace or silk having a residue of spirit gum. Repeat this process until the net or silk is clean. Small pieces may be lightly dipped into the plate of acetone and then brushed to loosen and remove the gum. When the piece or wig is clean, comb through it lightly and place it on a block or in its box until the next usage.

FEMALE WIGS

Female wigs are usually constructed of weft sewn to a netting base which is built on a thin silk frame, to size. Rarely does a female wig come with front hair lace. These wigs are usually designed so that the style of the "dressed" wig will cover the front and side hairline. In cases where the wig is designed to *expose* the hairline, the lace may be incorporated into the wig front and requires the same application described in this chapter. Most frequently, the female wig is held in place by the use of hair pins and bobby pins so that the wig is attached to the hair below. Additional falls, curls, and other feminine hairpieces are also attached by hair and bobby pins.

CHAPTER TEN

PROSTHETICS

The prosthetic piece is an artificial creation of a facial feature, completely formed and modeled, which may be added to the face. If handled carefully, it may last for additional usage, which is why a performer who intends to play the same role repeated times often prefers the prosthetic piece to applying putty nightly. The prosthetic piece is made of flexible plastic, foam rubber, or raw latex rubber from a mold. The flexible plastic and foam rubber pieces are far too complex to make. For our purposes, the raw latex rubber piece is most suitable. Pieces made from latex will serve extremely well.

To make a prosthetic piece, you first must make a mask of your face which will provide the specific forms of your features. Then you model in clay the feature you are planning to use and attach this to the mask. Using this clay model, you then make a mold. From this mold you pull the rubber latex feature. The form will fit perfectly onto your face, and you can apply and remove it easily. Each of these steps will be demonstrated here. To make a raw rubber latex prosthetic you will need the following materials:

petroleum jelly (Vaseline)
plaster of Paris
plaster of Paris bandages
cold dental impression material
towels
modeling clay
six rubber mixing bowls
two rubber spatulas
liquid latex rubber

MAKING THE MOLD FOR THE MASK

The first step in making a prosthetic piece is to take an impression of your face which will serve as the basis for all your future work. To make the mask, we first make a mold of the face. It is impossible to make a mask completely by yourself. One person must make the mask of another face, so I suggest you find someone else who also wants a permanent impression of his face, and take turns making the mask.

The mask is made while the model is lying prone. Set up a comfortable place for him. He must keep his face perfectly still throughout the process or it will be a failure. Drape towels around his head and neck and, if you take the impression on a couch or bed, put newspapers under and around the model to catch any splatter.

Set up a table to hold your materials and lay out the petroleum jelly, the impression material measured into six mixing bowls, spatulas, ten plaster of Paris bandage pieces cut into 6″ and 12″ lengths. When you start, you must move quickly because the impression material and the plaster both set very quickly. Be prepared to continue each step without pause until all phases are completed. Otherwise, your work will be spoiled and you will have to start over.

APPLYING THE IMPRESSION MATERIAL

With your fingers or brush, apply a small amount of Vaseline to the eyebrows, eyelashes, and to any exposed part of the hairline. Clean your hands. Mix the first amount of impression material with the prescribed

229. Measure out the impression material exactly, following precisely the instructions on the can.

230. Measure out the water at the directed temperature. The proper measuring cups are supplied with this particular impression material.

231. With the spatula, mix the material for the directed period of time.

amount of water at the proper temperature. (See Figs. 229 to 231.) You will be mixing the impression material as you work because it dries so rapidly. For this reason, I have suggested six mixing bowls. (In this demonstration, I used Elastic Impression Cream manufactured by Dental Perfection Company, Inc. of Glendale, California. However, there are many other materials available that will do the job just as well.)

First apply the impression material on one side of the forehead onto the temple; then on the other side of the forehead onto the temple. Using the spatula, drip the mixture onto the forehead and start to spread it with the spatula (Fig. 232). Try not to move the skin as you apply the material. The mixture should be soft enough to spread quickly and easily, like heavy batter. Use the spatula to keep it from dripping off the face. Keep the mixture at least ½″ thick on the face.

As soon as it looks as if the mixture will hold in place, mix the next batch and continue to apply more on other areas of the face (Fig. 233). Repeat the process until the entire face is covered. Do not carry the material beyond the front of the ears or beyond the hairline at the temples or forehead. You can carry it below the jawline, but no farther than the windpipe.

Around the eyebrows, apply the mixture in the direction of eyebrow growth. Around the eye socket, be particularly carefully to *pour* the mixture and use the spatula as little as possible. You want this area to remain as still as possible. (See Fig. 234.)

Place the mixture carefully around the nostrils. Be sure at all times that there are adequate breathing holes open (Fig. 235). If breathing is affected in any way, the model will become unsettled, so be careful and constantly reassure him.

APPLYING PLASTER BANDAGES

After the impression material has been applied, we now move to the plaster of Paris bandages (Fig. 236), which dry firmly enough to hold the plastic impression material. Do not wait for the impression material to set. Quickly wet one of the plaster of Paris bandages in the water (Fig. 237). Squeeze out the excess water and lay it on the mask (Fig. 238). Continue to apply other strips as shown in Figs. 239 and 240.

Let the plaster of Paris bandages dry, a period of roughly 10 to 20 minutes. The plaster of Paris will heat up as the drying process starts. During this time, talk to the model. Keep him reassured at all times.

COMPLETING THE MOLD

When the plaster of Paris outer bandages are firm to the touch, hold the mask with one hand and pull lightly at the skin around the edge of the mask to start the loosening process (Fig. 241). Ask the model to move his face under the mask, then ask him to sit up. Hold the mask in place all this time. As the model sits up and bends slightly forward, slip the mask off the face gently. Hold it with the plaster of Paris underneath, keeping the inner mold of impression material in place. (See Figs. 242 to 245.)

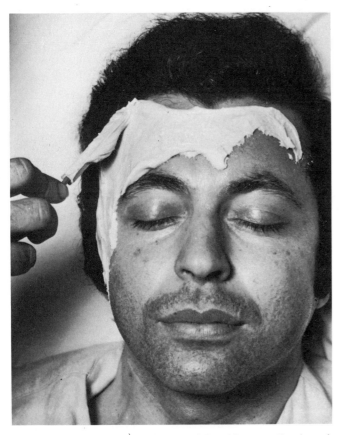

232. Apply the impression material with smooth, broad strokes of the spatula, first on the forehead and down onto the cheek.

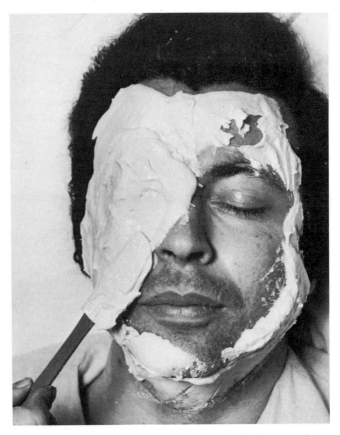

233. Carry the mixture down one side of the face and up under the chin.

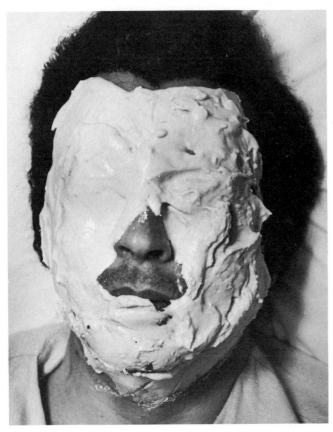

234. Around the eyes, pour in the material and avoid using the spatula. Build up the density of the impression material.

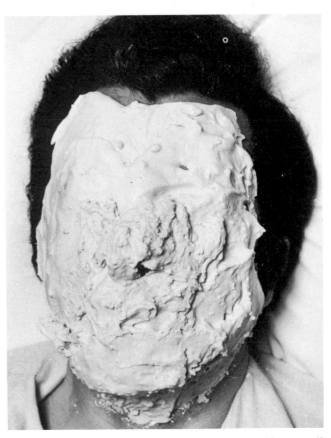

235. Make sure the nostrils are clear for breathing at all times.

236. The sections of plaster of Paris bandages should be pre-cut to 6″ and 12″ pieces.

237. Dip the bandage in water and quickly squeeze out the excess as you take it from the bowl.

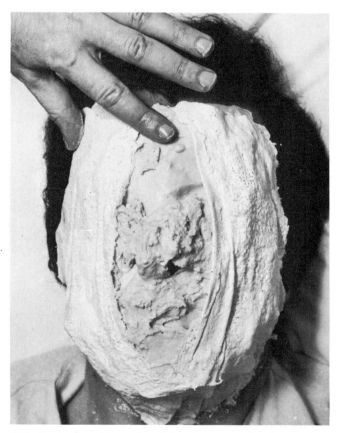

238. Apply the strips of wet bandage over the impression material to create a firm cradle.

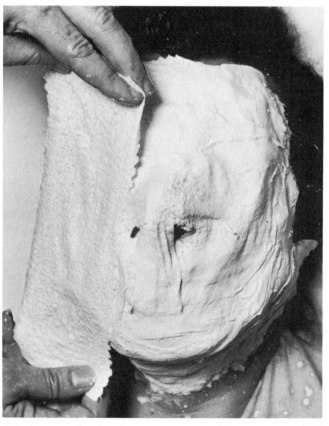

239. Lay on the bandages in alternate directions to bond them effectively.

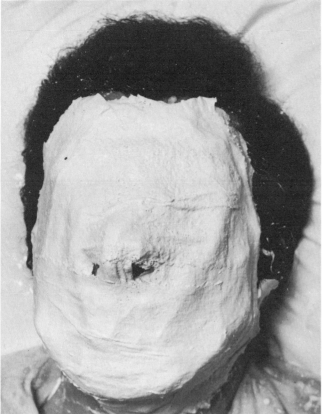

240. The bandages have been smoothed over with wet hands to join the plaster together. Always be sure to leave air holes at the nostrils.

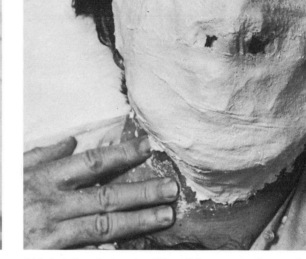

241. Let the plaster dry. When it is warm to the touch (about 20 minutes), begin to loosen the skin around the edge.

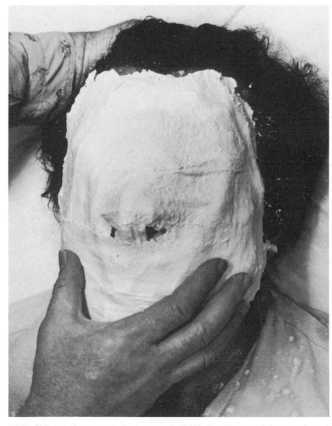

242. When the mask is loose, hold it in place with one hand and, supporting the back of the head with the other, help lift the model to a sitting position.

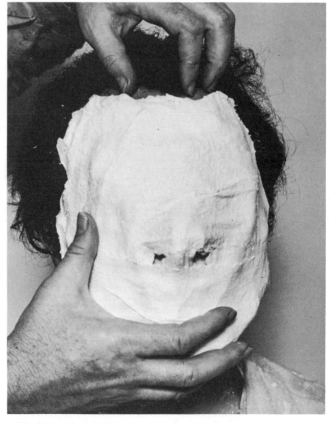

243. Once the model is seated, ask him to move his face beneath the plaster as an aid to the loosening process.

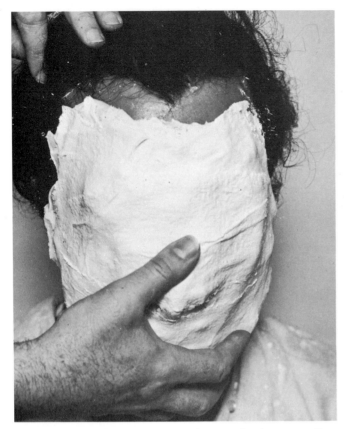

244. Ask the model to lean forward as you begin to ease the mask from his face.

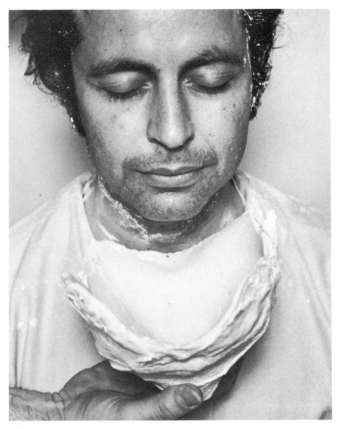

245. Remove the mask.

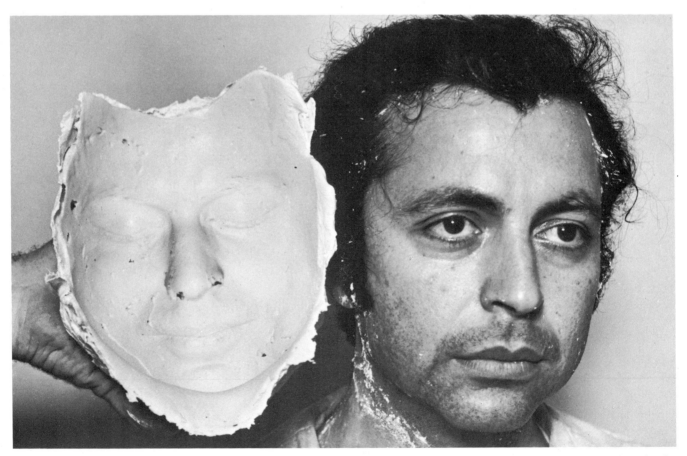

246. The mold for the mask is complete. Notice the negative form of the face in the impression material.

MAKING THE MASK FROM THE MOLD

You now have your mold (Fig. 246). From here you will make the positive mask. The positive will be made by pouring plaster of Paris into this mold. Look over the interior carefully for any bits of broken-off impression material or plaster. Carefully remove them. Insert two plugs of clay into the nostrils (Fig. 247) so that the plaster of Paris will not leak out. Set the mold on a table, placing some bits of modeling clay under it to hold it steady, and position it on an even level so that the shell will retain the liquid material like a soup bowl. (See Fig. 248.)

Into a clear mixing bowl, pour three cups of fresh plaster of Paris. Add water and mix. The mixture should have the consistency of pudding. If the mixture is too watery, add more plaster; if too thick, add water. Tap the bowl on the table to eliminate any air bubbles that may have formed in the mixture.

After the plaster of Paris is thoroughly mixed, pour about a cup into the shell (Fig. 249), then pick up the shell and swirl the plaster around so that it forms an initial inner coat on the interior of the shell (Fig. 250). If it is too heavy, spread the plaster over the mold with your spatula.

When the interior is coated, set the shell on the table and spoon in more of the plaster of Paris mixture (Fig. 251). Use your spatula to build up the thickness on all sides of the shell. Add more plaster until you spread at least 1″ to 2″ thickness over the whole mold. You may fill in the entire mold if you wish, but this is not really necessary. (See Fig. 252.)

The mold will harden in about an hour. When it is hard, pick it up, turn it over, and carefully separate the impression material and outer shell from the inner mold (Figs. 253 and 254). Examine the inner mask. If you have carefully followed these instructions, you should have a perfect reproduction of the face.

Now clean the mold of excess bits of plaster. If you find some small air holes, you can fill them with a touch of soft plaster of Paris. If there are some uneven lumps in the mold, you can easily scrape them away with a small knife (Fig. 255). Scrape carefully, because the plaster of Paris mold is still comparatively soft and can be easily cut in two. When you are satisfied, put the mold away to harden overnight. If you wish to preserve your mask permanently, give it two coats of shellac or varnish after the plaster has dried. Let the first coat of shellac dry thoroughly before applying the second. When this is completed, you are ready for modeling the artificial feature.

This mask will now be used to make a mold for the rubber piece. Now you will model the shape of the feature you are to wear. Restraint is the key here. The initial urge is always to make many more features than is necessary; each piece you build requires a separate mold-making process, which is time-consuming.

MODELING THE FEATURE

Setting the face mold on a table, place a small quantity of modeling clay on the feature you are going to alter. Here we will model a nose. Shape the clay on

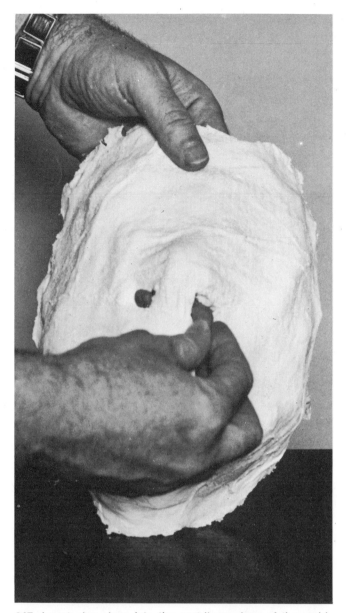

247. Insert clay plugs into the nostril openings of the mold.

248. Set the mask on a level surface, supporting it with the clumps of clay.

249. Mix the plaster of Paris as directed and pour in the first layer. Spoon in enough to cover the entire surface of the mold.

250. Swirl the plaster to cover the interior of the mold and bounce the mold to force out any air bubbles.

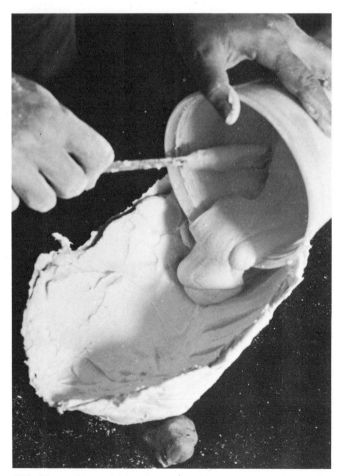

251. Place the mold back on the clay clumps and pour in more plaster of Paris.

252. Spread the plaster to a uniform thickness of at least 1″. Now let the plaster dry.

253. Once the plaster is dry, begin to peel away the mold from the face impression.

254. Continue to peel carefully in order to avoid breaking any part of the impression.

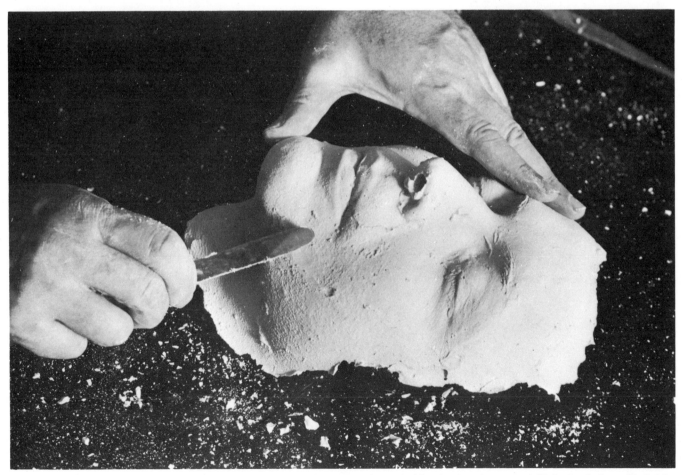

255. Scrape away any bumps or irregularities in the plaster and fill in the holes with fresh mixed plaster of Paris. Let the mask dry overnight.

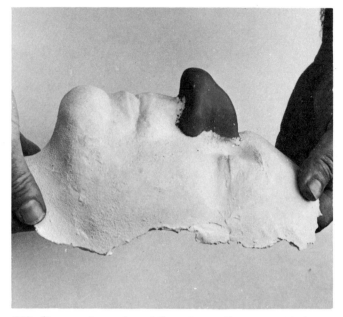

256. Place a piece of modeling clay on the nose and shape the form you want. Blend the edges into the mask.

257. Begin to construct a well around the feature with modeling clay.

258. Continue building the walls around the nose.

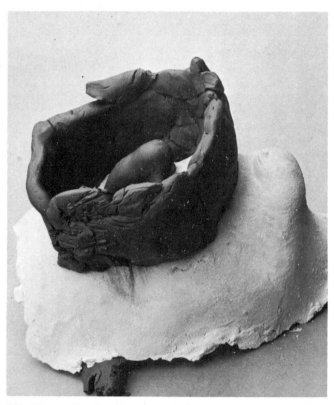

259. The walls should surround the feature, and be higher than the nose.

the nose to the shape you want (Fig. 256). Examine it carefully from all views, front, side, below. Avoid the urge to make the feature too large. The shape should fit naturally with the shape of your mask. Is this the shape of the feature you desire? If not, alter it any way you please. Blend the edges into the mask.

Treat the clay very much as you would nose putty. When you are satisfied that the built-up feature is what you want, create a pore texture by patting it with a piece of heavy, red artificial sponge, the type used by typists to moisten their fingers.

MAKING THE MOLD

The modeled feature will now be transformed into a mold from which you can make your rubber piece. Set the mask on the table and create a "well" around the feature with additional modeling clay (Fig. 257). Shape the well so that its walls are even all around and are higher than the feature itself (Figs. 258 and 259). Using a fingertip and a brush, coat the interior of the well and the feature with a light layer of Vaseline (Figs. 260 and 261).

Now prepare a mixing bowl with plaster of Paris as you did to make the mask. You will have to estimate the amount of plaster of Paris needed for this mold. (A full small mixing bowl should be sufficient as shown here.) Add water and mix the plaster well (Figs. 262 and 263). Shake out the air bubbles and pour a small quantity into the mold (Fig. 264). Pick up the mold and swirl about the plaster so that all surfaces of the mold receive a thin coating of the plaster. When you are satisfied that all interior surfaces are covered, pour in additional plaster to within ¼" of the top of the mold (Fig. 265). (Obviously, if the walls of your mold have not been constructed to an over-all even height, the plaster will spill over the walls.)

Now let the plaster dry; first it will heat up, then harden. When the plaster is quite hard, remove the clay walls of the well (Fig. 266) and carefully separate the mold from the mask (Figs. 267 to 269). Now remove the clay nose from the interior of the mold (Fig. 270). Check immediately for air bubbles and fill in or chip away any parts that would impair your mold (Fig. 271). Put it aside to dry and harden overnight.

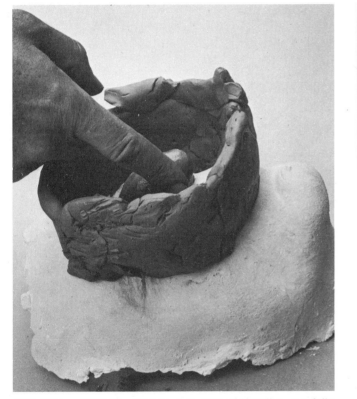

260. With a fingertip, apply a thin coat of Vaseline carefully on the nose.

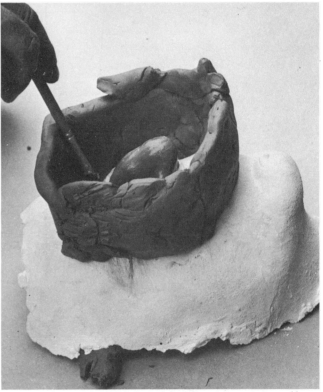

261. Use a brush to coat the rest of the interior with Vaseline.

262. Mix the plaster of Paris as directed.

263. Blend the plaster thoroughly, removing any air bubbles by gently tapping the side of the bowl.

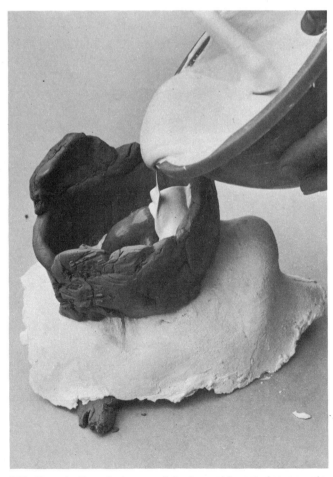

264. Pour in the plaster carefully to avoid capturing any air pockets in the mixture.

265. Pour in the rest of the plaster practically to the top of the walls of the mold.

266. When the plaster is dry and hard, remove the clay walls.

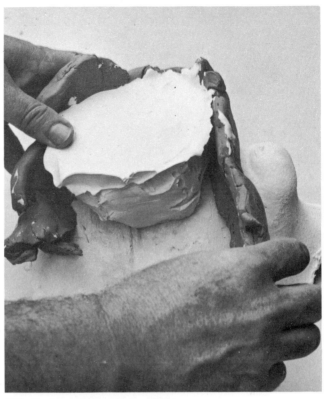

267. Peel away the clay carefully.

268. Holding the plaster firmly in two hands, ease the mold away from the mask.

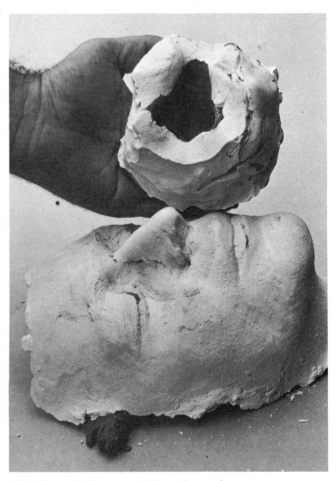

269. The mold is separated from the mask.

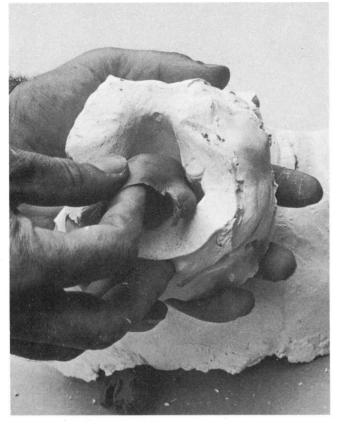

270. Now remove the clay from the mold. The Vaseline enables you to detach it easily.

271. Check the interior of the mold for any imperfections, such as bumps which can be smoothed down, or holes that can be filled with plaster. Let the mold dry overnight.

MAKING THE RUBBER PIECE FROM THE MOLD

Wash and scrub the mold clean of any residue of Vaseline or bits of clay or plaster. Dry the mold with a towel or tissues. Open the bottle of liquid latex and, using your Japanese writing brush or the brush from the latex container, paint a very thin coat of the rubber to the interior of the mold (Fig. 272). Carry this thin coating beyond the edge of the mold. Add a second layer of latex to the inside of the mold, but it's preferable that you don't continue the edge quite as far as you did the first time.

Allowing about ten minutes for the latex to dry between each application, apply successive coats of the latex and build up the piece so that it will hold its shape and have body. This process calls for at least ten or fifteen layers of the latex, but experience will help you determine exactly how many layers you will need for the latex to hold its shape.

Replace the cover or lid on the latex bottle when you are not actually using it. Exposure to air will cause the liquid to vulcanize and harden. In fact, if you store your latex for a long period of time without using it, you will note a progressive deterioration and hardening of the liquid. It should be a milky or off-white color and not much thicker than the consistency of buttermilk. If it is cracked or thick, do not bother using it. Get a new supply if you want a good piece.

When you have applied enough layers of the latex to make the piece, set the mold aside for the proper drying. When the milky white color of the latex has turned to a light tan (Fig. 273), the rubber has vulcanized. This process may take from two to six hours, depending on the number of layers of latex you have applied.

Once the latex has dried thoroughly, powder the interior of the mold with a powder puff (Figs. 274 to 276). Then carefully peel away the latex from the walls of the mold (Fig. 277), powdering the exterior of the rubber piece between the plaster as you peel. The powder protects the rubber from adhering to another area of rubber. When you have removed the rubber piece, check it carefully. Make sure the nose has been completely powdered. Then brush off the powder and trim the edges of the piece to the size you want (Figs. 278 to 282). The mold is now permanent and you can make additional pieces with it if you so desire.

APPLYING THE RUBBER PIECE

Before you apply the rubber piece, make sure the area is cleansed of makeup and is dry. You can put base on your face before it has been applied or afterwards. Apply spirit gum to the area where the piece will be attached (Fig. 284). Position the piece carefully and then tap the edges into place with a clean fingertip (Fig. 285). If an edge bunches up, gently peel it away and let it fall into place properly. After the piece is in place, press the edges down with a brush handle or cloth until the nose is completely adhered (Fig. 286). Apply the makeup base to the piece and paint it to conform with your total makeup (Figs. 287 and 288).

272. After cleaning the mold of residue clay or Vaseline, paint a thin layer of latex rubber on the interior surfaces of the mold.

273. Allowing each layer to dry between applications, continue to apply latex until you achieve the desired thickness. Then allow the latex to dry for several hours until the rubber vulcanizes. The latex will turn tan in color.

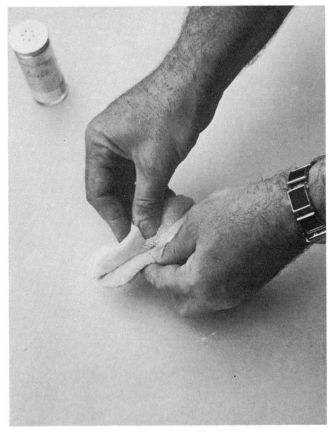

274. Shake powder onto the puff.

275. Rub the powder well into the puff.

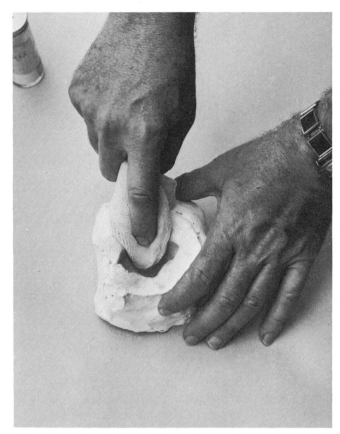

276. Powder the interior of the mold, completely covering the rubber piece.

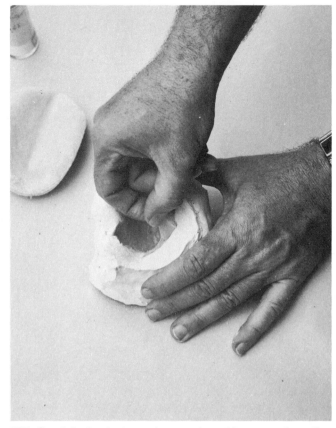

277. Carefully begin to peel away the rubber nose from the mold.

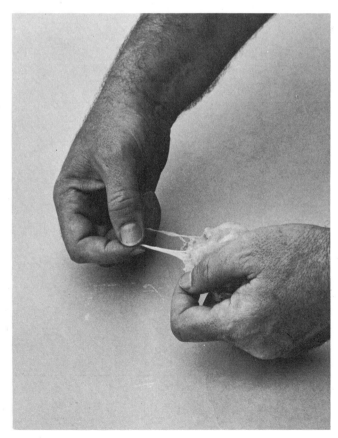

278. After you have removed the nose from the mold, peel off excess edges.

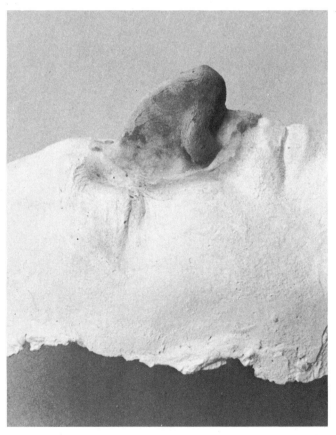

279. Place the nose onto the mask to be sure you have obtained a correct fitting.

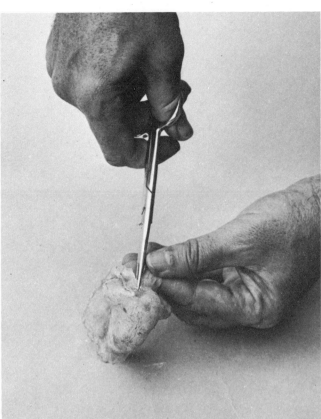

280. Trim off excess rubber around the nostrils so that you will have air holes.

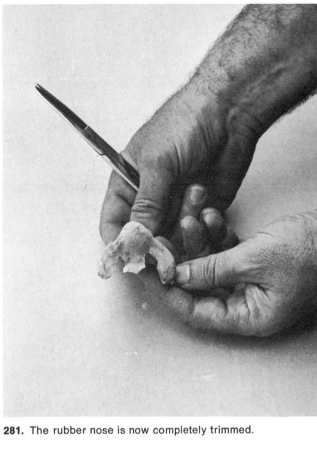

281. The rubber nose is now completely trimmed.

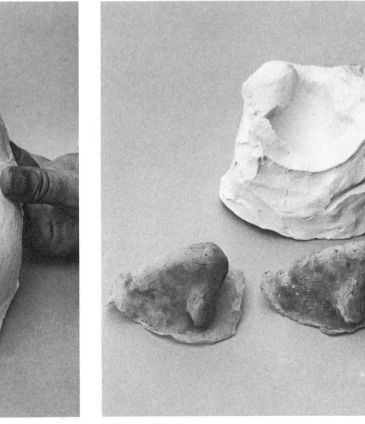

282. Place the nose back on the mask for a final fitting.

283. Once you have made a mold, you can use it repeatedly to make as many noses as you need. Keep the mold clean and in good condition and it will be continually useful.

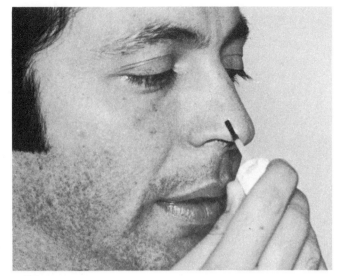

284. To apply the prosthetic piece, first brush on spirit gum to the areas of the nose that the rubber will attach to.

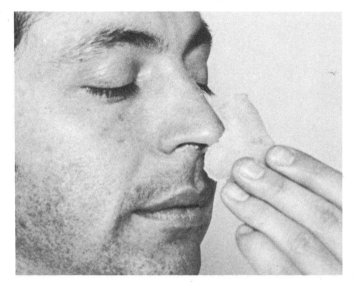

285. Place the rubber nose in position.

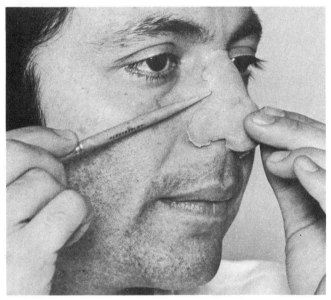

286. Press firmly on all edges of the piece until the rubber nose is glued in place.

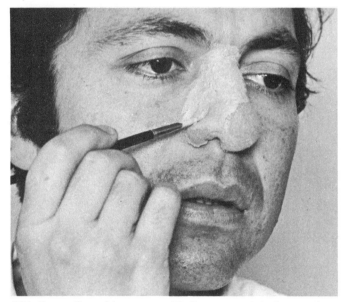

287. Cover the rubber nose with the appropriate base color and blend this into the base.

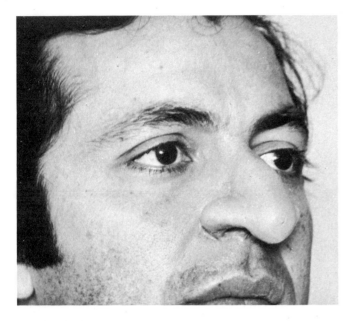

REMOVING THE RUBBER PIECE

To remove the piece after the performance, dab at the edges gently with a clean cloth dipped in acetone. Rub against the edges until you can loosen enough of the piece to grasp. Then carefully lift away the piece as you continue dabbing with the cloth soaked in acetone. When the piece is completely loose, lift it away (Fig. 289), and cleanse the edges of any residual spirit gum. Powder the piece and put it away for another use if it can be used again. Cleanse the rest of your face in the usual manner.

288. (Left) Notice how well the edges blend into the face. The nose has not yet been shaded.

289. (Below) To remove the piece, apply acetone to the edges to loosen the nose, then carefully peel it off the face.

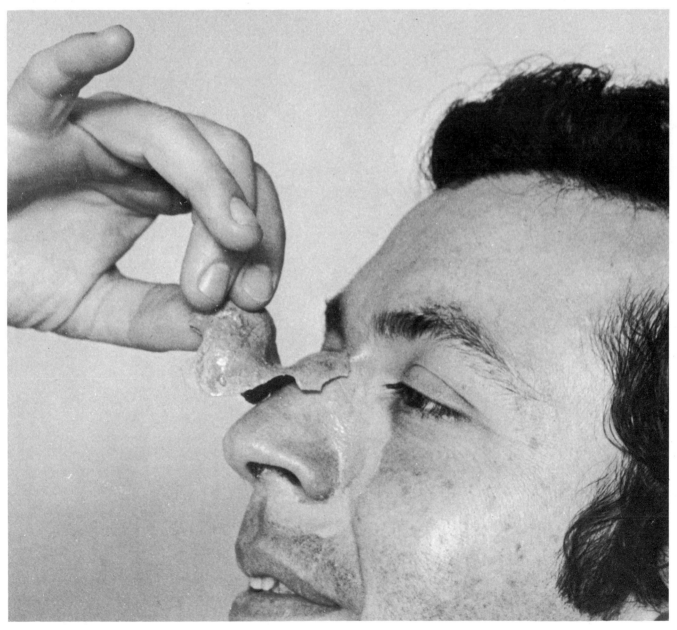

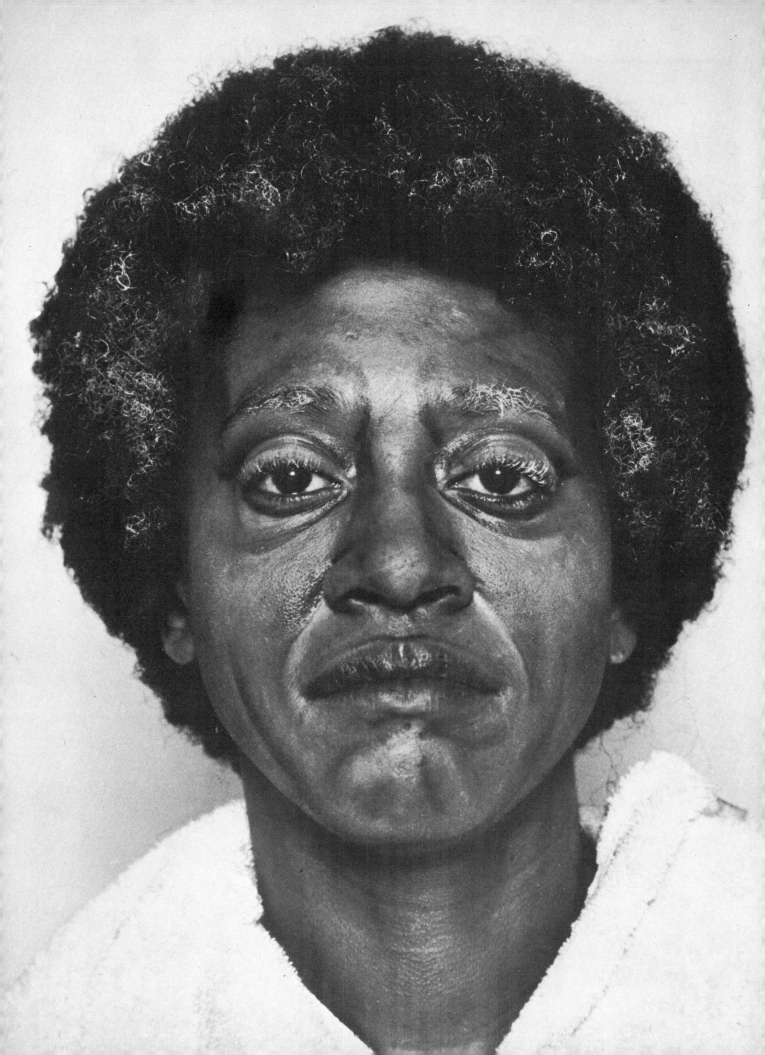

CHAPTER ELEVEN

THE BLACK PERFORMER

The black performer has always been taken for granted on the American stage. He has been used as a stereotype, and caricatured unmercifully. Some of the finest artists of our time have never had the opportunity to develop or to show the range of performances they were capable of assuming. Ignorance of the proper use of makeup for the black artist has been one of the factors in holding him back.

The most important contribution I can make to the black performer is to convince him that all of his makeup problems differ from those of the white performers in only two respects: (1) The black performer usually requires a different shadow mixture and highlight color; (2) The black performer may use his own skin color as a base color more successfully than is possible for the Caucasian. In every other respect—blending technique, use of optical illusions, and all other tools of makeup—the black performer uses exactly the same procedures as have been described throughout this book.

DETERMINING THE MAKEUP COLORS

Just as we have seen for the white performer, the black performer must first determine the skin color he wants to project to the audience. Is it your own skin color, or is it lighter or is it darker?

If the base color is determined—and the black performer need not use a base color—a satisfactory shadow mixture must be selected. If you have chosen a dark skin tone, the shadow mixture could be equal parts of maroon, brown, and black, made lighter or

darker as needs dictate. The highlight varies from the colors used by white performers to a highlight as dark as the base used for classic Greek.

In general, the black performer has greater latitude in selecting a base color than the white performer has. His own skin color can frequently be used as a base color. The greatest difficulty for a black performer whose skin is very dark is in making up a skin tone that is considerably *lighter* than that of his own natural color. The very dark skin tones tend to "bleed" through the base, making the very light tone difficult to achieve. Yet there is a solution to this.

It was my good fortune to have done the makeup for the renowned actor Canada Lee when he appeared in *The Duchess of Malfi*, on Broadway in New York City. It was the first time a Negro performer had been asked to play a Caucasian part.

Lee's skin coloring is quite dark and it did bleed through the normal grease paints available. I explored and discovered a remarkable cosmetic, called Lydia O'Leary's "Covermark," a makeup invented to cover birth marks and severe skin discolorations. It is completely opaque. Using this cosmetic, I determined the base color, shadow mixture, highlight, and rouge.

I applied a nose, wig, mustache, and beard, details that enhanced the Caucasian face. The makeup was so successful that Mr. Lee passed by his own brother backstage and wasn't recognized!

GRECIAN MAKEUP TECHNIQUE

To develop your skills in stage makeup, you must follow the same stage-by-stage development of technique outlined in this book. The Grecian techniques and principles are particularly important. The Grecian reveals the way to modify and alter features, retaining or creating the illusion of youth. The black performer uses the same base, shadow mixture, and rouge, and follows the same procedure for measuring and altering the features. The end result may appear more mask-like and unreal than it would for the Caucasian, but the skills developed in the Grecian technique are equally valuable for both black and white artists. Don't pass it by.

AGING

In learning how to develop and paint for age, the black performer should try various base colors and their complementary shadows and highlights, and also become skilled in using his own skin tones as a base, applying the shadows and highlights directly to it. (See Figs. 290 to 296.)

If putty is used to build up a feature, an appropriate base color must cover it and blend into the base or skin tone, just as was seen in Chapter 7.

With practice and application of the principles demonstrated in this book, the black artist should have open to him a vast range of roles that will allow expression of all his talents.

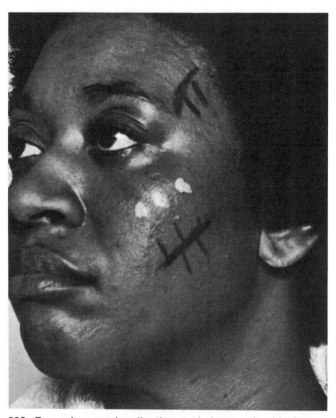

290. For aging—as in all other techniques—the black performer follows the same stages as the white artist. The temple and cheek sinkings are placed.

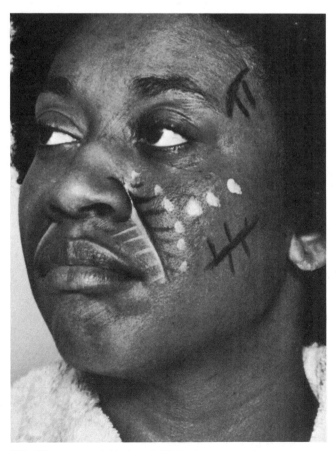

291. The nose wrinkle is established.

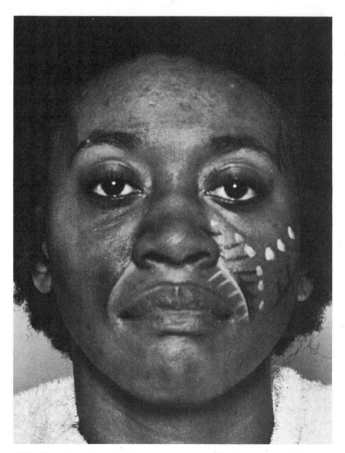

292. The temple, cheek, and nose wrinkle have been blended on one side.

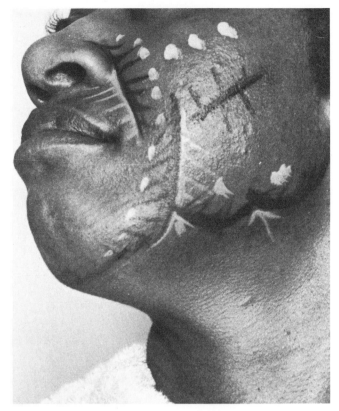

293. The jowls are placed with shadows and highlights.

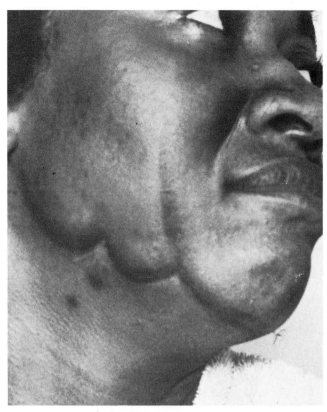

294. The jowls have been blended.

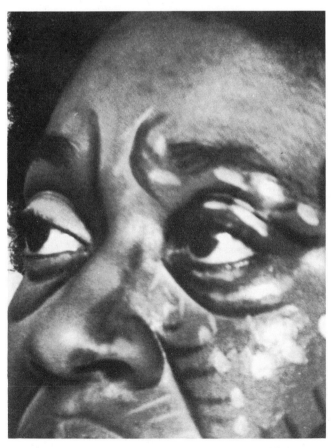

295. The upper and lower eye shadows and highlights are placed.

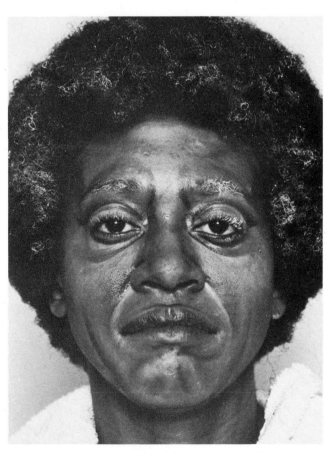

296. The aging is complete with the addition of graying to the hair, eyebrows, and lashes. For a more detailed description of aging, see Chapter 4.

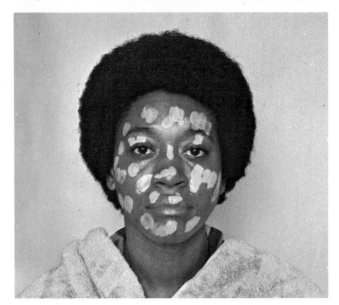

The base color has been spotted on the face.

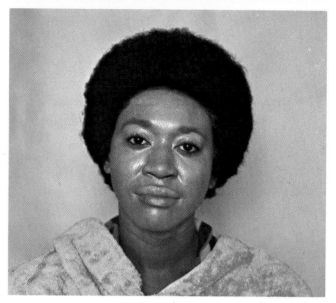

The base color is spread evenly.

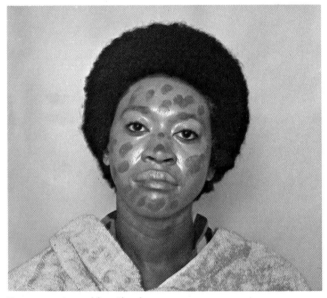

Rouge spots redden the base.

The rouge has been blended into the base.

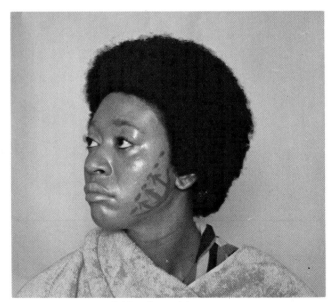

Note placement and blending of jaw rouge.

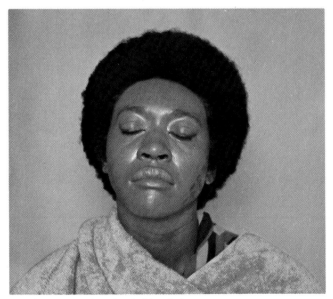

The jaw rouge has been blended.

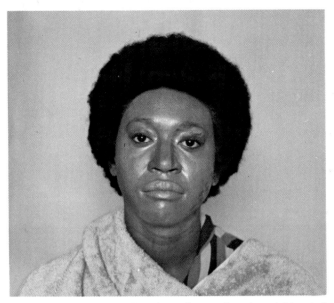

The nose and eye shading have been placed and blended.

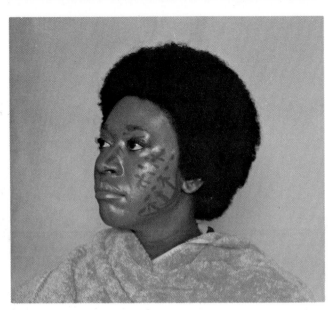

The cheek rouge is placed.

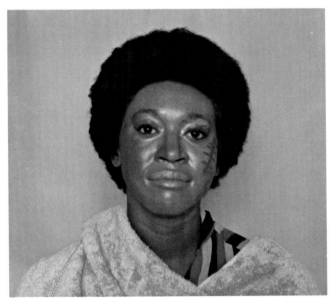

The cheek rouge is blended.

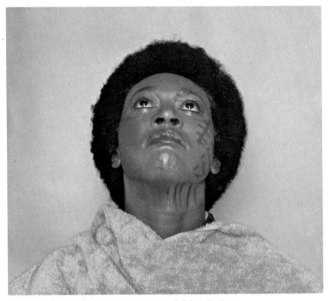

The neck shading is placed and blended.

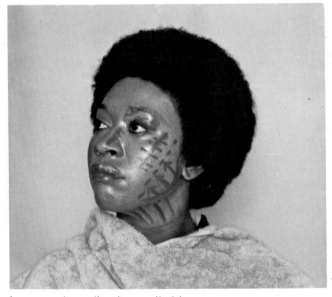

A new eyebrow line is penciled in.

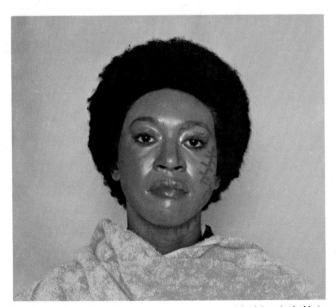

All the makeup has been placed and one side blended. Note the painted lips.

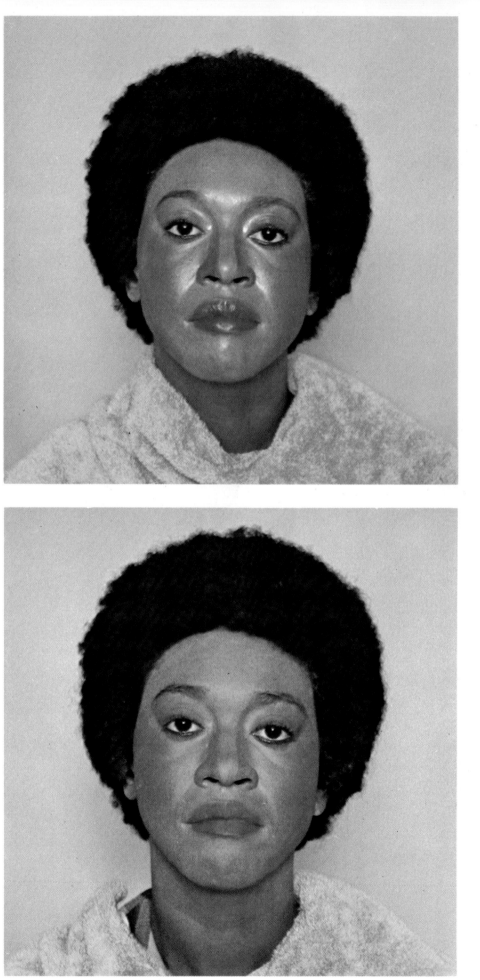

The complete makeup has been blended.

The complete makeup is now powdered.

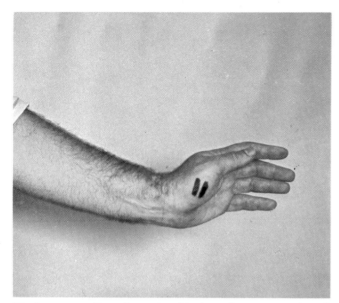

Shadow proportions for aging black performer: equal parts brown and black.

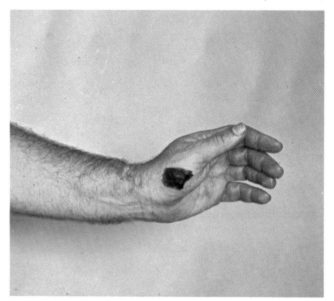

The shadow mixture has been completed.

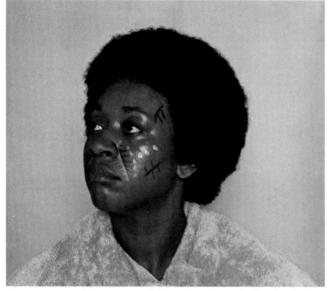

Placement and direction of the temple and check sinking, and nose wrinkle as well.

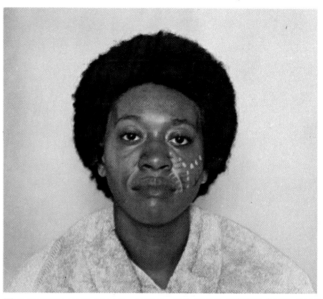

The temple and cheek sinking and nose wrinkle have been blended.

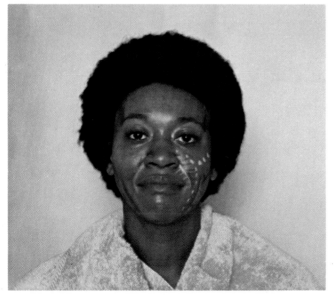

The placement and blending of the chin wrinkle.

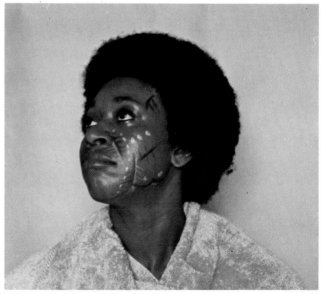

The placement of the jowls.

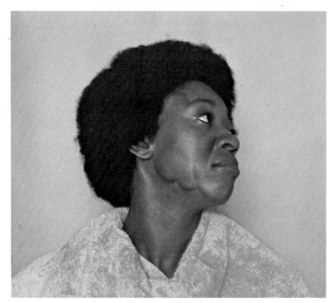

The jowls have been blended.

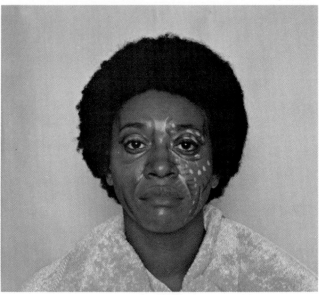

The blending and placement of the upper and lower eye.

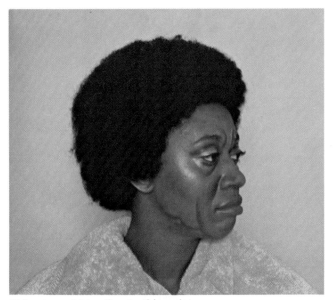

Side view of blending to this point.

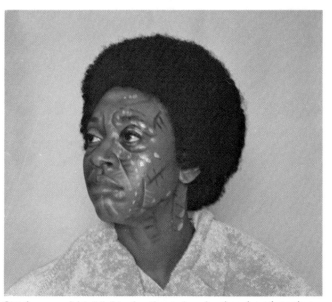

Shadows and highlights for the aging forehead and neck are placed.

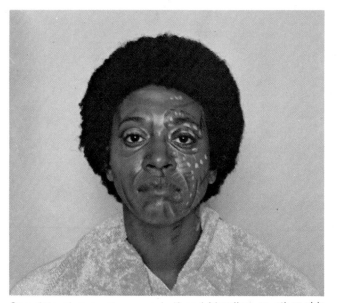

Complete placement on one half and blending on other side of the face.

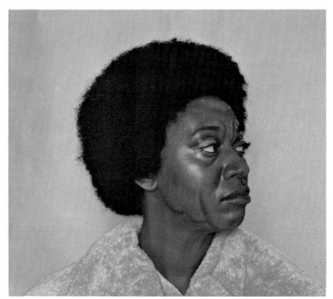

Complete blending, profile view.

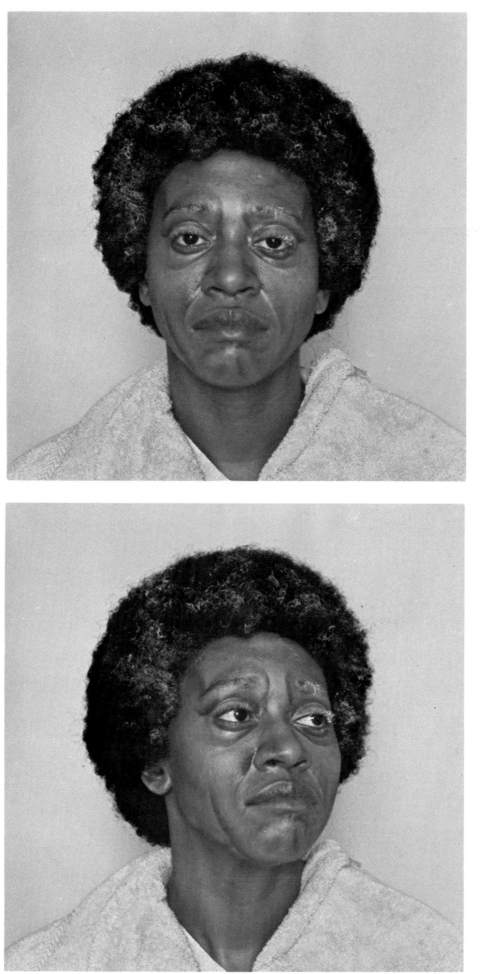

Graying has been added and painting is complete

Three quarter view of completed age for black performer.

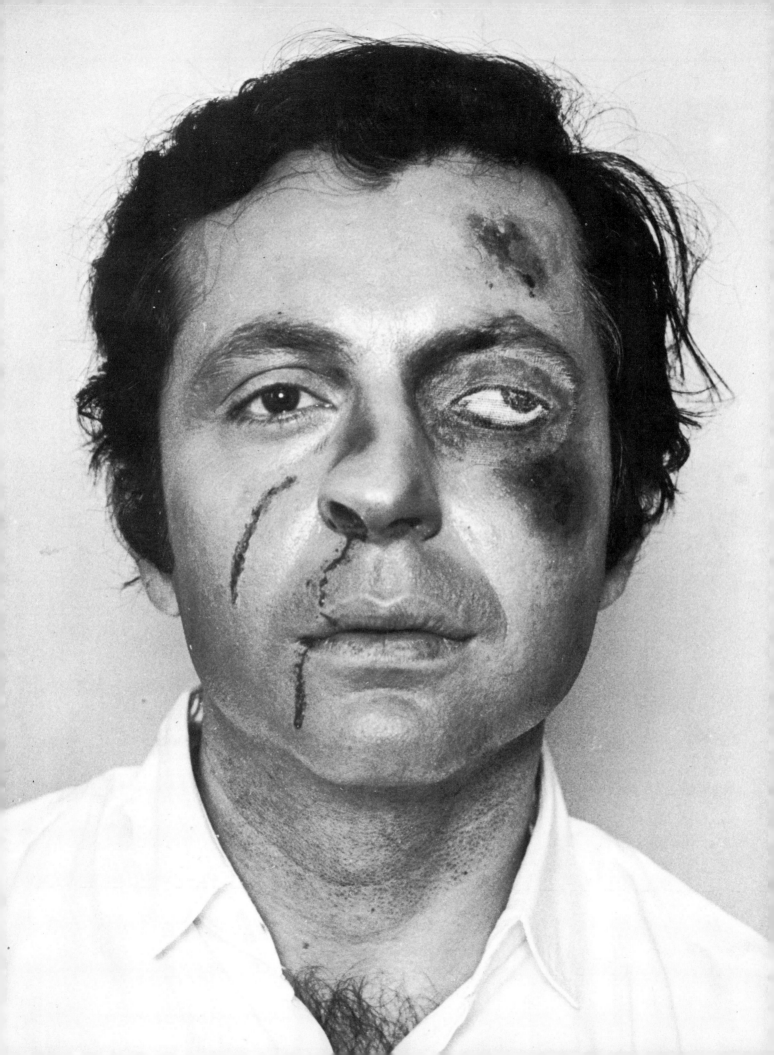

CHAPTER TWELVE

SPECIAL EFFECTS

Variations from the usual appearance, such as bruises, scars, broken nose, unshaven look, are vital to the context of a total characterization. These are considered special effects. The spectacular success of the "monster" period of film-making has created a false aura about these "special" make-ups. Creating the effect of horror is always much easier than it looks. In general, any extreme makeup technique requires a certain amount of *physical* work, but the real effort and creativity is in making up the subtle changes, the realistic modifications of the performer. Special effects in makeup are fun, but they are not nearly as difficult as the techniques we have dealt with so far.

There are some special effects which can be useful to you on occasion, but use them moderately and with care. Don't destroy a good characterization because you get carried away with the sensational effect of a scar, bruise, or wound. You must consider these effects within the dramatic context of the part.

ABNORMAL EYE

The ability to create the illusion of a damaged eye gives the performer an enormous variety of effects to add to his repertory. Obviously, there are many types of damaged eyes, scarred and bloody, for example. The macabre effect of a lifeless, dislocated pupil is what we will demonstrate here.

Cut a section of cotton bandage gauze to the size of the eye socket. (See Figs. 297 to 300.) After checking to be sure the gauze will fit the eye, draw the outline of the eye on the bandage (Fig. 301).

Glue the gauze in place with spirit gum or surgical adhesive (Figs. 302 and 303). After applying the gauze in place, wait for the gum to dry, then paint the base color and eye structure (both top and bottom of the eye) onto the gauze (Figs. 304 and 305). Draw in the pupil of the eye (Fig. 306).

The final effect is one of a permanently fixed, unnatural stare which can be made as unreal as your painting skill allows. You will be able to see through the gauze so that you can move about on the stage.

BROKEN NOSE

The broken nose can be fun because it requires skill to create an interesting and real effect. Aside from the usual paint, you will need the top of a rubber nipple from a baby's pacifier. (If finding one is too difficult, use a piece of soft sponge rubber.) The nipple will be cut and inserted into the nostril of the broken nose.

First, select the direction you want the break to go. On one side of the break, using the appropriate shadow mixture, carry the nose shadow in an arc from the eyebrow onto the mid-bridge of the nose. Then sharply arc it away and down to the bottom of the eye. Blend this shadow application into the area where the nose joins the face so that it blends into the base.

On the other side of the nose, start the shadow from about the corner of the eye. Arc it strongly onto the bridge of the nose and sharply arc it back to the top of the nostril. Blend this paint down to where the nose joins the face and then make it disappear into the base. This is the side on which you insert the nipple. (See Fig. 307.)

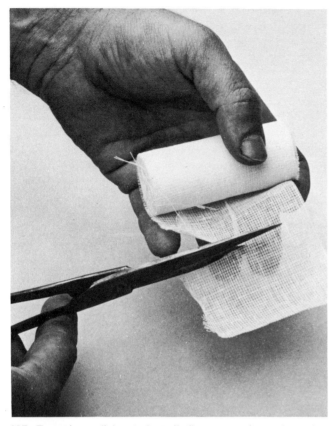

297. To make a dislocated pupil, first cut a piece of regular bandage to an oval large enough to cover the area of the eye.

298. Trim the bandage to approximate the eye shape.

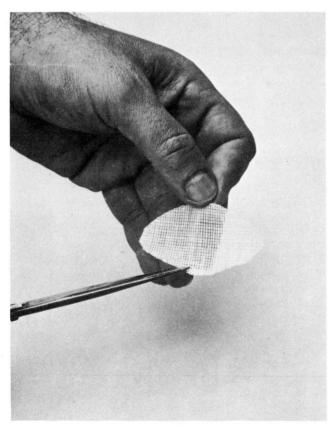

299. Clean up any stray edges of bandage.

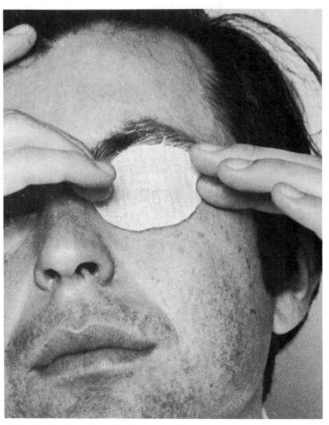

300. Fit the bandage to the eye. It must cover the eye socket completely from the eyebrow to the cheekbone. You must be able to move the eye fully beneath the gauze to avoid any discomfort while you perform.

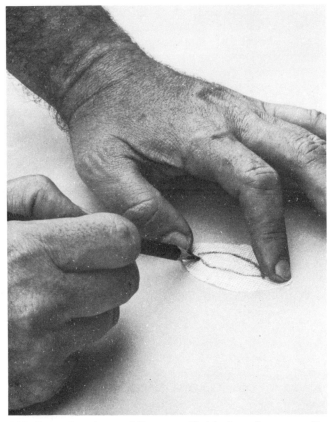

301. Draw the shape of the eye with black eyebrow pencil.

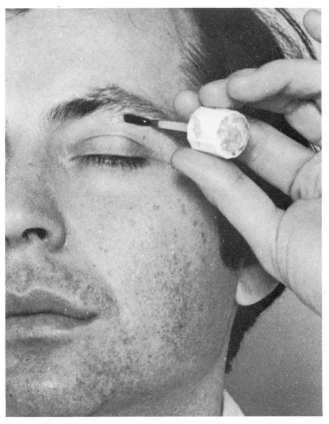

302. Apply spirit gum to the area around the eye. Avoid any contact with the eyelid or lashes.

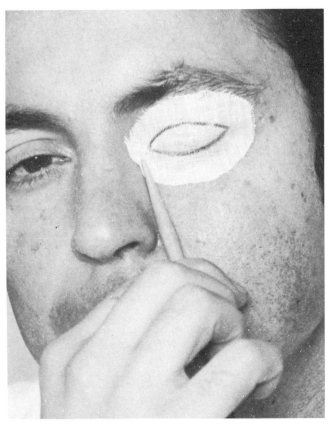

303. Place the bandage patch onto the eye and press firmly but gently for adhesion.

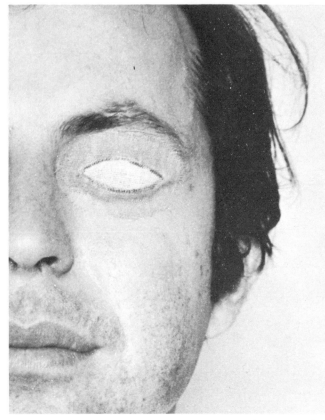

304. When the gum is dry, apply the matching base onto the patch and blend it into the skin color.

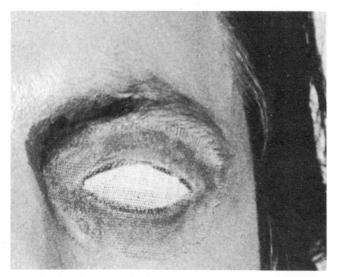

305. Apply whatever shading or aging effect is appropriate to the makeup.

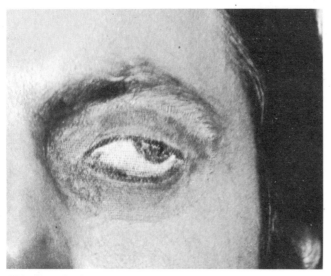

306. Draw in the pupil, coloring it however you want to match the other eye.

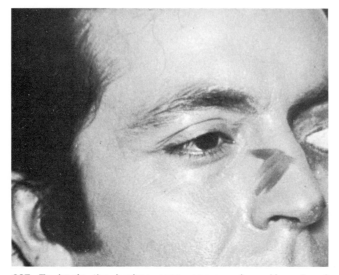

307. To begin the broken nose, carry a sharp V angle of shadow onto the bridge of the nose. Blend the shadow down to where the nose joins the face.

Take the pacifier and snip a tip off the first bulb (Fig. 308). Then cut the bulb away from the holder (Fig. 309). With the small finger inserted into the hole of the pacifier, press the pacifier into the broken nose (Fig. 310). The bottom of the nipple must not extend beyond the nostril. The nipple distorts the nose and yet allows you to breathe through the nostril.

Once the nipple has been inserted, shade the side of the nose opposite. Carry a strong highlight starting from the eye socket horizontally across the nose and then onto the nostril with the nipple. (See Fig. 311.)

BLOOD

Blood can be made by mixing red vegetable coloring with light glycerin until the desired consistency is achieved. You can also use some moist rouge with the glycerin if you need only a small quantity. If you want to buy blood already prepared, Max Factor's Technicolor Blood is the most suitable.

BRUISE

A bruise evolves over a short period of time. If the skin was not broken when it was bruised, a fresh blow shows no effects. Physical damage is noticeable immediately after the accident only if the surface of the skin has been broken. In these instances, blood makes the wound very apparent. If there is damage to the muscle or bone structure beneath the skin, it will form a lump and in time the damaged blood vessels and capillaries will discolor the skin surface and create a bruise. The small bruise that turns into a lump is barely distinguishable from any great distance. Only when it discolors can it be effectively made up for theatrical purposes.

The illusion of a bruise can be created by using first a blue-gray soft liner. Apply this, using the same illusion as you used in painting the cheek in Chapter 3, and illustrated diagramatically in Fig. 8C in Chapter 2. This will give the impression of swelling. To create a lump or roundness, apply the blue-gray paint darkest in the center of the appointed bruise and spread it out in all directions to blend into the base. When you have shaped the bruise for the desired size with the blue-gray, add a maroon soft liner to the surface, heaviest in the center of the bruise and blending out to simulate the purple discoloration of the bruise. Do not carry the color out all the way, as you did the blue-gray, and don't blend it perfectly evenly, because you want a splotchy effect. Bruise discoloration is irregular. Once you get the full effect of swelling, which has been completed with the maroon soft liner, you may add a few spots of moist rouge for blood or you may also use a few drops of theatrical blood. (See Fig. 313.)

SCARS

A scar is a healed cut in the flesh. In healing, the flesh is rejoined irregularly. To project into a theater, a thoroughly healed scar needs to be enormous! Most scars,

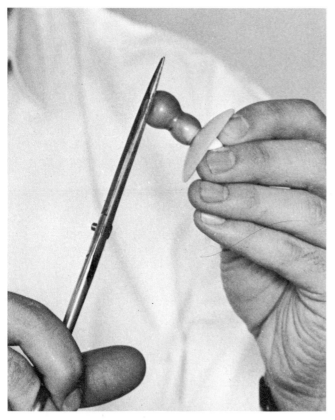

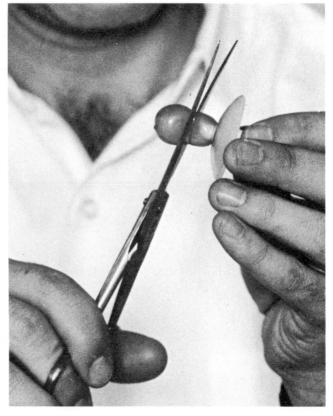

308. Cut off the tip of the pacifier.

309. Cut the bulb away from the pacifier.

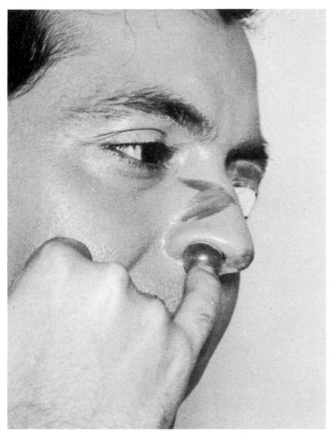

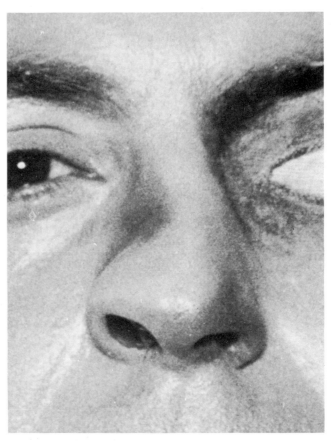

310. With the small finger, insert the pacifier into the nostril. This will distort the nostril, yet allow you to breathe. If it is uncomfortable, get a smaller pacifier or use the nipple from a baby's bottle.

311. Shading has been applied to the side of the nose opposite to the break. Shadow has been added at an angle, carried to the bridge of the nose, onto the nostril.

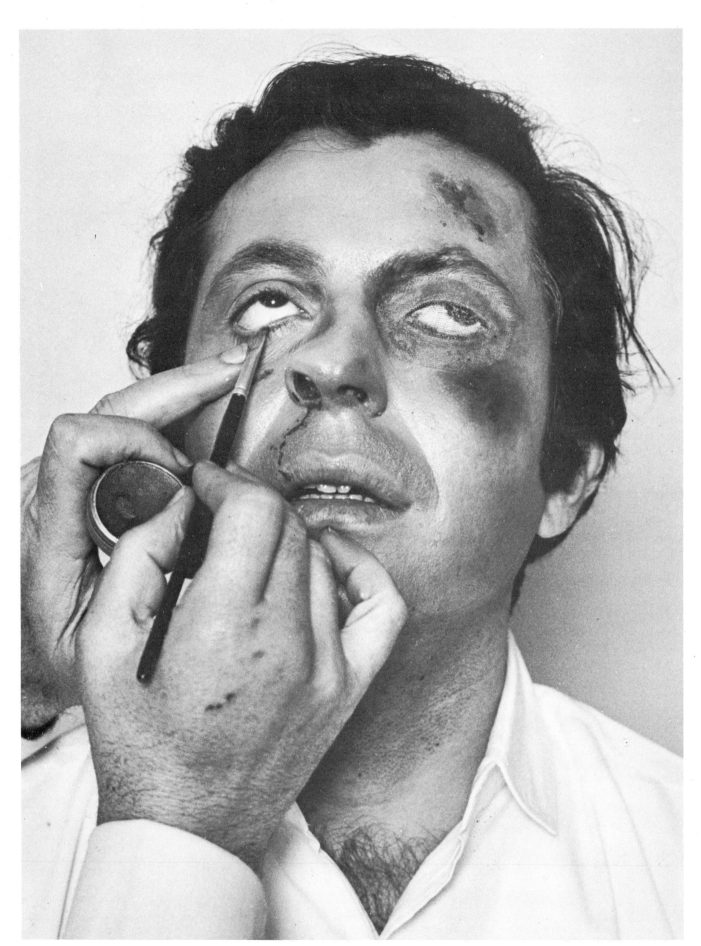

312. To create the effect of a bloodshot eye, rouge is applied to the inner lid.

when healed, show little more than a slight welt, which is a bit lighter in color than the surrounding skin. You can sketch in a scar, using highlighter and shadow, with the brush, to create an irregular welting. You can *build up* a scar with putty, mortician's wax, latex, surgical adhesive, scar plastic, or collodion. Collodion is a plastic material which seals the skin and creates a natural welting of a scar. Latex and surgical adhesive are painted in successive layers, building up the effect of scar tissue. Putty, mortician's wax, and scar plastic can be modeled to create these illusions. Whichever material you use, apply it along the scar line; let it dry. Add rouge, maroon brown, or blood for a fresh cut. For a healed scar, use regular shadow plus highlight. Keep scar lines uneven and be careful not to overdo it. Use restraint rather than gore. (See Fig. 313.)

BURNS AND WOUNDS

In creating burns and wounds, you want to give the illusion of lost skin surface, either in raw state or healing. Wounds resemble larger scars and may be created using most of the same materials on a larger scale. They can be particularly effective with surgical adhesive. Apply and spread adhesive, painted over the area that is to be the wound. Let it dry partially and then begin to pick at the adhesive, making holes in the application, giving the wound the desired irregular skin surface. Lift some of the adhesive away from the skin. Color it with the blue-gray and maroon liner, applied unevenly. (See Fig. 313.)

These big, spectacular effects are not at all as difficult as they seem at first, and they do not demand a fraction of the skill needed to paint a really subtle aging. Don't be impressed with big effects. Use your brain, try to develop your eye and knowledge of historical periods, and apply your slowly developing skills with patience and pleasure.

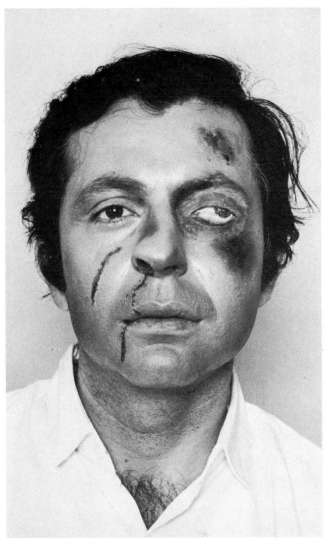

313. All the special effects discussed here are illustrated on this face: bruise on right cheekbone, burn on forehead, scar on left cheekbone, and blood.

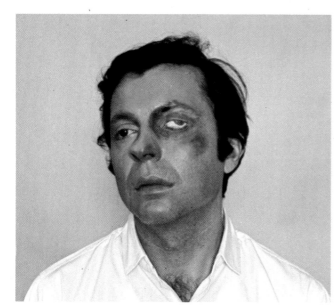
Placement of blue-gray for cheek bruise.

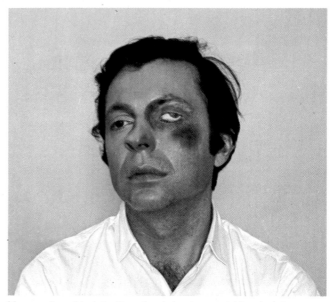
Maroon is added to the cheek bruise and blended in.

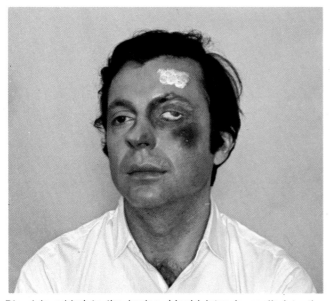
Blood is added to the bruise. Liquid latex is applied to the forehead to create a burn.

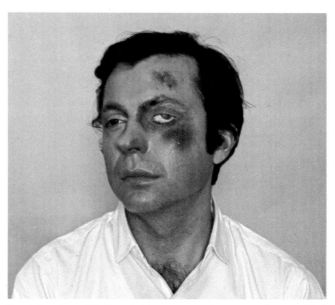
The latex has dried and blue-gray and maroon liner added to complete the burn.

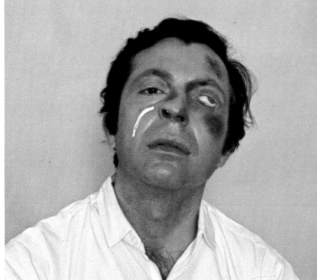
Latex is placed on the cheek to create a scarline.

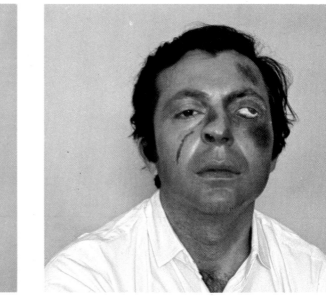
Latex has dried, and maroon and rouge colors the scar.

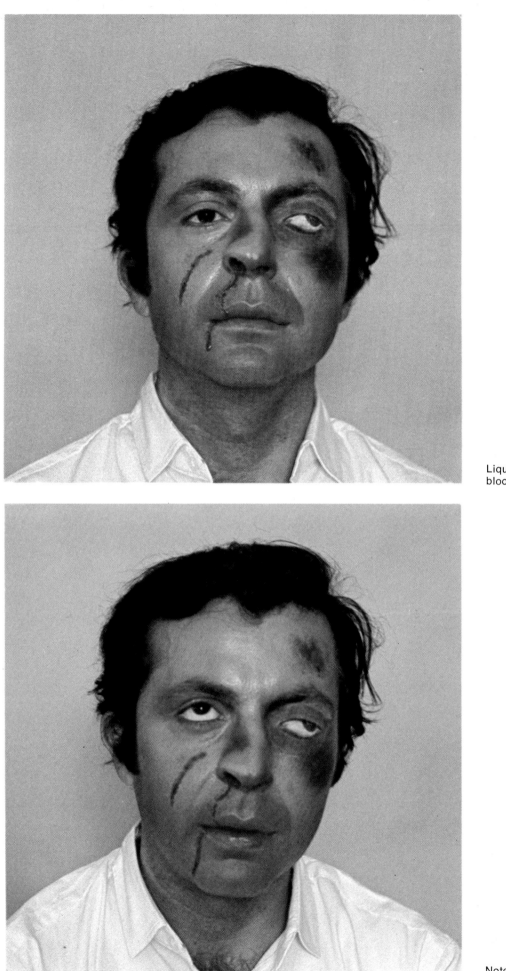

Liquid rouge was used to simulate blood from the nostril and mouth.

Note left eye appears bloodshot.

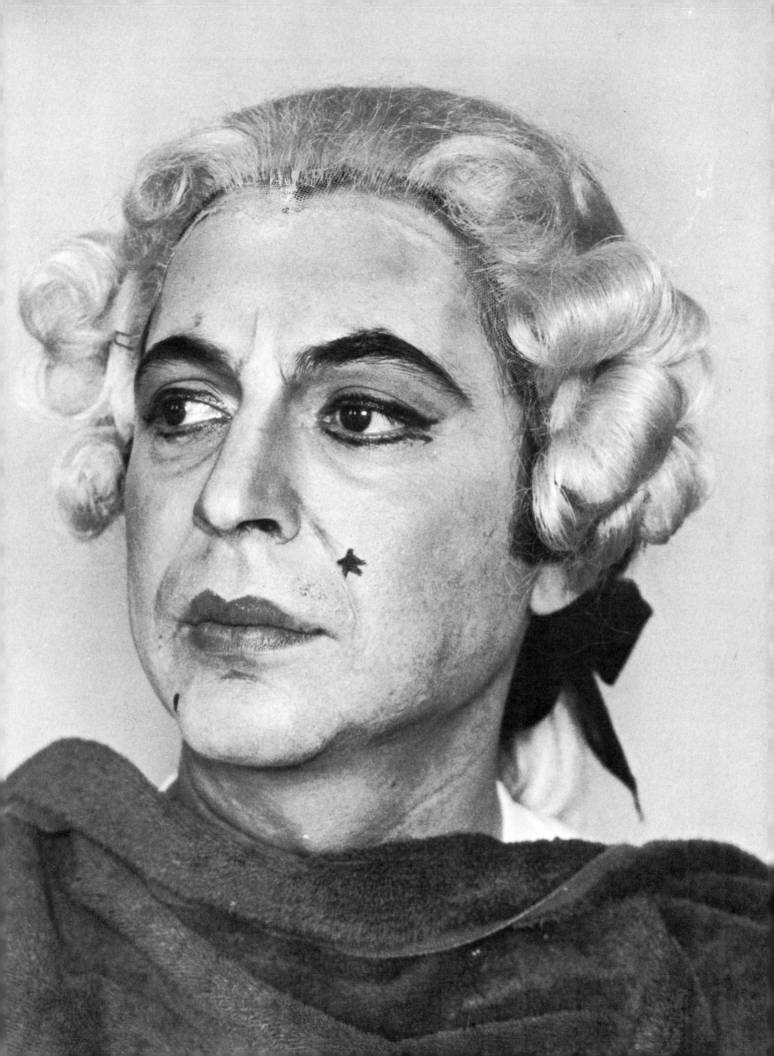

CHAPTER THIRTEEN

RESTORATION

Historical periods are generally characterized by costume and hairstyle alone. The makeup remains the same for all periods; only the accessories change. The Restoration is an exception to this, for in this period the individuals of the day wore makeup themselves, in addition to a wide range of wigs. This fact makes the makeup a particular problem because the performer must convey age and character through stage makeup and yet retain the effect that the character himself has deliberately made up in keeping with the style of the day. (In a contemporary role, the female performer has the same problem when the role is of an older woman who wears makeup to conceal her age.)

Understanding Restoration makeup is also important because a large body of plays and operas have been written in and about this period and these works are frequently performed today. Making up for the seventeenth century role should be a part of every performer's repertoire.

MAKEUP AS FASHION OF THE DAY

The bewigged and powdered popinjays used heavy white zinc oxide to cover their faces. Smallpox had ravaged Europe, and a person who had escaped with a clear skin was considered handsome and beautiful for that reason alone. For those less fortunate, the

heavy white base covered pock marks, a too-heavy application of rouge simulated health, and elaborate black beauty marks concealed venereal sores. Elegant wigs covered closely cropped heads and vast amounts of perfume concealed the odor of unbathed bodies. The historical explanation for the makeup is hardly as attractive as the paintings of the day suggest, and not nearly as appealing as the lovely figures we all remember from the movies depicting that romantic time.

RENDERING THIS IN STAGE MAKEUP

In spite of the rather sordid explanation for Restoration fashion, it is unnecessary for you to actually recreate the overly painted look of the period, unless it suits the role.

For a makeup base, use either hard or soft grease, and create a very pale, light skin color. If you are playing a youthful role, use a light brown shadow mixture for the nose and eyes. Use rouge carefully on the cheeks. Blending the color off on a light base will take skill. Paint and outline the lips in a pale red color. Black eyebrow pencil is used for the brows and beauty spots, and complete the makeup with a wig.

For age, you will need to use a light brown or blue-gray for your shadow mixture. Remember, even if you are playing the role of an older character, the fact that he is wearing makeup will subdue the effect of age.

This makeup calls for delicacy in blending. Working on a light base is a challenge and the painted effects can be delightful.

314. Conveying character through the Restoration makeup is a problem. The style of the period was to wear makeup, and theatrical effects must be created within the illusion that the character *is* wearing the makeup of the time.

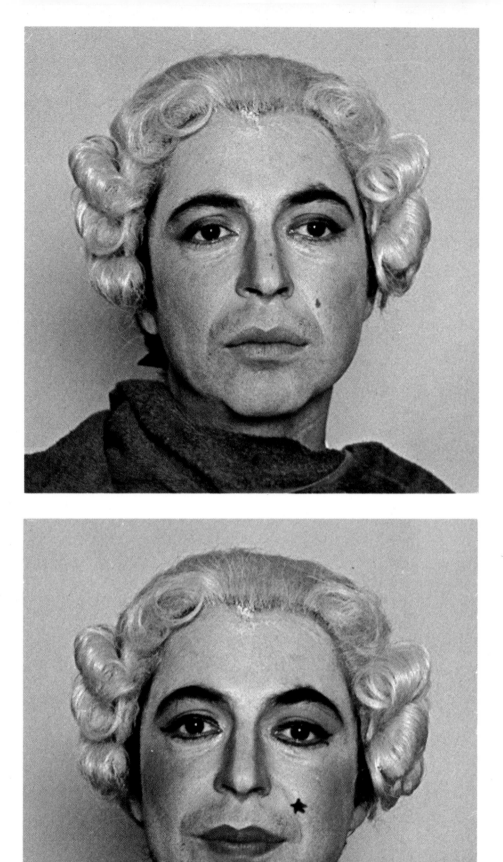

The base, with eye and cheek shading blended is shown.

The fop is created by exaggerating the Resoration makeup. Note bizarre beauty mark.

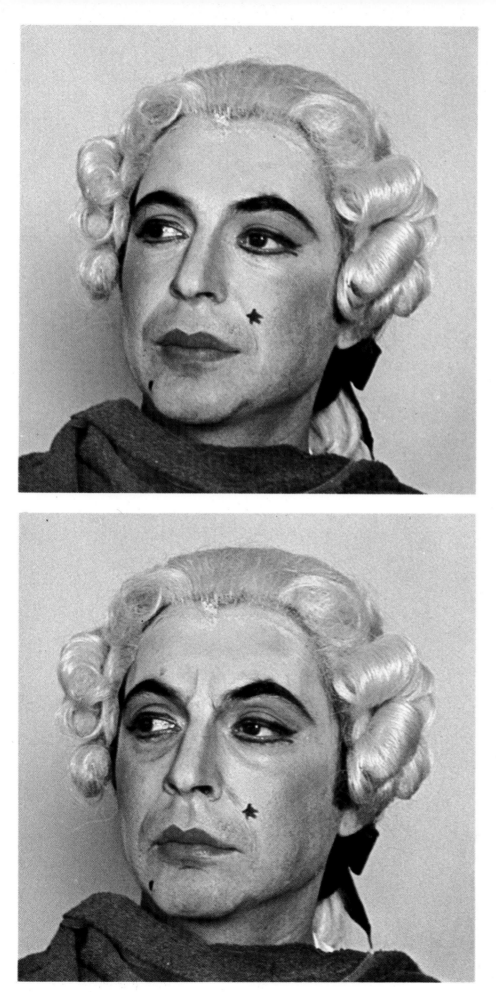

Three quarter view of completed Restoration.

The same angle is shown, with age added to the Restoration makeup.

This photograph of Baccalone shows a more extreme aging effect. Note how the colors bring alive this makeup, and how this work encompasses so many chapters of this book.

CHAPTER FOURTEEN

COURSE OF STUDY

A specific plan of study is very necessary to the reader who wishes to develop enough skill to utilize this book fully and for the teacher who intends to present his course in makeup techniques in a progressive manner. Obviously, the information in this book is of value regardless of the way in which it is used. Nevertheless, experience has taught me that a plan of sequential study, plus an allocation of specific time per work session and space between work sessions is essential to the development of intellectual knowledge and then to the slower development of painting skill so vital to improvement and progress.

Please do not think that I am recommending an *inordinate* amount of time to develop your skills. After many years of teaching, I have found that time is absolutely vital to the slow progression of learning makeup techniques.

I recommend that each work session be about two hours. Less time than that will not allow for much accomplishment. More time tends to make the session tiresome. I further recommend two work sessions per week. More sessions will not help because time is needed for you to absorb the work you have done and fewer sessions mean that you will forget the skills attained from one session to the next.

In all work sessions, allow about five minutes for setting out your material at the beginning and ten to fifteen minutes at the end for cleaning and packing up.

If you approach this work as a course of study, you will make better and more consistent progress than if you stab at it, hit or miss. The following list is the way I suggest you attack this study, so that you can progress from the simple and basic techniques to the more complex skills without suffering frustration or impairing your skills in any way.

GRECIAN TECHNIQUE

1st Session: Analyze face; make notes. Cleanse face and apply base. Apply jaw rouge. Check for errors. Cleanse and repeat.

2nd Session: Apply base and jaw rouge. Make up top of one eye, then top of other eye. Check for errors. Cleanse and repeat.

3rd Session: Apply base, jaw rouge. Make up top of both eyes, nose, and eyebrows. Check for errors. If necessary, repeat eyes and nose.

4th Session: Apply base, jaw rouge. Make up top of eyes, nose, bottom of eyes, eyebrows. Check for errors. If necessary, re-do nose or eyebrows. If not, proceed to try cheek rouge.

5th Session: Apply base, jaw rouge, top of eyes, nose, bottom of eyes, eyebrows, cheek rouge.

6th Session: Repeat work of last session and add mouth. Check for errors.

7th Session: Repeat work of last session, add under-jaw and powder. Criticize.

8th Session: Repeat all of the above to completion.

9th Session: Adapt and modify a classic Grecian makeup to more realistic and contemporary usage.

AGING TECHNIQUE

10th Session: Apply base. Create temple sinking; cheek sinking. Cleanse and repeat.

11th Session: Apply base, temple and cheek sinking, nose wrinkle, and highlight each side. Check and repeat.

12th Session: Apply base, temple and cheek sinking, nose and jowl wrinkle. Check and repeat if necessary.

13th Session: Apply base, temple and cheek sinking, nose and jowl wrinkles, above the eye sinking, and, if time allows, below the eye bag and pouch.

14th Session: Repeat last session and add jowls, mouth, and chin structure.

15th Session: Repeat last session and add brows and forehead.

16th Session: Repeat last session and add neck and powder.

17th Session: Repeat last session and add graying to hair. Evaluate.

EXTREME STOUT

18th Session: Apply base, nose, and cheek. Cleanse and repeat.

19th Session: Apply base, nose, cheek, and eye.

20th Session: Apply base, nose, cheek, eye, chin, and jowls.

21st Session: Repeat last session and add mouth, temples, and forehead.

22nd Session: Complete full stout painting, powder, and criticize.

23rd Session: Repeat last session.

EXTREME LEAN

24th Session: Apply base, temple, cheek sinkings. Cleanse and repeat.

25th Session: Apply base, temple and cheek sinking, eye, and nose.

26th Session: Apply base, temple and cheek sinking, eye, nose, mouth, jowls.

27th Session: Repeat last session and add forehead, neck, and eyebrows.

28th Session: Repeat last session, complete painting, and powder.

BUILDING UP FEATURES WITH PUTTY

29th Session: Apply putty nose for stout. Check. Cleanse and repeat.

30th Session: Apply stout nose. Apply base and shading. Check and repeat if necessary.

31st Session: Apply putty nose for lean. Check. Cleanse and repeat.

32nd Session: Apply lean nose. Apply base and shading. Check and repeat if necessary.

BEARDS AND WIGS

33rd Session: Pull wool clumps, shape, cut, and apply beard. Trim and examine.

34th Session: Blend wool clumps. Shape, cut, apply, trim, and examine beard.

35th Session: Apply straightened wool or hair beard for duration of session. Trim and examine.

36th Session: Apply straightened hair or wool for complete beard. Blend, trim, and examine.

37th Session: Apply cloth and lace wigs, mustaches, and beards.

38th Session: Complete makeup for extreme stout with nose, mustache, beard, eyebrows, and wig.

39th Session: Repeat last session.

40th Session: Complete makeup for extreme lean with nose, mustache, beard, eyebrows, and wig.

41st Session: Repeat last session.

PROSTHETICS

42nd Session: Take impression of face and make face mask for mold.

43rd Session: Model false feature; make mold for feature.

44th Session: Make rubber piece.

45th Session: Apply rubber piece and complete the makeup appropriate to it.

SPECIAL EFFECTS

46th Session: Complete effects for scars, wounds, bruises, damaged eye.

RESTORATION

47th Session: Complete Restoration makeup; check and repeat.

WORLD'S GREATEST ROLES

For an instructor, it is invaluable to give the entire class the problem of making up a specific character. Have each student draw up two lists stating on each his analysis of the physical factors he intends to show with the makeup. The instructor holds the second list and when the work is completed, each student in turn stands before the class, his list is read, and the class and instructor criticize the work for success or failure and suggest how to improve it. Here are six characters for male and female students which could be used with success, but any others that best suit the needs of the class or department are equally acceptable.

48th Session: Antony and Cleopatra

49th Session: Oedipus and Medea

50th Session: Cyrano and Roxanne

51st Session: Stanley Kowalski and Blanche du Bois

52nd Session: Faust and Marguerite

53rd Session: Papagano and Papagana

Obviously, this recommended course of study is simply a guide. Some of you will be able to keep to this schedule and progress reasonably well. Others will need more time than indicated. Do not be concerned if you are unable to keep up with this schedule. Everyone has a different ability in developing the tactile skill and perception necessary for makeup painting and modeling. In my experience, I have never seen anyone who was unable to progress with patience and practice; some progressed faster than others. Any student who was serious could achieve a respectable skill at makeup technique.

CHAPTER FIFTEEN

GALLERY OF MAKEUP EXAMPLES

In concluding this book, I wanted to present you with a wide variety of interesting makeup examples; some of them are very skillfully achieved, others less so. With a critical eye you can distinguish the effective jobs from the ones poorly conceived. I also felt this gallery could serve as a reference: you can examine how some performers have elected to interpret different roles, again, some with great imagination, others with very little imagination. I have attempted to select a range of roles and performers so that you can see the many directions you can turn, using the text of this book.

Some of the photographs in this gallery are retouched, mainly to conceal obvious wig lines or makeup painting. In the captions, I have indicated the retouched photographs; those that are unretouched are also identified. The photographs you have been using for the demonstrations throughout this book are not retouched. I felt it was important for you to see all the painting, the line of the wigs, the pattern of the lace. The photographs in this gallery, however, were not taken necessarily for instructional purposes, and the work may be more difficult to analyze.

Although this book is devoted exclusively to makeup for the stage, I *have* included some photographs of performers made up for film (a different makeup technique). I have selected these photographs mainly to illustrate various wigs and hairpieces which are suitable to the theatrical performer as well. I felt their value merited admission to the gallery.

Jean Madeira as Carmen. (retouched) For this role, the actress must have dark gypsy skin tone, full voluptuous lips, strong eyebrows and heavy lashes. Photo, Sedge LeBlang, The Metropolitan Opera.

Roberta Peters as Queen of the Night in *The Magic Flute.* (retouched) Note the makeup effects of this exotic character: heavy eyelashes and eyebrows and a sharply defined mouth. Photo, Sedge LeBlang, The Metropolitan Opera.

Mia Slavenska in *Aida.* (retouched) Although this performer has a lovely face, this makeup is simply too soft to project a very strong effect to the audience. Photo, Sedge LeBlang, The Metropolitan Opera.

Mildred Miller in *Rosenkavalier.* (retouched) In the opera there are a number of instances where the role of a man is played by a woman. Here the character is wearing a convincing Rococo wig. Photo, Sedge LeBlang, The Metropolitan Opera.

Helen Traubel in *Rosenkavalier.* (retouched) This is a fine performer who has overlooked her makeup. She has applied only lipstick and lashes, but nothing more comes across. Photo, Sedge LeBlang, The Metropolitan Opera.

Alicia Alonso in *La Fille mal gardée.* (retouched) Heavy eye work and lipstick, and little else, are typical of a dancer's makeup. Photo, Sedge LeBlang, The Metropolitan Opera.

Performer in *The Book of Job.* (unretouched) The pattern of stained glass was carefully worked out beforehand and only meticulous painting could have transformed this into a successful reality. It certainly has been accomplished here. Performed in Pineville, Kentucky.

Blanche Thebom as Baba the Turk in *The Rake's Progress.* (retouched) Note the use of hairpieces: wig, exaggerated false eyelashes, and beard. Women should learn to apply beards to be prepared for parts such as this one. Photo, Sedge LeBlang, The Metropolitan Opera.

Edward Caton in *La Fille mal gardée.* (retouched) Men should also learn to make up as women. The strong caricature makeup projects the prissy old maid, particularly successful when played by a fine male dancer. Photo, Sedge LeBlang, The Metropolitan Opera.

George London as Count Almaviva in *The Marriage of Figaro.* (retouched) Here is an example of Restoration makeup put to good use. The white cast in the base has not limited the projection of character. Note the beauty mark. Wig, Ira Senz. Photo, Sedge LeBlang, The Metropolitan Opera.

Jan Peerce in *The Masked Ball.* (retouched) Here is an example where the Restoration makeup could have been used, but was neglected. No effort was made to do a Restoration painting. Wig, Ira Senz. Photo, Sedge LeBlang, The Metropolitan Opera.

Cesare Siepi as Padre Guardiano in *La Forza del destino.* (retouched) Note the cloth front wig and the fine mustache and beard. However, the makeup itself consists of nothing but pencil lines. Photo, Sedge LeBlang, The Metropolitan Opera.

Jerome Hines as Ramfis in *Aida*. (retouched) Although the makeup work here is very heavy and lacks refinement, the performer had a concept by exaggerating the sneering quality of the character. Wig, Ira Senz. Photo, Sedge LeBlang, The Metropolitan Opera.

Jerome Hines in *Don Carlo*. (retouched) The performer's face is virtually sculpted in putty: note the work around the cheek and nose in particular. Even the eyebrows have been built up with putty. Wig, Ira Senz. Photo, Sedge LeBlang, The Metropolitan Opera.

Jerome Hines as Mephestopheles in *Faust*. (retouched) Another example of a heavy hand, yet a successful dramatic effect. Wig, Ira Senz. Photo, Sedge LeBlang, The Metropolitan Opera.

Jerome Hines as Don Basilio in *Barber of Seville*. (retouched) The performer is wearing here a cloth front wig. Note the putty work on nose and chin. The proportions of these features conform to those of the over-all face. Wig, Ira Senz. Photo, Sedge LeBlang, The Metropolitan Opera.

Alois Pernerstorfer as Sparafucile in *Rigoletto.* (retouched) This is a heavy-handed makeup job: pencil lines have been applied with very little imagination, turning this into an obvious makeup job. Photo, Sedge LeBlang, The Metropolitan opera.

Jerome Hines as Boris Godounov. (retouched) Note the use of wig, putty nose, and wool beard. The work is heavy, yet a good dramatic effect has been achieved. Obviously, an image of the character determined the makeup work done. Wig, Ira Senz. Photo, Sedge LeBlang, The Metropolitan Opera.

George London in *Aida.* (retouched) The performer is wearing a lace front wig and a wool beard. A dark base was used to simulate the skin tone shown here. Wig, Ira Senz. Photo, Sedge LeBlang, The Metropolitan Opera.

George London in *Tales of Hoffmann.* (retouched) Note cloth front wig. Wig, Ira Senz. Photo, Sedge LeBlang, The Metropolitan Opera.

Salvatore Baccaloni as Varlam in *Boris Godounov.* (unretouched) Note the good work on the putty nose. By encircling the left eye in a dark tone and subduing the right eye, one eye appears considerably more dominant than the other. Wig, Ira Senz. Photo, Herman Buchman.

Salvatore Baccaloni in *Gianni Schicchi.* (retouched) Here a hairpiece has been used for the sideburns. Pieces for the eyebrows add expression to the well made up eyes. Heavy putty work is used for the nose. Wig, Ira Senz. Photo, Sedge LeBlang, The Metropolitan Opera.

Gerhard Pechner in *La Forza del destino.* (retouched) Here a crepe wool beard has been applied as well as a cloth bald pate and eyebrows. The putty work on the nose, however, is the most effective detail. Wig, Ira Senz. Photo, Sedge LeBlang, The Metropolitan Opera.

Lorenzo Alvary as King Dodon in *Le Coq d'or.* (retouched) The performer is wearing an effective cloth bald wig, wool face hair, and a well made putty nose. Photo, Sedge LeBlang, The Metropolitan Opera.

Performer in *The Book of Job*. (unretouched) Here various colors are broken up to give the illusion of a multiple colored stained glass. Even the wig and beards have been sewn to carry out the effect. Performed in Pineville, Kentucky.

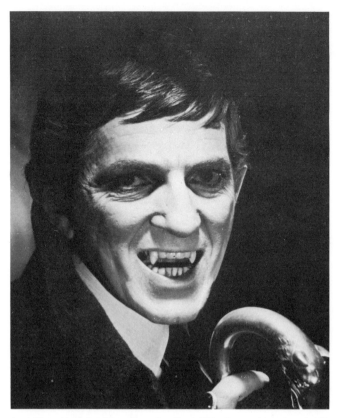

Jonathan Frid as Barnabas in *Dark Shadows*. (unretouched) The grotesque fangs are made by a dentist, then fit over the natural teeth for comfortable wear. Produced by ABC Television.

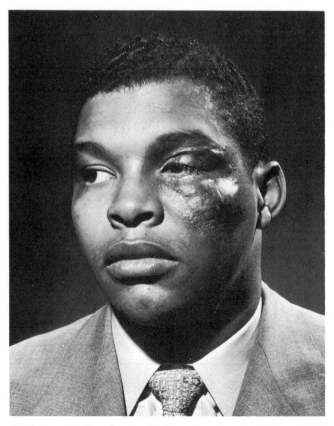

C. Wallace in *The Joe Louis Story*. (unretouched) The puffed eye was made with nose putty and the performer kept it on for a hot sixteen hour working day. Photo, Robert Ross.

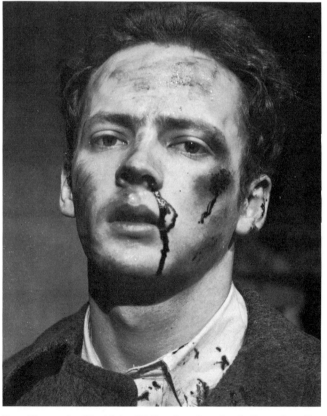

Ben Piazza in *World in White*. (unretouched) By using the methods described in Chapter 12, dirt, bruises, and blood are easily created. Produced by CBS Television.

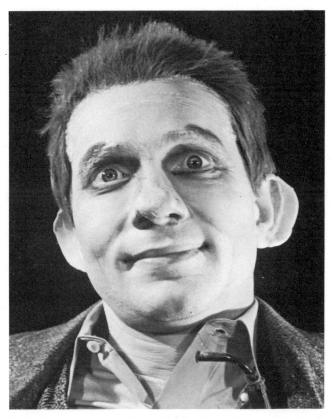

Michael Gorrin in *Uriel Acosta.* (unretouched) Here is an example of good use of cloth front wig, putty nose, and wool beard. Photo, Ralph Samuels, courtesy Michael Gorrin.

Michael Gorrin in *The Good Soldier Schweik.* (unretouched) For this performance, the actor wore not only a putty nose, but putty ears as well. Note also the bald front wig. Photo, Lewis Gorin, courtesy Michael Gorrin.

Michael Gorrin in *Chains.* (unretouched) The wool beard here is designed for a young man and the effect is superb. Photo, Lewis Gorin, courtesy Michael Gorrin.

Michael Gorrin in *The Magician.* (unretouched) The lace beard here is designed for the effect of an old man. Photo, Lewis Gorin, courtesy Michael Gorrin.

Vladimir Popov in *Three Sisters.* (retouched) The effect of old age has been enhanced by the use of white beard and wig. Photo, Moscow Art Theatre, courtesy Sol Hurok.

Alexei Gribov as Firs in *Cherry Orchard.* (retouched) This effect of old age does not rely much on makeup. Sometimes, hairpieces alone can accomplish a great deal. Photo, Moscow Art Theatre, courtesy Sol Hurok.

Yuri Leonidov as Yasha in *Cherry Orchard.* (retouched) The way in which the hair is combed, parted off-center, suits this nineteenth century period. Photo, Moscow Art Theatre, courtesy Sol Hurok.

Boris Smirnov as Lenin in *Kremlin Chimes.* (retouched) Matching the face of a historical figure presents its own problems. Here the wig and hairpiece portray Lenin. Photo, Moscow Art Theatre, courtesy Sol Hurok.

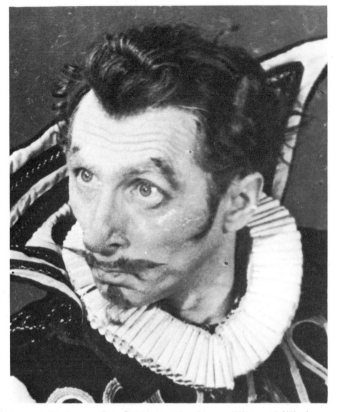

Sergei Theits as Dr. Caius in *The Merry Wives of Windsor.* (unretouched) The appearance of little makeup here is deceptive. The shading is subtle and therefore not very evident. Photo, Mossoviet Theatre, courtesy Yuri Zavadaski.

Sergei Theits in *The Old Man.* (unretouched) Although well painted, pouches and wrinkles are not conspicuous because the beard and wig dominate the job. Photo, Mossoviet Theatre, courtesy Yuri Zavadaski.

Boris Livanov in *Dead Souls.* (retouched) The concept here is splendid: the nose and sidewhiskers enhance this character. Compare this with the following photograph. Photo, Moscow Art Theatre, courtesy Sol Hurok.

Boris Livanov as Zabalin in *Kremlin Chimes.* (retouched) The painting of age in this case has been excellent, further enhanced by the use of wig-mustache, putty nose, and white wig. Photo, Moscow Art Theatre, courtesy Sol Hurok.

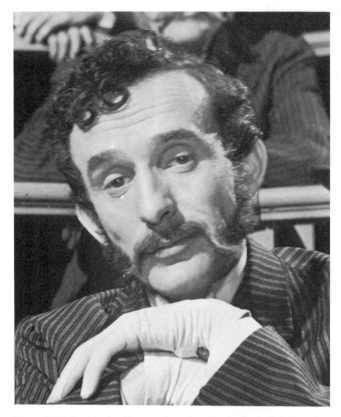

From *Within Man's Power*. (unretouched) Curled hair, plus lace sideburns and mustache give the period effect of a rakish young man. Wig, Ira Senz. Photo, Robert Nordbye, courtesy Nicholas Webster.

From *Within Man's Power*. (unretouched) The same actor has aged in the play: wearing now a different mustache and hair style, grayed hair, to create the older look. Wig, Ira Senz. Photo, Robert Nordbye, courtesy Nicholas Webster.

From *Within Man's Power*. (unretouched) Here again in the same play the lace toupee plus face sideburns and mustache give the appearance of a young man. Wig, Ira Senz. Photo, ACKAD, courtesy Nicholas Webster.

From *Within Man's Power*. (unretouched) The same actor, with toupee removed, hair grayed, gray mustache, and age painting, to give the effect of the character in later years. Wig, Ira Senz. Photo, ACKAD, courtesy Nicholas Webster.

(unretouched) The beard here is the actor's own. The lace toupee and mustache have been attached. The painting is very light. Wig, Ira Senz. Photo, Charles Haas, courtesy Thomas A. Lipton, Inc.

(unretouched) Here the hair has been curled for the effect of the period. Lace sideburns and mustache have been added. Wig, Ira Senz. Photo, Charles Haas, courtesy Thomas A. Lipton, Inc.

(unretouched) The hair here is the actor's own, and the fine lace beard and mustache have been added to match. Photo, Charles Haas, courtesy Thomas A. Lipton.

(unretouched) This beautiful lace front wig creates the effect of the period quite naturally. Wig, Ira Senz. Photo, Charles Haas, courtesy Thomas A. Lipton, Inc.

(unretouched) Study this photograph for the effective use of layered straightened hair. Photo, ACKAD, courtesy Nicholas Webster.

(unretouched) This is an example of an English judge's full bottomed wig. Courtesy Wig Creations, London.

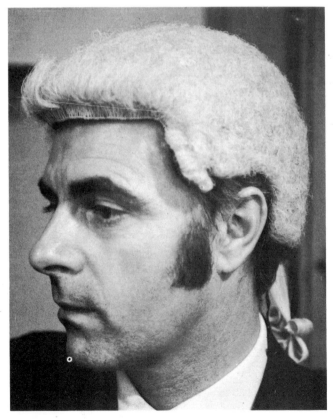

(unretouched) Here is an English judge's bench wig. Courtesy Wig Creations, London.

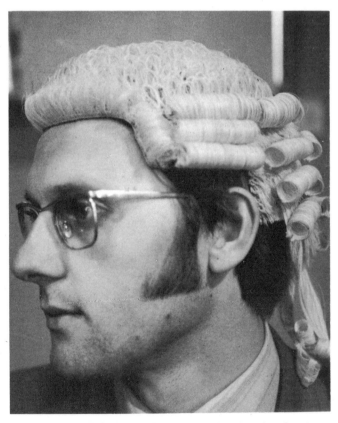

(unretouched) This is an English barrister's wig. Courtesy Wig Creations, London.

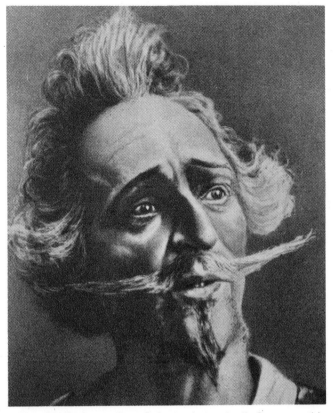

Fydor Chaliapin as *Don Quixote.* (retouched) Compare this interpretation of Don Quixote with that of the one shown in Chapter 6. You will see that the principles apply in both characterizations.

Fydor Chaliapin as *Ivan.* (retouched) This profile view reveals a long beard shaped for a dramatic effect. Note also the subtle shaping of the nose, a shape totally different from the actor's own.

Fydor Chaliapin as an old man. (retouched) Notice the skillful way in which this performer has created the effect of old age, particularly successful in the eye work.

Fydor Chaliapin as an old man. (retouched) A totally different effect of age is created in this work. The versatility of this man's work is enormous.

LIST OF SUPPLIERS

M. Stein Cosmetic Co.
430 Broome Street
New York, New York
(manufacturer and supplier of Stein Cosmetics and Stein
  Permawax, a mortician's wax)

Max Factor & Co.
1665 North McCadden Place
Hollywood, California
(manufacturer and distributor of Max Factor cosmetics)

L. Leichner Ltd.
Leichner House
Acre Lane
London SW2, England
(manufacturer and distributor of Leichner cosmetics)

Lydia O'Leary
41 East 57 Street
New York, New York
(manufacturer and distributor of Covermark)
Norcliff Labs
Fairfield, Connecticut
(manufacturer and distributor of Albolene)

M. Grumbacher, Inc.
460 West 34 Street
New York, New York
(manufacturer of artist brushes)

Wig Creations Ltd.
25 Portman Close
Baker Street
London W1, England
(manufacturer of wigs and hairpieces; rent wigs and
  hair goods for theatrical use)

Ira Senz Wigs
580 Fifth Avenue
New York, New York
(manufacturer of wigs and hairpieces; rent wigs and
  hair goods for theatrical use; supply all brands of
  theatrical makeup)

Thayer Labs, Inc.
Metuchen, New Jersey
(manufacturer of Duo Surgical Adhesive)

Charles Meyer
11 East 12 Street
New York, New York
(manufacturer of Meyer Mascara)

Johnson & Johnson
New Brunswick, New Jersey
(manufacturer of Fast Setting Bandage)

INDEX

Edited by Susan E. Meyer
Designed by James Craig and Robert Fillie
Demonstration photographs by Susan E. Meyer
Black and white photo processing by Dan Becker Labs
Composed in nine point Helvetica by Atlantic Linotype Corp.
Printed and bound in Japan by Toppan Printing Co., Ltd.